The Theory of African Literature

Implications for Practical Criticism
Chidi Amuta

Institute for African Alternatives
Zed Books Ltd
London and New Jersey

The Theory of African Literature was first published in 1989 by
Zed Books Ltd., 57 Caledonian Road, London N1 9BU
and 171 First Avenue, Atlantic Highlands, New Jersey 07716
with The Institute for African Alternatives, 23 Bevenden Street, London N1 6BH

Copyright © Chidi Amuta 1989
Cover design by Andrew Corbett
Typeset by EMS Photosetters, Rochford, Essex
Printed and bound in the UK by Bookcraft Ltd., Bath.

British Library Cataloguing in Publication Data

Amuta, Chidi
  The theory of African literature:
  implications for practical criticism
  1. English literature. African writers.
  1945- – Critical studies
  I. Title
  820.9'96

ISBN 0-86232-546-3
ISBN 0-86232-547-1 Pbk

Library of Congress Cataloging-in-Publication Data

Amuta, Chidi, 1953–
  The theory of African literature : implications for
practical criticism/Chidi Amuta.
    p.   cm.
  Bibliography: p.
  Includes index.
  ISBN 0-86232-546-3 : $39.95.
  ISBN 0-86232-547-1 (pbk.) : $12.50.
    1. African literature – History and criticism –
Theory, etc. 2. Criticism – Africa – History – 20th
century. 3. Literature and society – Africa –
History and criticism. 4. Politics and literature –
Africa – History – 20th century. 5. Marxist
criticism. I. Title.
  PL8010.A53   1989   809'.889'6–dc19   88-14302.

The Theory of African Literature

For **Tosin**
the woman
who made the great crossing . . .

and became
my wife.

Contents

Preface   vii

Introduction   1
The Dialectical Imperative in African Literature   1

1. Ideological Formations in the Criticism of African Literature   12
Criticism, Ideology and Society: A Dialectical Overview   13
The Class Position of the Critic   16
Aspects of Bourgeois Criticism   18

2. Traditionalism and the Quest for an African Literary Aesthetic   33
The Intellectual Climate   34
An African World View: Illusion or Reality   37
Pitfalls of Traditional Aesthetics   41

3. Marxism and African Literature   52
Marxist Aesthetics: An Open-ended Legacy   52
Politics and Ideology in African Literature   56
African Literature and the National Question   61
The Class Question: African Literature or Literature of the
    African People?   68
Beyond Orthodox Marxism: The Framework for a Post-Marxist
    Theory of African Literature and Culture   72

**4. A Dialectical Theory of African Literature: Categories and
    Springboards**   77
Dialectics and Cultural Theory   77
Categories for a Dialectical Theory of African Literature   80
Springboards for a Dialectical Theory of African Literature
    and Culture   89

5. Issues and Problems in African Literature: A Dialectical Revision   103
African Literature: Beyond Definition   104
African Literature and its Audience   107

The Language Question 112
Commitment and Alignment 114
Continuities from the Past 117
Aesthetics and Critical Values 120
The Limits of Literature 121
Implications for Practical Criticism 122

6. **History and the Dialectics of Narrative in the African Novel** 125
Problems in the Sociology of the African Novel 125
The Materialism of Cultural Nationalism: Achebe's *Things Fall Apart* and *Arrow of God* 130
Proletarian Consciousness and the Anti-Colonial Struggle: Ousmane's *Gods Bits of Wood* 136
Class Struggle and the Socialist Vision: Ngugi's *Petals of Blood* 143

7. **Drama and Revolution in Africa** 154
Politics and Ideology in Contemporary African Drama: Theoretical Observations 154
Historical Reconstruction and Class Struggle in Anti-Imperialist Drama: *The Trial of Dedan Kimathi* and *I Will Marry When I Want* 157
Contemporary Contradictions and the Revolutionary Alternative: *Once Upon Four Robbers* and *Morountodun* 167

8. **Poetry and Liberation Politics in Africa** 176
Poetry and Politics: The Dialectic of Commitment 176
Private Experience as Public Protest: Dennis Brutus's *Stubborn Hope* 178
The Poetic Essence of National Liberation: Agostinho Neto's *Sacred Hope* 185
Poetry as Political Polemic: Odia Ofeimun's *The Poet Lied* 191

9. **Beyond Decolonization** 197

Select Bibliography 200

Index 205

Preface

If the primary motive were to add to the list of books of literary criticism in the sense in which traditional academic convention has come to conceive of that most abused of disciplines, this book might never have been written. On the contrary, the ideas set out here simultaneously constitute an act of rebellion, a political statement, a personal testimony and an intellectual intervention in that order.

This book is the culmination of my efforts to unlearn and confront the ignorance of the last ten years on the nature of African literature and its relationship to the society that informs it. A disturbing but conspicuous feature of the fast-accumulating postulations on and exegeses of African literature is the near absence of a consistent and organic theoretical focus. Where any attempt has been made to transcend this limitation, the natural recourse has been to quaint domestications of theoretical paradigms and models from the bourgeois West. The closest one gets to an authentic theoretical viewpoint is the works of the vast army of traditionalist aestheticians who almost invariably insist on a selective resuscitation of poetic norms and values from pre-colonial African cultures as an alternative to the hegemony of bourgeois Western formulations. The most prominent achievement of the latter group to date is embodied in *Towards the Decolonization of African Literature* by Chinweizu et al.

While one of the primary objects of this book is to confront and transcend the kind of reductionism and romantic simplification represented by the Chinweizu formation, my definitive concern is that assessments of African literature based upon idealist and humanistic notions derived from fixed traditional (Western and African) prescriptions of art are not only defective but ultimately dysfunctional in the contemporary African context.

What is urgently called for, in the words of Biodun Jeyifo, is "a rigorous act of materialist literary interpretation . . . to recover 'real' meaning from the metaphysical fogs and abstracted empirical details" which currently befuddle discourse on African literature. In this respect, it is my insistence that it is the socio-economic, political and ideological contradictions which define the life and historical experiences of the African people that must form the basis of a new and more functionally relevant theoretical approach to African literature. The crucial intervention which this volume sets out to institute is that of bridging the widening chasm between whatever slender theory there is and actual critical practice. There is a proliferation of essays that sequester literature from society, thereby betraying the putative socio-historical involvement of much of African literature.

In several ways, therefore, this book is a prolegomenous exploration of the possibilities of and categories for a radical, dialectical and therefore "scientific" theory of African literature. The challenge which I try to pose in these pages to the African cultural intelligentsia is that of reviewing some of the received axioms and categories of our current discourse. If the ideas that have kept us in a perpetual state of underdevelopment are to be assailed and subverted, we must look in a different direction for philosophical inspiration. In place of Plato, Aristotle, F. R. Leavis, I. A. Richards, Northrop Frye, Gerald Moore, Izevbaye etc., the conceptual inspiration of this volume is derived from Marx, Engels, Plekhanov, Mao, Trotsky, Eagleton, Fanon, Onoge, Ngugi, Cabral and kindred spirits.

The positing of an alternative theoretical framework also implies a quest for a new idiom of critical discourse, a meta-language. In this respect, I have tried here to eschew the bald orthodoxy and nauseating lack of lexical creativity that has come to constitute the benchmark of much of the plangent barbarism that passes in the name of leftist discourse in the Third World.

The challenge of the contemporary African situation is that of confronting reality at the level of praxis informed by relevant and systematic theory. All else is conjecture.

I have since learnt that writing a book is necessarily a collaborative effort. My indebtedness to various authors and thinkers, living and dead, is registered throughout the length of this work. I am particularly grateful to Biodun Jeyifo of the Department of Literature in English, University of Ife, who taught me the rudiments of the radical approach to literary study and whose immense intellect has remained a great source of inspiration. Special thanks to my friends: G. G. Darah, Eme Ekekwe, Ikenna Nzimiro, Princewill Alozie, Godwin Nwabueze, Al-Amin Mazrui and Charles Nnolim whose vigorous debates on the issues raised in this book helped to clarify some of my conceptions. My students, both at the University of Ife and the University of Port Harcourt, have provided invaluable encouragement through their endless questions and often incisive discussions on the relationship between African literature and the realities of imperialism and neo-colonialism.

Lastly, and by no means the least, I thank James D. Williams for having the courage to unravel the "mysteries" of one of the world's worst handwritings and producing this manuscript in the process.

Finally, what I have appended here is not just a catalogue of debts and gratitudes but a testament of fellowship, love and abiding solidarity. I know that in the process of working on this project, I have once again stretched the patience of my family and the charity of friends. I can only hope that this book can compensate for these denials and negligences. Let me carry the burden of whatever "errors of rendering" that it may contain.

Chidi Amuta
Port Harcourt

Introduction

The Dialectical Imperative in African Literature

A fundamental crisis of consciousness and confidence defines the present condition of scholarship in African literature. This crisis, we must quickly add, is mostly qualitative rather than quantitative, for there is now an undeniably formidable mass of postulations, commentaries, reviews and valuations ostensibly devoted to a greater understanding of African literature. On closer examination, however, this copious output runs in inverse qualitative relationship to the demographic increase of African and "Africanist" literary scholars and their entrenchment at the helm of establishments in universities and cultural centres all over the world where Africa happens to form the subject of academic inquiry.

The extent of the crisis in question is so far-reaching that of late, key members of the bourgeois literary academy have had not only to express concern about the health of their profession but have even begun to doubt the very justification for an apparently irrelevant undertaking like literary criticism in the contemporary African context. Albert Gerard recently summarized these concerns when he lamented:

> Many of us are dismayed at the endless accumulating trite essays about Negritude and colonial atrocities, about the culture clash between tradition and innovation, and about endogenous corruption in what is bizarrely called post-independence Africa (meaning postcolonial). We are also aware that sympathy with Africa in the golden sixties, combined with unprecedented prosperity in the Western world, enabled a disquieting number of nonentities to obtain academic appointments on the basis of slender achievements.[1]

This acknowledgement of incoherence and superficiality has deepened into a distress call informed by a nagging doubt about the very relevance of literary criticism as it is practised in the African context. Hear Abiola Irele:

> We . . . have a situation in which literature is taught and commented upon in our universities purely as a professional engagement, as part of an industry that functions as an end in itself.[2]

These anguished cries, it needs to be emphasized, are the logical consequences of a critical tradition based on false premises and limited objectives. They sound the obituary of the accepted bourgeois tradition while inaugurating the challenge for a more rigorous materialist understanding of the relationship between African societies and their literary products.

The roots of the present crisis and disillusionment are not difficult to locate. The criticism of African literature as we have come to know it has been bedevilled by such ailments as (a) a false idealist, static and undialectical conception of African society, (b) a faulty notion of the essence and nature of literature, (c) a near absence of clear theoretical moorings and (d) a preponderance of subjective (often intuitive) exegeses of isolated texts.

In the bulk of discourse on African literature and culture, Africa is still conceived of as an undifferentiated socio-cultural continuum which has remained more or less oblivious to the passage of time. Mostly a feature of the now fossilized anthropological scholarship of the sort associated with Janheinz Jahn, Ulli Beier and others, the pet clichés in the intellectual armoury of this school include such expressions as "African culture", "African personality", "African society" and the like. In this totalizing fixation with Africa as a vast homeland of the exotic, the linguistic, ethnic and class heterogeneity of Africa is conveniently forgotten. Accordingly, the time referent of this school is usually some primordial stage of unspoilt innocence, what I have referred to elsewhere as "the era of raffia, calabash and masquerade culture".[3] In an attempt to substantiate their viewpoint with literary evidence, critics and scholars in this formation as recent and supposedly sophisticated as Chinweizu et al. often garnish their commentaries with carefully selected quotations from oral and written sources that confirm their essentially primitive idyllic view of Africa.

Equally disquieting is the notion of literature that informs bourgeois criticism of African literature in general. The redundant debate that raged at conferences and seminars in the early 1960s over an accurate definition of African literature testifies to the incoherence and idealism in question. The emphasis was to identify the "African writer". It is also instructive to note that the quest for a definition was confined to written literature. This was understandable given the class configuration and aesthetic socialization of those engaged in the quest. They were mainly university-based teachers and writers employed as salariats in the various arms of the neo-colonial governmental structures. The much more fundamental question of what constitutes literature in the first place was never raised, since Victorian Europe had, through colonialist education, handed down a fixed script-based notion of literature. It is my contention that the initial controversy over the identity of African literature and the African writer was a logical off-shoot of the doubts sponsored by colonialist supremacist ideology about the very humanity of the African. This unnecessary controversy was the beginning of a whole series of diversions.

If there was then no consensus on the definition of African literature and the precise identity and stature of the African writer, there was, however, no doubt in the minds of both the African élite and their Western counterparts as to who an African was. To the Western mind, the African was and has remained a product of "the heart of darkness", an incarnation of several racially-defined pathological limitations. To the Western-educated African, on the other hand, the African just happens to be the darkest species of *homo sapiens*, the victim of centuries of denigration and exploitation. The Western stance produced what Achebe has aptly termed "colonialist criticism", a critical fashion whose standards of evaluation are furnished by a racial criterion.[4] On the part of African critics, the natural response to colonialist criticism has been a whole tradition of defensive intellection characterized by fevered defences of both African literature and the racial identity of its producers. This conflict of interests led to the birth of a certain belligerent criticism with an artificial conflict between African and Western critics of African literature, each laying claims to a monopoly of intelligent hermeneutics. The crux of the controversy, which filled the pages of *African Literature Today*, no. 7, had to do with whether a European critic could produce a fair and valid evaluation of African literature. The quarrel gravitated around the vague question of whether to use "Western" or "African" aesthetic criteria. There are of course no such criteria, for aesthetic values and criteria are the products and instruments of specific groups and classes in specific societies. It is a fairly familiar fact that there is a definite socio-historical axis to critical values. Disagreements over the relative value of works in a given body of literature often emanate from larger disagreements well outside the province of literature and criticism. The quarrel was, therefore, essentially an intra-class one, between bourgeois Western scholars and their African counterparts, over whose false consciousness should gain the upper hand. It needs to be underscored that this controversy had nothing to do with any honest attempt to increase our knowledge of African literature.

As in most conflicts among the bourgeoisie, African critics and their Western counterparts settled for compromise. The compromise took the form of liberal relativism. The relativist position emphasizes, among other things, that literature is *literature* (human, universal), that there is either good or bad criticism, that political and racial considerations have only tangential, if any, import for the sacrosanct realm of literary criticism and that all evaluations of works from a given body of literature are all *good* for as long as they are based on logical and intelligent perception. Bernth Lindfors, the prolific American critic of African literature, is the prime pontiff of this position:

> Literary criticism is a fickle and uncertain area in which no one has the final word. There are never any right or wrong answers as in elementary mathematics or physics; there are only good and bad arguments based on different interpretations of the same data.[5]

This liberal recourse to absolute relativism opened the floodgates for yet a further aberration in the criticism of African literature. This was the birth of what could conveniently be termed "intuitive" criticism, a mode of criticism that relies almost exclusively on the subjective intuitions of the critic as the source of judgemental values. This lazy school of criticism naturally lent itself to the complacencies of a fledgling promotion-hungry intellectual culture. It is relatively easy to pick on individual texts in African literature and appreciate them as isolated systems of signification with assorted meanings depending on the emotional disposition, aesthetic socialization, world view or interest of the individual critic. Your reading of *Things Fall Apart* would be no less credible and *good* if you are a heathen, white racist, catholic, agnostic, atheist or just a plain imperialist intellectual opportunist for as long as you meet the requirements of disinterested objectivity and sound argument! In this tradition also, the individual texts are treated as isolated phenomena, pearls secreted by equally astral but "gifted" individuals inhabiting the celestial world of the creative imagination. The curriculum vitae of an average professor of African literature is likely to be replete with fragments of literal and reductionist readings of texts by varied authors in no particular relationship, essays not held together by any discernible theoretical framework and executed in singularly inelegant prose. These series of amputated reviews and empirical claptrap, mainly sponsored by European- and American-based journals like *African Literature Today* and *Research in African Literatures*, constitute the bulk of what has come to be promoted by imperialist media and publishing houses as the mainstream of African literary scholarship. This mass of pedestrian effusions does have a certain *value* nonetheless. It has become a ready commodity in the hands of profit-hungry publishing houses intent on satiating the rabid appetite of vast armies of certificate-conscious students in African and European universities and colleges. For this writer, the disquieting anticlimax of every lecture on African literature has always been the students' stock question: any commentaries? It is the accumulation of these trite reviews that has built up the impression that literary criticism in the African context is not a serious, socially relevant undertaking.

Against the background of the foregoing limitations and inadequacies, a cardinal preoccupation of this book is to place in historical and ideological perspective some of the major statements and positions in the criticism of African literature to date. In pursuit of this necessary preliminary operation, one cannot but run into unavoidable collisions here and there with the interests, values and careers whose ideas constitute the pillars of Africanist bourgeois scholarship. No apologies need to be offered in this respect, for one of the requirements of radical dialectical criticism is a preparedness to "wrestle" with other intellectual formations through what Fredric Jameson calls "ideological analysis". If the reader of this book approaches this aspect of it with a negative attitude, he is more likely to condemn it as yet another exercise in the now fashionable demolition of acknowledged reputations. On the contrary, by placing the various "renowned" critics and their works in proper ideological perspective, one is clearly acknowledging the vital contributions that have been made to the understanding of African literature by scholars as varied as Gerald Moore, Abiola Irele, Dan Izevbaye, Isidore Okpewho, Chinweizu, Arthur Gakwandi, Lewis Nkosi and others. It needs to be additionally emphasized that much as the works of some of these scholars form the targets of the polemical assault of the first part of this book, we are implicitly paying tribute to the value of these works in crystallizing the contradictions that define the contemporary African condition at the level of intellectual labour. The intellectual products of society are no less valuable in exposing the essential contradictions of life in that society than other areas of experience.

A common denominator of African literary scholarship, as we indicated earlier, is a disturbing theoretical anaemia. It is true that the metacritical intelligence can group the critical practices of leading scholars of African literature in terms of their ideological affinity (see Chapter One) on the basis of the values and world views they express and represent, but it is difficult to see them as products of definable schools of critical thought informed by any consistent theoretical foci. Only perhaps our emergent Marxist criticism begins to approximate this requirement despite the serious limitations in its present manifestations.

Literary study as one of the disciplines devoted to the specialized understanding of the different aspects of human society needs a rigorous theoretical thrust if it is to be taken as seriously as the other disciplines from which it differs only in terms of the ontological peculiarity of its object of study. This recognition has since dawned on the Western and Eastern cultural academies: hence the plethora of theories – Freudian psychoanalysis, phenomenology, semiotics, structuralism, new criticism, formalism – that assail us from all directions. Characteristically, our cultural intelligentsia have endlessly appropriated these theoretical tools and applied them, often indiscriminately, to aspects of African literary culture. As ready-made conceptual tools with infinite practical applications, these theories are not fundamentally different from other finished products of the advanced industrial societies – yam pounders, brewing machines, automobiles, armoured tanks etc. – with which Africa is being discouraged from original development. True to type, the underbelly of each of these items always has a bold inscription: CAUTION! The same applies to the various critical theories.

The wilful suspending of the instinct for rigorous theorizing is the most conspicuous mark of underdevelopment in the field of African cultural scholarship in general and literary criticism in particular. In making this observation, one is mindful of the attempts by some scholars to adapt literary theories, especially from the bourgeois Western repertoire, for speculating on and exegetizing African literature. While acknowledging the truism that ideas are universal tools in the service of humanity, human societies have an inherent specificity which necessitates that ideas for their understanding and engineering be made relevant to their immediate needs at specific moments. As a vital component of the critical enterprise, the interpretations of the literary products of a given society can only command validity if they are rooted in theoretical paradigms that either organically derive from or are most directly relevant to the objective conditions of life in the society in question. Such a theoretical paradigm must, in addition, derive its relevance from its commitment to the freedom of members of the society, for freedom is the precondition for art which critical theory only intervenes to ratify and corroborate.

Thus, formulations and interpretations of African literature predicated on such abstractions as structuralism/semiology, Freudian psycho-analysis, American new criticism and other mystifications cannot but remain tangential and irrelevant to a proper understanding of it. The reification of thought in advanced capitalism which these tendencies represent does not begin to relate to Africa's largely peasant economies. This is why I am afraid that a brilliant scholar like Nigeria's Sunday Anozie may well be squandering his otherwise formidable intellectual armoury in appending footnotes to the copious esoteric scriptures of Roland Barthes et al.[6]

It is the intellectual limitation of and the ultimate pedagogical dangers posed by the foregoing trends that provided the initial impetus for this book. More immediately, it was the appearance of two other volumes which, ostensibly, set out to put paid to the theoretical indeterminacy and cultural alienation in African literary scholarship that quickened this impetus. I am referring specifically to Chinweizu et al.'s *Toward the Decolonization of African Literature* and Wole Soyinka's *Myth, Literature and the African World*. Although addressed to different aspects of the same problem in prose styles of differing turgidity, both works are united by a common ideational and politico–intellectual compulsion: the need to "shake off the yoke of Eurocentricity which history has pressed upon the shoulders of Africa". The upshot of these authors' articulation of the problem is the emergence of a certain decolonization rhetoric, the outlines of which are given fuller treatment in Chapter Two of this book.

A common feature of this position is a certain elevation of cultural decolonization to the realm of an exclusively superstructural proposition. In our view, genuine decolonization does not simply mean a regression to the poetic norms and metaphysical cosmology of simple African peasant communities nor does it mean the symbolic re-naming of streets in Africa's urban centres after contemporary heroes and "illustrious ancestors"; it does not even reduce itself to the exclusive use of African languages as the media of communication in African politics and letters: all these are implicated in the mental decolonization process which in itself represents the external psycho-social manifestation of a deeper, more titanic struggle – the anti-imperialist struggle. A correct reading of this book, therefore, must be anchored on its informing insistence that much as decolonizing the African mind is a challenge requiring urgent intervention, that challenge cannot be sequestered from the more crucial task of disengaging the social and economic structures that inform African culture from the deadly tentacles of those economic and cultural value systems that sponsored the colonization process in the first place. The thesis around which this book is woven is, therefore, this: *African literature and its criticism testify to the historical contradictions that define the African situation. In order to resolve these contradictions in the direction of progressive change, literary criticism must be predicated on a theoretical outlook that couples cultural theory back to social practice. In this respect, literary theory and practice must form part of the anti-imperialist struggle, thus demystifying literary criticism and reintegrating it into the social experience and practice of which literature itself is very much part.*

The anti-imperialist struggle is not a simple unidirectional process. It is a complex set of struggles on different fronts with a common objective. It is at once a struggle against psychological timidity foisted by centuries of dehumanizing denigration, against the entrenchment of colonialist economic structures as roadblocks to genuine development, against the tyranny and endless buffoonery of an insensitive ruling class presiding over societies riven by class inequalities, against the hegemony of irrelevant alien ideas, and against the growing sophistication of the ideological tentacles of global imperialism. Literary theory and criticism in Africa cannot feign indifference to these concerns. As I write this introduction, black youth and nationalists in South Africa are engaged in the critical stage of their titanic struggle against one of the world's most diabolical systems – apartheid; as I write this also, nearly a dozen African countries are at the brink of economic collapse as a result of "debts" ostensibly owed to the IMF and Western banks; at this moment also, the decimation of thousands of drought-stricken Ethiopians by hunger is being converted into an object of showmanship and diplomatic doublespeak; as I write this also the United States government is busy sending military assistance to terrorist squads in Angola and Mozambique to shoot down governments freely chosen by the people ostensibly in a bid to contain "the spread of communism and communist ideas". Terry Eagleton places these concerns in a more frightening global perspective when he writes:

> It is estimated that the world contains over 60,000 nuclear warheads, many with capacity a thousand times greater than the bomb which destroyed Hiroshima. The possibility that these weapons will be used in our life-time is steadily growing. The approximate cost of these weapons is 500 billion dollars a year, or 1.3 billion dollars a day. Five per cent of this sum – 25 billion dollars – could drastically, fundamentally alleviate the problems of the poverty-stricken Third World. Anyone who believed that literary theory was more important than such matters could no doubt be considered eccentric, but perhaps only a little less eccentric than those who consider that the two topics might be somehow related.[7]

The African equivalent of this sense of outrage is expressed in what I have elsewhere characterized as the anti-imperialist consciousness.

The translation of this consciousness into a theoretical potential in the field of literature calls for a holistic paradigm. Such a paradigm is, in our view, furnished by a dialectical theory of literature. Such a theory must pay attention to the complex relationship between literature and the equally complex set of relationships in its informing society. It must also study the various components of the literary event as approximations to what I choose to refer to as the "dissonant harmony" of social experience which is the ultimate source of literary form. Thus, *context*, *content* and *form*, the main cardinal dialectical co-ordinates of literature, are seen as functions of variable relationships. The perception of this flow of interaction requires a cast of mind that is in itself dialectical in the terms in which Yu Kharin conceives of it:

> Only from a dialectical position can one comprehend the objective world and the universal laws for its development. These fundamental laws include the laws of the unity and struggle of opposites, the law of the transition of quantitative changes into qualitative ones and back again and the laws of the negation of negation.[8]

For the dialectical intelligence, conflict and qualitative change are permanent features of reality. Accordingly, literature is a product of people in society and a producer and reproducer of the cognitions and values of society; in short a social institution, a superstructural manifestation of a fundamentally material process, the process of creation of ideas and values within limits prescribed by the social essence of language. Literature is, in addition, one (only one!) of the instruments for the sharpening and mobilization of social consciousness in pursuit or negation of qualitative change, an instrument for the preservation or subversion of the existing order.

The most urgent problem which a dialectical theory of African literature (or any literature, in fact) must face is one of an operational methodology: how to theorize and how to use the fruits of theory as hermeneutical tools for exegetizing individual texts or literary events. The multi-dimensionality of the "tasks" (Nkosi) which constitute the themes of African literature and which inhere in the very sociality of literature itself compels an interdisciplinary social-science-related approach. No comprehensive knowledge of African literature is to be gained from an astral notion of literature which insists on seeing it as a self-justifying undertaking. Anthropology, history, sociology, psychology, political economy etc. are all actively implicated in the essence of African literature. In effect, a dialectical theory of African literature, because of the historical predication of that literature, must eschew the redundant traditional divisions between the disciplines in the social sciences on one hand and those in the humanities on the other. Warns Cliff Slaughter on the need for an integrated approach in any historical–materialist-based theory of culture:

Historical materialism does not substitute itself for the detailed work of investigators in specialized fields, but it does reject those ahistorical divisions between the different social sciences and between social sciences and humanities which obstruct a critical material analysis of society and culture.[9]

Even if such liberal accommodation is made, we are still faced with the practical problem of harmonizing knowledge gained from these "service" disciplines into a coherent and consistent methodology suited to the demands of literary study as a field of study made distinct and peculiar by the *fictive essence* of literature itself.

Because the starting point of a dialectical theory of literature is the recognition of the very sociality of literature, its approach is necessarily sociological. Here a note of caution is called for, for there are now several kinds of sociology inquiry. We must guard against that notion of sociology which views the group essence of social life in terms of normatively constituted categories and abstractions specifically evolved to suit the cultic professional requirements of liberal value-free scholarship. Raymond Williams warns against the negative implication of this kind of *sociology* for literary study:

> To have a sociology concerned only with abstract groups, and a literary criticism concerned only with separated individuals and works, is more than a division of labour; it is a way of avoiding the reality of the interpenetration, in a final sense the unity, of the most individual and the most social forms of actual life.[10]

Beyond adopting the sociality of literature as a point of departure, a rigorous sociology of literature perceives the context of literature, its *content* and *form* as dialectically interconnected areas for comprehending the social essence of literature. The experiences which constitute the content of a work of literature are mediations of processes in the macro-society which we refer to as *context* in this book. Form as the vehicle through which we encounter these processes is an organic extension of the mediated experience. Therefore, the notion among bourgeois critics that sociological criticism (especially in its radical manifestation) eschews formal considerations is false. On the other hand, the very categories with which the sociological critic discusses the form of literature (character, diction, setting etc.) may not differ from those used by traditional bourgeois criticism. But in the view of the sociological critic these categories are in themselves active, historically produced and determined semantic tools for understanding active, humanized processes, not lifeless labels for dissecting laboratory specimens! Thus conceived, a dialectical sociological theory of literature is at once a method as well as an aesthetic.

Given the anti-imperialist imperative which we have already underscored as the challenge of the contemporary African intellectual scene, a dialectical sociology of African literature must of necessity be ideologically partisan. Marxism, to the extent that it begins from stressing the primacy of sociality as the basis of human existence and proceeds therefrom to proffer a scientific theory of society that rejects exploitation and inequality, offers a natural anchor for all theories of culture predicated on the desire for freedom. And Africa cannot be exempt from this historical necessity. Here again we come face to face with the cynicism of African bourgeois scholars.[11] The ready charge is that Marx and Engels are as alien to Africa as Max Weber and Northrop Frye. In the specific context of literary criticism, I have stated elsewhere that

> the crucial distinction between bourgeois criticism on the one hand and the radical alternative on the other is basically a philosophical one; it is predicated on the mode of perceiving reality. It is fundamentally an opposition between idealism and materialism. It is additionally a distinction between liberal idealism and dialectical materialism. The fact that Marx and Engels came to articulate and systematize dialectical materialism into a coherent socio-political philosophy is hardly central to the *relevance* of their "scientific" theories for the comprehension and transformation of human society anywhere in the world.[12]

More pointedly, the attraction of Marxist theory for radical African intellectuals resides in its opposition to imperialism which Lenin recognized as "the highest stage of capitalism". Accordingly, Marxist criticism represents for this writer not only the springboard for the anti-imperialist struggle in the area of literature and culture but also a theoretical weapon for a *total* understanding of literature in its essential social resonance. As Onogu has observed,

> Marxist criticism goes beyond a content and form analysis of artistic works, to a consideration of the very institutional processes of art creation and art criticism. Marxist critics are concerned to struggle for a democratization of the structures of artistic production and criticism.[13]

While using Marxism as a general underlying framework, I have tried to explore the pronouncements of writers like Fanon, Ngugi and Cabral for theoretical pillars towards a domestication of the classical axioms of Marxist cultural discourse to the historical particularities of the African and Third World situations.

The adoption of a Marxist framework in African literature creates several areas of challenge. These include questions about literature and the national question, literature and emergent class formations, literature and history, the stubborn continuity of oral forms in modern written literature. In pursuit of answers to these myriad questions, our modest effort falls into three broad divisions:

1) an attempt to explain the main ideological characteristics and motivations of the major critical statements on African literature to date,

2) a tentative outline of a dialectical theory through a materialist redefinition of the issues and problems in African literature,

3) the application of the dialectical paradigm in the interpretation of texts freely chosen from the three conventional forms of written literature.

I make no pretension here to be addressing a so-called "grassroots" audience, a pretension which has often been used to couch a basic inability to pursue cultural discourse in a rigorous manner. This book is addressed to an audience of essentially tertiary level scholars, students and informed readers in the belief that those on whom historical circumstances have conferred the responsibility of interpreting and leading in the struggle to change the African reality must be equipped with rigorous theoretical tools to neutralize their class alienation.

It is hoped that this volume will contribute to the task of raising alternative questions about African literature and culture in particular and the position of Africa in the world in general.

Notes

1. Albert Gerard, "Is Anything Wrong with African Literary Studies?", in Bernth Lindfors (ed.) *Research Priorities in African Literatures* (Munich/New York: Alans Zell, 1984), p. 20.
2. Abiola Irele, "Literary Criticism in the Nigerian Context", *The Guardian* (Lagos) 15 June 1985, p. 9.
3. Chidi Amuta, "Criticism, Ideology and Society: The Instance of Nigerian Literature", *Ufahamu*, vol. 12, no. 2, 1983, pp. 116–138.
4. Chinua Achebe, *Morning Yet on Creation Day* (London: Heinemann, 1975), pp. 3–18.
5. Bernth Lindfors, "The Blind Men and the Elephant", *African Literature Today*, no. 7, 1975, p. 54.
6. Sunday Anozie's obsession with structuralism and his insistence on reading structuralist models into African literature has come under attack from various African and Africanist scholars. See Abiola Irele, "Sunday Anozie, Structuralism and African Literature", *The Guardian* (Lagos) 8 March 1986, p. 13.
7. Terry Eagleton, *Literary Theory: An Introduction* (Oxford: Basil Blackwell, 1985) p. 194.
8. Yu A. Kharin, *Fundamentals of Dialectics*, trans. Konstantin Kostrov (Moscow: Progress, 1981) p. 119.
9. Cliff Slaughter, *Marxism, Ideology and Literature* (London/Basingstoke: Macmillan, 1980) p. 6.
10. Raymond Williams, *Problems in Materialism and Culture* (London: Verso, 1980) p. 29.
11. These charges constitute a regular feature of polemical encounters between radical African scholars and their more complacent bourgeois opposites.
12. Chidi Amuta, *Confrontations: Radical Perspectives on Nigerian Literature* (Oguta: Zim Pan-African, forthcoming) Preface.
13. Omafume Onoge, "Towards a Marxist Sociology of African Literature", *Ife Studies in African Literature and the Arts*, no. 2, 1984, p. 15.

1 Ideological Formations in the Criticism of African Literature

Literary and art criticism is one of the principal methods of struggle in the world of literature and art.   **Mao Tse-Tung**[1]

All criticism must include in its discourse . . . an implicit reflection on itself; every criticism is a criticism of the works *and* a criticism of itself. In other words, criticism is not a table of results or a body of judgements, it is essentially an activity, i.e., a series of intellectual acts profoundly committed to the historical and subjective existence . . . of the man who performs them.
Roland Barthes[2]

In the nearly three decades of its emergence and consolidation as a distinct academic undertaking, scholarship on African literature (especially in the form of criticism) has displayed astonishing self-neglect. Although quite copious in exegetical output, criticism has not looked sufficiently inwards in order to rediscover its real motivations, challenges and social relevance. This is not to suggest an absence of metacritical undertakings. But such effort as has been made by Abiola Irele, Dan Izevbaye, Albert Gerard and others has been articulated within an intellectual context that takes bourgeois criticism for granted as a specialized form of discourse whose practitioners must abide by certain rules. The socio-historical determination of criticism has not quite been at issue until very recently.

It was perhaps Wole Soyinka who, in his 1980 inaugural lecture at the University of Ife, forcefully challenged African literary critics to the fundamental task of concretely positioning their profession in a social and historical context. His articulation of the challenge was characteristically pungent:

Very little . . . has been attempted in studies of the critic as a socially situated producer, and therefore as a creature of social conditioning, a conditioning which in fact offers no certitudes about the nature of his commitment to the subject which engages him, his motivations, indeed, about the very nature of his social existence.[3]

This chapter sets out to explore this vital area, as a prologue to the rest of the volume. My specific task here is to identify, revise and criticize the discernible ideological standpoints that have come to characterize critical discourse on and evaluations of African literature to date for the following reasons: firstly, to highlight the dangers inherent in the growing and unrestrained constrictive professionalism and academicism in the criticism of African literature; secondly, to attempt an analytical exposition of the informing social theories behind the different ideological positions which different critics on the literature in question have assumed, with a view to indicating the direction of critical consciousness; and thirdly, to underline the place and role(s) of the critical intelligence in our contemporary socio-political discourse and praxis. These objectives are however pursued in the context of a clear theoretical conception of the nature and overall epistemological status of criticism in general and literary criticism in particular.

Criticism, Ideology and Society: A Dialectical Overview

Criticism as a product and process of active interrogation of human sociality and its cultural manifestations is of an ancient lineage. Its *raison d'être* would appear to be the human awareness of sociality and the imperfections which are inherent in the various relationships into which people must enter with one another. In its most fundamental expression, criticism as a social practice circumscribed by the existence of language is hardly detachable from the rest of social discourse. It is integral to discussions about the prospects of rain in the next planting season, about the best blacksmith in the hamlet, the need to separate church and state, the status of best-sellers, the anti-nuclear movement as well as whether or not Third World countries should continue to spend the greater parts of their gross national product on servicing doubtful debts or about whether Achebe or Soyinka will ever get the Nobel prize in literature! Because criticism is indubitably integral to the social evolution process, its fates and fortunes trace nearly the same trajectory as social history. The issues that form the object of criticism, its forms and functions as well as its specific ideological predilections are contingent upon the current preoccupations of society itself. In other words, the series of critical acts in a society across time are in themselves structurally analysable along a diachronic paradigm. Thus, criticism does have a history; specific fashions and trends in social and cultural criticism come into being, become dominant and fade away as a result of specific and determinate historically identifiable causes. This is the *socio-historical axis* of criticism as a constitutive social practice.

Even as a specialization, literary criticism thus derives from an instinct that predates the existence of the literary text or the literary event. As Eagleton rightly observes,

> criticism has a history, which is more than a random collocation of critical acts. If literature is its object, it is not its sole point of genesis; criticism does not arise

as a spontaneous riposte to the existential fact of the text, organically coupled with the object it illuminates.[4]

The crucial "point of genesis" and ultimate conditioning factor of literary criticism is to be sought in the very class heritage of society itself. The class position of the critic, his self-perception in and mode of insertion into the prevailing class formations of his society influence and even determine the ideological colouring of his critical products. In this context, we conceive of ideology simply as "a relatively formal and articulated system of meanings, values, and beliefs, of a kind that can be abstracted as a 'worldview' or a class outlook".[5] Consequently, if we examine the range of critical reflections on the literature and art of a society across time or even in a specific epoch, it becomes possible to make discriminations among them in terms of ideological leanings. Precisely, as members of the cultural academy preoccupied with literature, we are critics, just as architects, engineers, or doctors are professionals, each practising a specialized calling from a definite ideological position and attitude to society. What distinguishes the calling of the literary critic is the very nature of the subject – literature – a truthful illusion.

It is, therefore, possible and, in fact, imperative that the notations "liberal", "conservative", "radical", "leftist" and so on, should also be applied to positions which critics and their products assume. This is the *class-ideological axis of criticism*.

In the global history of ideas, an understanding of the dialectical interrelationship between the two axes of criticism (the *socio-historical* and the *class-ideological*) is crucial to a comprehension of the role of criticism in the cultural front of the larger struggles that define social existence in different societies and in different epochs. A random sample of specific critical traditions in world culture would corroborate this observation.

In most traditional or pre-colonial African societies in which the production and consumption of literature were part and parcel of communal self-assertion and self-projection, the critic was hardly distinguishable in the arena from the rest of the audience or the performer. In fact, the three functions could be (and were often) played out simultaneously by one and the same person. An example that I can readily call to mind is the very dramatic annual Ekpe festival dance in Ngwaland which features masquerade displays, choral processions and widespread audience participation in the form of dancing and chanting.[6] At the height of this euphoric display of communal self-fulfilment at the bounty of harvest, it is usual for an individual dancer to step aside, admire a fellow dancer of outstanding ability and join others in carrying the distinguished performer shoulder-high amidst hilarious applause and approving comments. Days and weeks after the festival, domestic and public gossip in farms and other places of gathering are enlivened by critical reflections on outstanding or unsatisfactory performance at the recent festival. Performers derive their fame and acclaim from a cross-section of such informal evaluations. This is criticism at its most organic and instinctive profundity, for here it derives from and is part of the ritual of communal living. Solomon Iyasere makes a similar observation in respect of oral performance culture among the Edos of Nigeria and generalizes as follows:

> The role of the critic in the African oral tradition was a complex one. He was not a literary technician in search of ossified precision and foreign patterns and designs, but a spontaneous entertainer, a historian and a wordmaster – in short an artist. Criticism was not divorced from the creative process but an essential part of and adjunct to it. Creativity and criticism enjoyed a symbolic relationship. Critical evaluation and the composition of a work of art were regarded as facets of the same process and, in most cases, aspects of the same moment.[7]

Similarly, the wave of anti-feudalist and anti-establishment strikes, student unrest and general armed struggle associated with the revolution in China earlier in the 20th Century culminated in, among other things, the 1919 Cultural Revolution. The basic tenets of this revolution questioned accepted literary traditions, fashions and aesthetic values. Most young writers were agreed that "literature must stop being esoteric and start serving the whole society".[8] The attendant literature eschewed the traditional penchant for idolizing the philosopher-king and celebrating events around the court. Instead, the new literature dwelt on the experiences of commoners within the emergent revolutionary society with its heavy emphasis on egalitarianism, communalism and a certain romantic simplicity. Examples of this trend can be found in such works as Lao Xiang's story "A Village Lad Drops Out of School" and Jiang Chi's "On the Yalu River". The thinking behind this radical development in Chinese literary consciousness was articulated into a coherent artistic manifesto in Mao Tse Tung's "Talks at the Yenan Forum on Literature and the Arts".[9] The theoretical positions and critical canons articulated in this document acquire meaning and significance mainly within a framework that defined for literature a pragmatic functionalism in China's revolutionary struggle against her imperialist aggressors, especially the Japanese.

In pre-Athenian and Athenian Greece a critical response to the Homeric epics and the great tragedies was a heightened and integral aspect of audience participation in the literary event. Professor Bowra writes:

> Much of their art was popular in the sense that it was performed before large crowds in the open air. But even so they never made the mistake of judging the intelligence of an audience by that of its lowest members. Poetry, being a serious affair, demanded attention and concentration, and the Greek audience responded to the claims on them, becoming good listeners and intelligent critics.[10]

Consequently, even Plato's poetics and metaphysics of static universals spared a thought for literary art in relation to society. Compelled by the need to safeguard the moral health of his imaginary polis from the possible corrupting influence of the poet as an artificer of illusions, Plato jettisoned the poet from his ideal republic and thereby inadvertently inaugurated the form and content dichotomy in Western critical discourse and aesthetic epistemology.

Accordingly, the reality of medieval Western society was the primacy of the Christian God in the order of things. This state of affairs was dramatized by the supremacy of the Catholic church in Rome and the prevalent conception of humankind exclusively as candidates for salvation whose life on earth had to be spent in pious and miserable self-immolation. Scholasticism, the dominant intellectual tradition of the period, although it had little time for sustained and orchestrated poetic enunciations, produced in St. Augustine and St. Thomas Aquinas the outlines of a poetics that emphasized the subliminal immanence of the divine in all natural objects and therefore in all imitations of nature. At best, scholastic aesthetics were essentially formalistic and emphasized Christian morality. Further on in the history of the Western world, the romantic period was characterized by a sense of revolt against the ossifying rationalism of the preceding neo-classical intellectual tradition and the unsettling ecological and moral repercussions of the nascent Industrial Revolution. The response of literature to this pressure took the form of a revolutionary celebration of the natural, the rural, the youthful and innocent so characteristic of the poetry of Blake ("Songs of Innocence"), Coleridge and Wordsworth as opposed to the rigid argumentative poetry of Dryden, Pope and Samuel Johnson before them. Critical response to this poetry was polarized between the extreme aestheticism of the "art-for-art" school of Shaftesbury, Hutcheson, Diderot, Sulzer etc., on one hand and the emphasis on the realistic and the didactic of the post-Hegelians, Compte, Proudhon and Shelley, on the other.

In all the foregoing instances, we find that criticism and critical theory are ways of dialoguing both with the specific literary works as well as the issues that define the state of consciousness in the ambient social world. It is against this general theoretical background that we now proceed to examine the forms which critical attention on African literature has assumed over the years.

The Class Position of the Critic

As a further prelude to the identification of the major manifestations of bourgeois criticism of African literature, it is necessary to situate concretely the critics of African literature – especially the Africans among them – in a socio-economic and political context. The literary critic is a member of the cultural arm of the neo-colonial intelligentsia which in itself is a product of colonial education. The critic is to be located mainly in the universities and earns a living as a salariat in the neo-colonial economy. In common with counterparts in most of the other disciplines, s/he belongs to something of a *parasitic* elite. This is not just in the sense that the critical "products" have had tangential practical relevance to the material circumstances of the majority of Africans but in the sense that the critic is like a tick on the body of the cattle of literary creativity. If this is an indictment, it has more to do with the *manner* in which critics have practised their calling as well as the overall *Weltanschauung* that has largely informed their perceptions.

In terms of class affiliation, the African critic is a member of the intellectual arm of the neo-colonial bourgeoisie. Although he may not own property or employ labour, the relatively easy access to power and privilege which his Western higher education confers on him would tempt us to place him in the group that Claude Ake loosely refers to as "exploiters by class position".[11] As an intellectual, he falls under what Gramsci categorizes as "traditional" intellectuals.[12] But as a member of the neo-colonial bourgeoisie, he is only a nominal, even marginalized member of the petty bourgeois class.

In more specific terms, we can now identify two dominant formations (ideologically, that is) in the emergent tradition of African literary criticism. Here Nkrumah's categorization of the intellectual elite in neo-colonial Africa is of particular relevance. The first formation of critics whom we refer to as "bourgeois critics" throughout this book would tend to correspond to those whom Nkrumah says provide intellectual and ideological legitimation for "the privileged indigenous class".[13] At his most liberal, the bourgeois critic is the cultural equivalent of the advocates of "mixed economy" for African countries, displaying an unquestioning acquiescence to the values of bourgeois society. The danger posed by this type of critic arises from the fact that owing to a certain lack of proper political education and commitment, they may in fact be unaware of whose values they are promoting or espousing. Often disoriented by Euro-American higher education, mystified by the captivating myths of Greco-Roman civilization and drunk with the canons of biblical morality, bourgeois critics end up seeing themselves as humanists in the universal idealist sense.

In the context of their immediate national society, they come to see themselves solely as university teachers, scholars whose business is with the education of genteel "taste" and the cultivation of "civilized" values through the subjective interpretation of literature as an illusion. They are likely to be found arguing, quite trenchantly, for a separation of politics from the noble calling of humane letters. As we shall see later, however, this position runs counter to and detracts from the historical predication of modern African literature and the avowed socio-political commitment of nearly every African writer of note.

The Euro-American variants of the bourgeois critic of African literature are to be located in more or less the same socio-economic structures. They are either university-based intellectuals operating from the numerous

African studies institutes in Europe and America or just plain schizoid "fugitives" fleeing from the economic and emotional aridity of cultures haunted by the evil repercussions of capitalism. They are either permanently resident in Africa or frequently visit conveniently chosen and designated "centres" of African literary and cultural activity. Their main sources of funding range from "generous" fellowships – Rockefeller, Ford, Rhodes, Smuts, Fulbright etc. – to incomes from outright employment in African universities under the annual exchange programmes or some other mutually convenient arrangement. The important point to note about these critics is that in addition to being purveyors and major conduits for the export of bourgeois critical ideology, they carry with them cultural values that are products of centuries of an unequal relationship between Europe and Africa. These values, often rooted in European supremacist mythology, have combined with the key axioms of bourgeois ideology to condition their major pronouncements on African literature.

The alternative to the bourgeois tradition of criticism in African literature is to be located in a radical, revolutionary consciousness among a minority of African and Africanist intellectuals. Critics in this formation fall within the group of what Nkrumah calls "revolutionary intellectuals",

> those who provide the impetus and leadership of the worker–peasant struggle for all-out socialism. It is from among this section that the genuine intellectuals of the African Revolution are to be found.[14]

Therefore, the distinction between bourgeois critics of African literature and their radical, anti-imperialist counterparts is one of world view and ideological orientation; it is not that of means of livelihood, for all African literary critics, as members of the neo-colonial intelligentsia, subsist mainly on public patronage through grants, subventions and salaries channelled through universities, research institutes and other cultural affairs outfits. To the extent that bourgeois criticism of African literature is informed by the main constituents of liberal ideology – individualism, subjectivism, relativism – the critical products of its practitioners will, on the surface, appear divergent and multifarious without, however, undermining the fundamental commonality of their ideological origin.

It is against the background of this broad conceptual framework that we can begin to grasp the various sub-formations and concrete manifestations of bourgeois criticism of African literature to date.

Aspects of Bourgeois Criticism

Colonialist Criticism

Aptly designated by Chinua Achebe, colonialist criticism is the elaboration of the cardinal axiom of colonialist ideology into a tradition of criticism with specific application to the emergent literature of the erstwhile colonized – in this case, Africans. A supremacist arrogance predicated on racial prejudice is the informing impulse of this brand of criticism which Achebe characterizes as

> a certain specious criticism which flourishes in African literature today and which derives from the same basic attitude and assumption as colonialism itself . . . This attitude and assumption was crystallized in Albert Schweitzer's immortal dictum in the heyday of colonialism: *The African is indeed my brother, but my junior brother.*[15]

The practitioners of this critical fashion, which still persists up to the present day, are to be located among both Euro–Americans and their African protégés. Among the former, critical comments on and evaluations of African literary works are characterized by a certain patronizing condescension. At best, they view works of African literature from a certain evolutionary perspective with the underlying notion that the African literary genius is evolving towards a state of completion and perfection whose ultimate point of reference is "the great tradition" of some Western European literary culture. In the context of this evolutionary paradigm also, literary creative genius, which is a startling signal that the African is human after all, is grudgingly recognized to the extent that it must have been catalysed by the "benefits" of the so-called European civilizing mission in Africa. Thus, the endless quest for European influences on African writers is one of the ruses in the trick bag of members of this formation. At times, this quest for influences degenerates to the level of guessing and fictionalizing as we notice when Charles Larson sees the influence of James Joyce in Armah's *Fragments*.[16] These Europeans usually pretend to a certain keen interest in Africa and Africans which might astonish even Africans.

The African disciples of this mode of criticism operate from the same basic assumptions. The sources of the brain damage are easy to locate: colonialist education, lavish consumption of European literature, a quisling acquiescence to the fiction of European supremacy and an attendant self-hate which compels the critic to gaze perpetually westwards for signals of approval that his critical statements conform to the canons of a discourse consecrated by Western bourgeois academicians. When, therefore, a prolific African critic like Eustace Palmer examines the origins of the African novel, he loses sight of the historical conditioning and specificity of literary forms and apologetically confesses:

> The African novel grew out of the Western novel, and writers like Achebe, Laye and Ekwensi were much more influenced by Conrad, Hardy, Dickens, Kafka and George Eliot than by the African oral tale.[17]

Where colonialist criticism unconditionally acknowledges the artistic profundity of an African literary work, it is quick to confer on such a work a certain stamp of universalism. But in the discourse of devotees of this tradition, the word *universal* is innocuously synonymous with the bourgeois West. As Achebe rightly observes, the term universal is used as "a synonym for the narrow, self-serving parochialism of Europe".[18]

A variant of this universalizing scheme is an outright appropriation of literary works in the emergent corpus of the national literatures of different African countries into the mainstream of the literary tradition of one European country or the other. The criterion for such appropriation is the metropolitan language in which, for historical reasons, such a body of literature happens to be expressed. Thus, it becomes convenient for Bruce King to group the literatures of African countries of English expression as "new English literatures" or aspects of the literature of England in diaspora![19]

In terms of political sensitivity, colonialist criticism is undisguisedly hostile to African literature that displays a definite commitment to a political redefinition of the position of the African in the world, especially in relation to the West. Armed with the convenient liberal insistence on the need to sanitize literature of political and social concerns, the more daring pontiffs of colonialist criticism maintain that socio-political commitment is a mark of immaturity in African literature.[20] This position, however, has nothing to do with an honest fidelity to value-free scholarship, for where an African literary work has attacked European values with venom, such critics have retorted in a manner that leaves no one in doubt as to whose political values and interests inform (and of course whose money finances) their critical production. For instance, the same critics who had praised Ayi Kwei Armah for his scatological depiction of the moral depravity of contemporary Ghanaian and African polity in *The Beautyful Ones* and *Fragments* did not hide their discomfort when the same writer, with equal artistic deftness, in *Two Thousand Seasons* and *The Healers*, turned the searchlight mainly on the centuries of European brigandage in Africa. Understandably, therefore, Bernth Lindfors dismisses *Two Thousand Seasons* as a dangerous book to put in the hands of young Africans and evaluates *The Healers* in similar vein:

> Yet it is still a cartoon, still comic strip history. It will not persuade many adults because it falsifies far more than authenticates and in the process fails to avoid the pitfalls of oversimplification. Nevertheless, some grown-ups will be able to enjoy it at the level of popular fiction, for it is good cops-and-robbers, cowboys-and-indians stuff . . . But basically it is juvenile adventure fiction of the *Treasure Island* or *King Solomon's Mines* sort, the only major difference being that it is thoroughly African juvenile adventure fiction.[21]

The sinister motive and logic of Lindfors' assertion is obvious: he proceeds from negative assessments of Armah's first three novels by African critics to his own uncomplimentary remarks on the last two novels. The conclusion which he tempts us to swallow: Armah is a bad African writer! But we know better. No objective evaluation of African writers and their works is to be arrived at by critics whose political biases and aesthetic values are motivated from the *outside*.

Against this background, then, colonialist criticism is not to be dismissed as a dying intellectual tradition; it has metamorphosed and been recruited into the cultural arm of contemporary imperialism complete with a local middleman cadre and its foreign partners.

Art-for-art Criticism

Art-for-art criticism of African literature is an extension of imperialist assimilationist rhetoric on the part of modern Western critics. On the part of their African counterparts, this critical posture stems from a hangover of the colonial heritage which presumes that cultural values are *good* in themselves if they approximate a certain astrally and universally defined sense of the beautiful. The main thrust of this critical posture is the assumption that the object of art is the creation of beauty irrespective of the social ambience of the individual artist. At the back of this assumption is a certain universal conception of humanity whose reference point is usually bourgeois Western man. Whether they are Africans or Euro-Americans, advocates of this position draw from the same spring of idealist/formalist poetics in which literary creations are reducible to formalistic equations. Omafume Onoge has identified Dan Izevbaye and Eustace Palmer as the principal pontiffs of this school. In his essay, "Criticism and Literature in West Africa", Izevbaye conceives of the maturation of African literature in terms of greater jettisoning of socio-political preoccupations.

> As the literature becomes less preoccupied with social or national problems and more concerned with the problems of men as individuals in an African society, the critical reference will be human beings rather than society, and the considerations which influence critical judgement social ones.[22]

Although this excerpt speaks for itself, Onoge's diatribe on Izevbaye's brand of idealism deserves reproducing:

> Izevbaye's art-for-art advocacy is really for a depoliticised literary universe inhabited by abstract human beings with abstract moral values of an abstract religious pietism. A literary universe which, our prosaic logic compels us to add, must be created by astral writers and equally astral critics.[23]

Eustace Palmer's pronouncements on aspects of African literature, especially the novel, have borne the same stamp of historical decontextualization and liberal universal humanism. As recently as in his mistitled book, *The Growth of the African Novel*, his comments on the Nigerian novels of his choice dramatize Palmer's art-for-art obsessions. Writing about Ekwensi's *Survive the Peace*, a novel depicting the last moments of the Nigerian Civil War, Palmer is worried more by whether Ekwensi adheres to his Western conceptions of novelistic form.

> Ekwensi shows no sense of plot and structure, the novel consisting of isolated episodes only tenuously held together by the overriding theme. As far as characterisation goes, Ekwensi shows little psychological insight.[24]

The one-and-half-page discussion of this novel of over two hundred pages does not try to find out whether there is anything in the nature of the experience being depicted that necessitates the loose episodic structure of the novel or whether, in fact, the debilitating psycho–social effects of the Nigerian Civil War gave room for psychological depth on the part of individuals. It is our contention that such generalizations, in neglecting the social experiences that condition the literary works being discussed, fail to do justice to the very literary forms generated by those experiences, for the dialectical relationship between context, content and form cannot be reduced to the dictates of a borrowed stereotypical notion of form. Similar examples could be multiplied indefinitely in the series of amputated reviews that constitute the bulk of Palmer's otherwise enormous book.

A further trait of the art-for-art school of critics of the literature in question is the usual search for the ancestry, equivalents, affinities and precedents of stylistic trends in African literature in the Euro–American literary tradition. It becomes easy, for instance, for Bernth Lindfors to see Ekwensi's entire narrative art as deriving essentially from "third-rate American movies and fourth-rate British and American paper-back novels".[25] On the surface, the allegiance is to art; but the underlying worry is about the health of Western forms in the hands of African neophytes.

Because the main practitioners of this critical fashion operate from a liberal framework, their critical perceptions are usually subjective to a point of near absolute relativism. Consequently, they also represent the most widely published critics of African literature in terms of sheer output.

Cultural Anthropological Criticism
The transitional realm from outright colonialist criticism to the faintest recognition of the specific socio–cultural character and historical determination of African literature by critics of African literature takes the form of an unmediated obsession with cultural anthropology. The dominant traits and informing ideas of this trend in African cultural scholarship have been aptly characterized as the "Festac consciousness" which manifests concretely in the numerous festivals featuring revivalisms of calabash-and-raffia traditionalia. "Culture" in the parlance of the critics in this school is conceived of in the sense of static aspects of a society's material and spiritual achievement and characteristics at a particular stage in the process of social development. Thus conceived, the physical symbols of culture are seen exclusively in terms of museum pieces, chipped porcelain and survivals of animistic social existence to be recovered in long-abandoned caves and the ruins of great walls and moats.

The critical effort of this school takes one of two forms: it either laments the rupture of traditional African cultures as evidenced in the increasing Westernization of aesthetic consciousness in the works of leading African writers or tries to establish the presence and continuities of varying traditionalia – folklore, tribal customs etc. – in contemporary African literature. In the former category belongs much of Romanus Egudu's readings of Okigbo's poetry in his book *Four Modern West African Poets*. Bernth Lindfors' *Folklore in Nigerian Literature* and Oladele Taiwo's *Culture in the Nigerian Novel* belong in the second category. About the notion of culture that informs his book, for instance, Taiwo writes *inter alia*: "The 'culture' of the title refers to indigenous culture."[26] However, in his exegesis of the Nigerian novels of his choice, Taiwo dabbles into issues in contemporary culture thereby reaffirming the dynamism of culture and dangerously compromising the cardinal premise of his book.

A further offshoot of this critical tradition is what Biodun Jeyifo has described as "ethno-criticism" which, in addition to seeing African literary works in terms of the ethnicity of their authors, also resurrects decadent ethnic myths and traditionalia and tries to project these on to the screen of contemporary literary works.[27] In the writings of critics in this formation, one discovers the disquieting tendency in African socio–political life to see national achievements exclusively in terms of the ethnicity of individual contributors, a fact which undermines the emergent national character of African culture. It becomes convenient for a critic like Ernest Emenyonu, in his otherwise beneficial book, *The Rise of the Igbo Novel*, to conceive of the works of writers like Chinua Achebe and Cyprian Ekwensi (both writing in English) as belonging to Igbo ethnic literature.[28]

In the history of the criticism of African literature in English, the enduring significance of this school lies in its attempt to underscore the debt which the majority of first generation African writers like Achebe, Soyinka and Kunene owe to the oral traditions of their respective ethno–national cultures. Its basic deficiency lies in its predominantly ahistorical and static conception of culture. Its abiding value is to be located in the commendable background material which it furnishes for the study of African oral literatures especially.

Bourgeois Sociological Criticism

Bourgeois sociological criticism of African literature owes its rise to the rather reluctant realization on the part of some critics that the literature which forms the object of their enquiry is made peculiar by the fact that it is concerned with problems in African society at various points in its development. Abiola Irele was perhaps the earliest to experience this realization when he observed:

> We have a duty not only to make our modern African literature accessible to our people in terms which they can understand, but also in the process, to promote an understanding of literature, to widen the creative (as well as responsive) capabilities of our people . . .[29]

Irele wraps up his critical stance in what he refers to as the "sociological imagination" whose essential method is to

> correlate the work to the social background to see how the author's intention and attitude issue out of the wider social context of his art . . . and to get an

understanding of the way each writer or group of writers captures a moment in the historical consciousness of his society.[30]

There is a certain ambiguity in Irele's "sociological imagination" option. This arises from the fact that he insists on intuitive subjectivity as the definitive attribute of the critical intelligence while recognizing the objective social problems and processes which preoccupy the writer:

> Despite the technical requirement of critical judgements, they are, in the last resort, of a subjective character – relying on the personal responses of the critic as a reader . . . *A good part of criticism depends, therefore, on the intuition which is later corrected and given an intellectual formulation.*[31] (my emphasis)

The unconscious apostles of Irele's position display understandable timidity when confronted with the relationship between the structurally perceivable class and historical character of the immediate social reality and the literary works they choose to explicate. Oyin Ogunba's efforts in *The Movement of Transition* (a study of Soyinka's plays) provide a ready example. One of Ogunba's main areas of attention is the degree of faithfulness of the plays he studies to the Aristotelian unities and other technicalities of Western dramaturgy while acknowledging their immediate African social anchorage. Even in those of Soyinka's plays inspired by obvious and recent events in African history, Ogunba fails to establish confidently the relationship between these plays and their socio–political referents. What we get is a superfluity of equivocal statements like this one on *Madmen and Specialists*:

> *Madmen and Specialists* was produced after the Nigerian Civil War . . . and was probably first conceived when the playwright was in detention during the war. This particular war *appears* to be the focus of Soyinka's comments in this play.[32] (my emphasis)

The most annoying instance of this trend is, again, Romanus Egudu in his little-known book, *Modern African Poetry and the African Predicament*. Wearing the façade of a critic with a sociological bent, intent on relating modern African poetry to African society, Egudu however fails to tell us what exactly constitutes the "African predicament". In order to get a glimpse of his conception of the contradictions in contemporary African society, one has to retreat to his earlier book, *Four Modern West African Poets*, where he declares:

> Modern West African poetry deals essentially with the African predicament, which is an aspect of the tragedy of man's existence. It is the crisis of the past, the present, the future – the past being hideous, the present, confused and harassing, and the future uncertain and intriguing. The poetry is therefore born of anarchy, an anarchy of the mind and the spirit which is projected into the somewhat ordered chaos of poetic artistry.[33]

This obsession with the apocalypse manifests itself in the more recent book in the form of vague generalizations about the inadequacies of the status quo and so on. In the specific instance of his treatment of poetry on the Nigerian Civil War, for instance, Egudu's conceptual lapses become more evident. Whatever else it may have been, the Nigerian Civil War was a specific experience in the historical process of a specific national society. Its causes were specific and determinate in socio–political terms and it evoked definable and structurally analysable psychic and ideological responses in different Nigerians, including writers. But Egudu envelops all these in equivocal statements like this:

> The Nigerian Civil War (1967–70), which was the culminating point of the series of political crises in that country since 1962, has provided some of the Nigerian poets with the opportunity of manifesting through art the nature of their feelings about life and human values.[34]

Since the poets in question are Soyinka, Clark and Achebe, one may ask what these poets had been dwelling on before the war!

Egudu and his fellow bourgeois pseudo-sociological critics substantiate Jeyifo's charge that

> the state of African literary criticism is directly commensurate to the "publish-or-perish" rubric and the academic pecking order which constitute the peculiar form of the individual and class entrenchment of the African professional intelligentsia in the national neo-capitalist economy.[35]

The common shortcoming in the foregoing versions of the bourgeois sociological criticism of Nigerian literature has to do with the fact that the pronouncements of its chief practitioners are usually not predicated on solid empirical information on the social phenomena they see objectified in the literary works they analyse. Nor do they operate from any known tradition in sociological theory; they are neither functionalists nor reflexive sociologists.

For a more profound and rigorous manifestation of this critical position, we are compelled to turn to the work of Emmanuel Obiechina. In this connection, his contributions to date find expression in his extensive researches into Onitsha Market literature as well as in his important book, *Culture, Tradition and Society in the West African Novel*.[36]

In addition to drawing attention to the important linguistic and formal features of the phenomenal Onitsha Market pamphlet literature, Obiechina's substantive theoretical position with regard to this literature reveals his clear understanding of the vital place of class configurations in any meaningful discussion of culture and society. He contends that

> the different segments of society have different tastes, especially in the matter of what each reads. The middle classes determine their own literary interests just as working people seek their own level of literary enjoyment. It is one function of the literary historian to recognise and record and analyse existing cultural tastes

without prejudice, establishing the connectedness and underlying unity in the cultural situation.[37]

Obiechina goes further to provide an analytical and reasoned explanation of the emergence of this popular literature at the time and place it did. Among other factors, he ascribes the rise of popular pamphleteering in Onitsha to the absence of a black intellectual elite in the hinterland, the rise of popular journalism as well as the cultural and psychological outlook of the inhabitants of Onitsha, especially the Igbo people with what he calls their "mobile consciousness".[38]

In *Culture, Tradition*, Obiechina's exploration of the inter-relationship between culture, tradition, society and the novelistic mode in the texts of his choice is particularly illuminating. His conception of the categories of culture, tradition and society is unambiguous and dialectical: "The essential reality of contemporary West African culture is that within it oral tradition continues to exist side by side with encroaching literary traditions."[39] While appreciating the functionality of the essentially oral and, therefore, animistic and superstitious culture of Africa before colonial incursion, Obiechina, unlike the cultural anthropological critics, is at pains to confess that "belief in magic, witchcraft and the gods tends to be in inverse proportion to scientific progress and control of the environment."[40]

However, Obiechina does lapse occasionally into the cultural nationalist penchant for seeing many of the contradictions in contemporary African society in terms of the much-advertised "culture conflict" at the expense of a rigorous pursuit of the very determinants of the cultural question which, we contend, were inherent in the larger design of colonialist economic arithmetic. By and large, Obiechina's contribution to Nigerian cultural discourse could, to a lesser degree, be equated to those of Ian Watt in English literary scholarship.

A common denominator in most of these aspects of the "sociological" approach to African literature is that while being able to correlate specific social experiences with the content of a given literary work (or body of literature), they are informed by a rather amorphous and nebulous notion of society as well as an equally hazy theoretical knowledge of the precise relationship between the social and the literary. The crux of the problem is to be located in the contradiction inherent in their insistence on subjective intuition as *the* mode of perceiving the meaning of literature while simultaneously acknowledging society as an objective reality and the source of literary experience. But the objective reality of society is implicitly conveyed as consisting of scattered epiphenomena, without order and structure. The consequence is a mode of criticism which is close to aesthetic formalism and whose ancestry dates back to Taine and Nietzsche. Says Lukacs of this brand of *sociological* criticism:

> Thus the sociological approach to literature offers no escape from the narrow subjectivism of aestheticism. On the contrary, it draws criticism deeper into the morass. The constant vacillation between examining the content in literature

from an abstract social or political point of view and examining form from a
subjectivist point of view represents no real progress or constructive evolution.
The absence of a principled basis for criticism is merely intensified, for both
extremes open the doors to indirect and subtle domination by the capitalists who
own the press.[41]

The critic's dabbling into the realm of the social and political meanings of
African literature creates two other possibilities: the African writer takes
on the additional responsibility of literary criticism in order to clarify his
views and "correct" his critics thereby preparing the ground for a writer–
critic confrontation.

The African Writer as Literary Critic

The African writer's incursion into the embattled arena of literary
discourse and criticism can be understood as a function of two interrelated
motivations: one is an attempt to lay bare the peculiar social and
philosophical outlook that informs his own work(s); the other, an attempt
to use this outlook as a basis for evaluating the works of his fellow writers.
We are more concerned, in this chapter, with the latter area.

The social commitment and historical consciousness of the average
African writer is, by now, axiomatic. Therefore, when the writer takes on
the additional responsibility of criticizing the works of his fellows, he is
extending the frontiers of this commitment by intervening to challenge the
more scandalous deviations and distortions of the professional critics,
especially of the "sociological" variety. A common characteristic of the
critical pronouncements of most African writers is the propensity, mostly
unconscious, to evaluate the works of other writers and even attempt to
"correct" their world view and social vision according to the writer–critic's
own subjective world view. Lukacs illuminates this point when he observes:

> No matter how broad the horizon of his social and personal interests or how
> original and profound his intellect, the writer–critic generally approaches
> aesthetic problems from the point of view of the concrete questions arising in his
> own creative work, and he refers his conclusions . . . back to his own work.[42]

Thus Soyinka, an avowed mythopocist with a fundamentally religious
sensibility, reads Ousmane's *God's Bits of Wood*, an otherwise thoroughly
materialist novel, in purely mythic terms:

> As with all good epics, humanity is re-created. The social community acquires
> archetypal dimensions and heroes become deities. Even Penda the prostitute is
> apotheosized.
>
>   The remote, enigmatic Bakayoko is a promethean creation, a replacement of
> outworn deities who have the misfortune to lose their relevance in a colonial
> world. Amoral in the mundane sense of the word, Bakayoko appears to be
> sculpted out of pure intellect and omniscience.[43]

This mystificatory reading is in spite of the obviously "mundane", terrestrial and materialist preoccupation of the novel: a strike by exploited railway workers against their colonial masters which has both negative and redeeming implications for them and their families and at the end of which the revolutionary aspiration and will of the workers is vindicated.

At times, the critical practice of the African writer degenerates to the level of outright chiding and hectoring. This can be said of Achebe's reductionist reading of Armah's *The Beautyful Ones Are Not Yet Born* in which he chides Armah for mediating social reality through an aesthetics of negation:

> Armah is clearly an alienated writer complete with all the symptoms. Unfortunately, Ghana is not a modern existentialist country. It is just a West African state struggling to become a country. So there is enormous distance between Armah and Ghana. There is something scornful, cold and remote about Armah's obsession with the filth of Ghana.[44]

This judgement is again a negation of the simple theoretical point that a dialectical conception of art and society must contend with the fact of negation as a necessary launching pad for the inauguration of a positive and progressive view of society, a fact which Soyinka accurately strikes at in his response to the same novel. Says Soyinka: "beyond banal protests at such 'unflattering portraits' of a young nation, . . . [the novel's] pessimistic suggestion bears the possibility of its own hopeful contradiction, an accurate summation of society only too well understood by Armah."[45]

On a slightly different note, Ngugi's judgement of Soyinka's earlier work is predicated on a socio–political ideology which also corresponds to Ngugi's own artistic philosophy (his authorial ideology). Thus, in his assessment of *A Dance of the Forests*, *The Strong Breed* and *The Interpreters*, Ngugi faults Soyinka for his hazy political sensibility:

> Soyinka's good man is the uncorrupted individual: his liberal humanism leads him to admire an individual's lone act of courage, and thus often he ignores the creative struggle of the masses. The ordinary people, workers and peasants, in his plays remain passive watchers on the shore or pitiful comedians on the road.[46]

Underneath these conflicting positions is to be discerned a clear sense of struggle, of confrontation and ideological divergence which cannot be fully explained at the level of a purely superstructural conception of literature and its criticism. These differences of opinion attest to the absence of an ideological and, therefore, political consensus among African writers. It is also a subtle by-product of the invasion of Africa by the ethics of the market place if the writer as a producer of the literary art object is forced to scream: read me; don't read my neighbour!

The general theoretical point which is being underscored here is that when the writers of an epoch get involved in the criticism of the literature of their contemporaries, their value judgements also reflect the class and ideological conflicts which define social life and which they re-create in their own artistic works.

Writers versus Critics

If ambiguity and conflict define the arena of the criticism of African literature, nowhere else has it been so pronounced as in the series of polemical confrontations between major African writers and their more daring critics. Having come into prominence mainly through a Western-dominated tradition of criticism which packaged and presented him variously as "the custodian of the conscience of the race", the repository of social vision and crystallization of the aspiration for social justice, the average African writer acquired the mien of a deity. What with the hundreds of European critics, editors and researchers trooping in to interview him or inviting him to address a conference, the African writer was nurtured into a culture of messianism and was flattered into an over-exaggerated estimation of his socio–political importance. In the process also, the writer was bestowed with a feeling of superiority (not just primacy) over the critic, a point to which the critics themselves have unconsciously acquiesced by virtue of the theoretical and philosophical aridity of their products, a deficiency which makes them appear totally dependent on literary texts for their livelihood. In the process, both writers and critics reified their practice away from actual social life.

Thus when some critics summoned enough courage to subject the craft and social vision of specific writers to rigorous critical analysis, they were walking a terrain beset with landmines. First, they had to contend with the messianic ego of the writers: for in most religions, to affront the ego of a deity is always an act of senseless martyrdom! Consequently, in their polemical responses to their critics, key African writers have displayed characteristic condescension and oracular omniscience. For instance, when Soyinka woke up to find his reputation as a poet threatened by the daring irreverence of the troika of Chinweizu, Jemie and Madubuike, he invoked "the principle of imaginative challenge which is one of the functions of poetry" and dismissed the critics in question as a "three-headed pontifex maximus simplicissimus".[47]

While restating the centrality of the writer's ego in a possible explanation of the writer–critic controversy in African literature, it needs to be stated also that economic and ideological factors play a prominent role (even if unconsciously) in aggravating these conflicts. In a situation where ideas, in the form of books and articles, are also commodities whose value is reflected in the balance sheet of publishers and booksellers, "intellectual" disagreements cannot but be marred by remote considerations of marketability and the interests of those who own the principal organs for the dissemination of intellectual products. Thus the writer, while honestly defending his social convictions and artistic philosophy, may in fact be running down his colleagues and indirectly advertising his own works. In the process also, writers adopt *favourite* critics and deride those critics whom they consider *hostile* to their works. The consequence is a complexity of alignments and alliances among writers and critics whose ideological configurations cannot easily be disentangled from the economic and political factors that govern social life in the larger society in question. Again, Lukacs summarizes this contradiction in the following terms:

> For the writer, a "good" critic is one who praises him and attacks his neighbour; a "bad" critic is one who scolds him or promotes his neighbour. For the critic, the great body of literature represents a dreary livelihood that demands much effort and pain. In this atmosphere where no real criteria exist, where there are political and economic pressures from the capitalist employer, mounting routinism and sensationalism and inexorable competition constantly threatening financial and moral destruction, unprincipled cliques emerge for whose aesthetic and moral level no outsider can have any respect.[48]

In African literature, the veracity of this assertion is disturbingly stark, for the pattern of exchanges between writers and critics has often assumed the dimensions of a fratricidal verbal warfare occasionally degenerating to the level of adolescent name-calling: between Achebe and Nnolim over the source of *Arrow of God*; between Soyinka and the Ife-Ibadan School of Marxist critics over the former's obsession with obfuscatory mythologizing at the expense of ideological clarity; between Armah on one hand and Charles Larson and his other critics on the other over the latter's laziness and racial bigotry and more recently, between the Chinweizu school and everybody else.[49] The list could be multiplied infinitely.

In this intellectual free-for-all, certain underlying motivational factors crystallize. Disagreements and quarrels between African writers and their critics have revolved mainly around: appropriate values (often racial) for the judgement of our literature; the ideological imperatives for writers given the socio-historical challenges of Africa; matters of craft (levels of obscurity) given what *should* be the target audience of African literature; and the very qualification of the critics (as parasites on the literary artifacts) to pass judgement on matters of creativity and authorial vision.

The foregoing aspects of the criticism of African literature display, in their incoherence, the lack of theoretical mooring in much of the critical practice under discussion. Criticism should be guided by theory, and theory, in turn, by philosophy. In the absence of this chain of relationships, writers and critics of the same epoch and even of the same broad class and ideological origins will display incoherence and indeterminacy in their pronouncements on literature and culture. In the process, their attention may be distracted from the real nature and scope of their historical challenge while undue attention is paid to rivalry and contests for supremacy.

If we look for the closest approximation to a critical ideology, at least in terms of a body of critical pronouncements informed by a broad but uniform world view in African literature, it is to be sought in the erection of the pre-colonial ("traditional") African world into a classical universal embodying philosophical, moral and aesthetic *constants*. In the thinking of "traditionalists", it is against this absolute that all aspects of contemporary African experience and cultural practice must be actively and constantly related and measured in order to highlight their essential difference from elements of Western culture and civilization. This is the main thrust of what I call *traditionalist aesthetics*, to which we turn in the next chapter.

Notes

1. Mao Tse-Tung, "Talks at the Yenan Forum on Literature and the Arts", in *Selected Works*, vol. 3 (Peking: Foreign Language Press, 1967) p. 88.

2. Roland Barthes, *Critical Essays*, trans. and ed. Richard Howard (Evanston: Northwestern University Press, 1972) p. 257.

3. Wole Soyinka, "The Critic and Society: Barthes, Leftocracy and Other Mythologies", Inaugural Lecture, University of Ife, 1980, p. 3.

4. Terry Eagleton, *Criticism and Ideology: A Study in Marxist Literary Theory* (London: Verso, 1978) p. 17.

5. Raymond Williams, *Marxism and Literature* (Oxford: Oxford University Press, 1977) p. 109.

6. The Annual Ekpe festival dance drama has its origins among the Ibibios of Nigeria's Cross River State with whom the Ngwas of Imo State share a common border.

7. Solomon Iyasere, "African Oral Tradition – Criticism As Performance: A Ritual", *African Literature Today*, 11, 1980, p. 173.

8. Kai-Yu Hsu, *The Chinese Literary Scene* (Harmondsworth: Penguin, 1976) pp. 12–13.

9. Mao Tse-Tung, "Talks at the Yenan Forum".

10. C. M. Bowra, *Ancient Greek Literature* (London: O.U.P., 1967) p. x.

11. Claude Ake, *Revolutionary Pressures in Africa* (London: Zed Press, 1978) p. 62.

12. Antonio Gramsci, *Selections from Prison Notes* (London: Lawrence and Wishart, 1982) p. 9.

13. Kwame Nkrumah, *Class Struggle in Africa* (New York: International Publishers, 1970) p. 38.

14. Ibid., p. 39.

15. Chinua Achebe, *Morning Yet on Creation Day* (London: Heinemann, 1975) p. 3.

16. Ayi Kwei Armah, "Larsony or Fiction as Criticism of Fiction", *Positive Review*, 1 (1978), pp. 11–14.

17. Eustace Palmer, *The Growth of the African Novel* (London: Heinemann, 1979) p. 5.

18. Achebe, *Morning Yet on Creation Day*, p. 9.

19. Bruce King, *The New English Literatures* (London/Basingstoke; Macmillan, 1980).

20. See, for instance, Dan Izevbaye, "Criticism and Literature in Africa" in Christopher Heywood (ed.) *Perspectives on African Literature* (London: Heinemann, 1971) p. 30.

21. Bernth Lindfors, "Armah's Histories", *African Literature Today*, no. 11, 1980, p. 95.

22. Izevbaye, "Criticism and Literature".

23. Omafume Onoge, "Toward a Marxist Sociology of African Literature", *Ife Studies in African Literature and the Arts*, no. 2, 1984, pp. 7–8.

24. Palmer, *The Growth of the African Novel*, p. 60.

25. Bernth Lindfors, "Cyprian Ekwensi: An African Popular Novelist", *African Literature Today*, no. 3, 1979, pp. 2–4.

26. Oladele Taiwo, *Culture and the Nigerian Novel* (London: Macmillan, 1976) p. 28.

27. Biodun Jeyifo "Ethno-Criticism or the Ethnic Criteria in African Literary Criticism", *Positive Review*, vol. 1, no. 3, 1979, pp. 40–42.

28. Ernest Emenyonu, *The Rise of the Igbo Novel* (Ibadan: O.U.P., 1978).

29. Abiola Irele, "The Criticism of Modern African Literature" in Heywood (ed.) *Perspectives on African Literature*, p. 30.

30. Ibid., p. 25.

31. Ibid., pp. 11–12.

32. Oyin Ogunba, *The Movement of Transition* (Ibadan: University of Ibadan Press, 1975) pp. 203–204.

33. Romanus Egudu, *Four Modern West African Poets* (New York: NOK, 1977) p. i.

34. Romanus Egudu, *Modern African Poetry and the African Predicament* (London: Macmillan, 1978) p. 104.

35. Biodun Jeyifo, "Literalism and Reductionism in African Literary Criticism: Further Notes on Literature and Ideology", paper presented at the Conference of Association of African Literary Critics, University of Ife, 1975.

36. Emmanuel Obiechina, *Culture, Tradition and Society in the West African Novel* (Cambridge: Cambridge University Press, 1975).

37. Emmanuel Obiechina, *An African Popular Literature: A Study of Onitsha Market Pamphlets* (Cambridge: Cambridge University Press, 1973) p. 1; see also *Literature for the Masses* (Enugu: Nwamife, 1971).

38. Obiechina, *Culture, Tradition and Society in the West African Novel*, pp. 7–8.

39. Ibid., p. 26.

40. Ibid., p. 33.

41. Georg Lukacs, *Writer and Critic*, trans. and ed. D. Khan (New York: Grosset and Dunlap, 1971) p. 198.

42. Ibid., p. 215.

43. Wole Soyinka, *Myth, Literature and the African World* (Cambridge: Cambridge University Press, 1976) p. 117.

44. Achebe, *Morning Yet on Creation Day*, p. 26.

45. Soyinka, *Myth, Literature*, p. 116.

46. Ngugi Wa Thiong'o, *Homecoming: Essays* (London: Heinemann, 1973) p. 65.

47. Soyinka, "Neo-Tarzanism: The Poetics of Pseudo-Tradition", *Transition* 48 (1975), pp. 38–44.

48. Georg Lukacs, *Writer and Critic*, p. 203.

49. In a bid to advance the tenets of his *Toward the Decolonization of African Literature* into a definitive literary ideology, Chinweizu has recently engaged radical and bourgeois writers alike in bouts of polemical wrestling matches. See, for instance, his recent outings in *The Guardian* (Lagos) 16 February and 2 March 1986.

2 Traditionalism and the Quest for an African Literary Aesthetic

It is important that we understand that cultural imperialism in its era of neo-colonialism is a more dangerous cancer because it takes new subtle forms and can hide even under the cloak of militant African nationalism, the cry for dead authentic cultural symbolism and other native racist self assertive banners.
Ngugi wa Thiong'o[1]

I feel the need to scream
the hard-scissoring nightmares of men
hiding behind ancestral masks
masks of illusions,
carved out of the wish to escape
    if only for a day
the saw-blade kiss of reality
Odia Ofeimun[2]

In this chapter, I try to locate the meeting point of the bulk of conflicting but mutually inclusive positions in the discourse of modern African literature and culture in what may be termed *traditionalist aesthetics*. This is a complex of theoretical standpoints and critical statements which seek to define the authenticity, standards of creative performance and critical evaluation of African literature in terms of values and models freely selected and adapted from the so-called "traditional", pre-colonial African cultural matrix. This ever-growing and now almost hegemonic intellectual tradition finds its most recent and most trenchant expression in what I call the *decolonization rhetoric* of the sort exemplified by the necessary but problematic book, *Toward the Decolonization of African Literature* by Chinweizu et al.[3] Paradoxically, this theoretical viewpoint finds legitimation in Soyinka's powerful but equally troublesome *Myth, Literature and the African World*.[4]

My basic contention is that for all its attractiveness and desirability as an intellectual "fashion", traditionalist aesthetics is fundamentally flawed by its inherent ahistorical, undialectical and ultimately idealist conception of the relationship between literature as an aspect of culture and the socio-economic processes which overdetermine other aspects of contemporary

African experience in particular. Therefore, to use traditionalist aesthetics as the exclusive and decisive point of departure for a rhetorical decolonization of African literature, or for the definition of an immutable aesthetic value system for that literature, is not only reactionary and diversionary but also, in itself, a colonial attitude. Additionally, it is a negation of the primordial social involvement of pre-colonial African art as well as the putative historical predication of modern African literature and art.

To this extent, the current hegemony and popularity of traditionalist aesthetics (especially among Nigerian students and their teachers) constitutes a formidable cognitive road-block to the emergence of a tradition of rigorous theorizing on African literature, thus condemning the literature in question and its critical discourse to a state of perpetual underdevelopment.

The Intellectual Climate

The perennial yearning for the lost ideals of racial infancy; the nostalgic groping for the nipples of the pristine African maternal breast; the selective resuscitation of ancestral myths, values and institutions; the indiscriminate appropriation and application of the tools of Western bourgeois rationalism to contemporary African culture; the endless quest for "traditional" criteria for the evaluation of a literature that has since lost its cultural innocence: these and their variants are the manifestations of the present crisis of consciousness and confidence in bourgeois intellection of modern African society and culture in general and literature in particular.

This conjunction of theoretical contradictions which has unfortunately been consecrated into the dominant intellectual tradition of Africa (in the field of culture at least) betokens an ambiguous sense of nostalgia which looks in two principal directions for inspiration: African cultural scholarship has looked insistently either back at traditional pre-colonial Africa or to the dominant (bourgeois) cultural tradition of the West for theoretical moorings. In either direction, a certain preoccupation with tradition in its idealist (static) sense seems central to contemporary discourse on African literature and culture. Whether our point of reference is literature or the figurative arts, dance or fashion, architecture or cuisine, the pendulum of discourse and controversy swings either to pre-colonial "Africa" or "the West".

While granting that the dilemma in question is historically inevitable, one is perturbed by a certain insidious ambiguity in the conception of the two opposing geo-cultural regions, namely Africa and Europe. The Africa that is usually projected is the pristine, unspoilt world of migrant herdsmen, naked tribesmen and dancing damsels; the highest indices of its achievement in terms of material culture are the ever-present Ife and Benin bronze heads, the Dogon masks, the terracotta relics, Nok culture, the great walls of Zimbabwe and so on. Accordingly, these achievements and relics are artfully insulated from history in its dynamic meaning. On the other hand, European models are carefully selected from the highest points in Western civilization usually dating from the Renaissance to the present era of guided missiles and computer chips. In an attempt to erect a comparative paradigm between "the two worlds", the Western and pro-Western media and intellectual establishment have consciously or unconsciously come to adopt an unbalanced North–South framework. Thus, for instance, a comparison of Western and African architectural models in Western scholarship and media would tend to compare say Igbo thatch huts with New York skyscrapers. In short, there is a basic reluctance on the part of the Western intellectual establishment and their African protégés to concede a certain measure of motion or dynamism to the African world.

The sense of intellectual anguish which lies at the root of these observations does not arise from what the West (or certain sections of it) have chosen to believe about Africa but from the more debilitating realization that prominent African intellectuals have tacitly acquiesced to this unbalanced comparative paradigm. Thus, we are assailed from all directions by indiscriminate bandyings of such clichés as "the African world", "African culture", "African values" etc. by African bourgeois scholars. Implicit in all this is a basic reluctance on the part of these scholars to see Africa not only as part of a changing world but also as a highly heterogenous and multivalent geo-political entity whose problems need to be confronted at the level of theories with practical value for both the present and the future.

There is a kind of defensive intellection which seeks to rationalize the African contribution to world culture exclusively in terms of the past glories of illustrious ancestors conceived in broad continental terms. It needs to be underlined that this kind of rationalization belongs in a general tradition of affirmative consciousness which is a continuation of the reflex response to the cultural denigration and psychological emasculation which were implicit in colonialist ideology. It is the appropriateness of this response in the heydays of nationalist politics and black collective race retrieval that confers historical importance on men like Caseley Hayford, Wilmot Blyden, Leopold Senghor and others. Negritude and allied philosophies with their inherent class limitations were the appropriate vehicles for the expression of that sense of racial injury. It also needs to be underlined that such affirmative philosophies had inherent *revolutionary* significance in the days when they were current.

The contemporary problematization of the question of an aesthetic reference point for African literature is a by-product of this tradition of black affirmative consciousness. But, the African literary intelligentsia came to the realization that they had a cultural task to perform rather belatedly and through a curious backyard route.

The emergence of African literature in the European languages was greeted by the European literary establishment with a spontaneous spate of reviews and critical essays characterized by a patronizing condescension couched in glamorous eulogy. Underlying these critical celebrations was a certain nebulous universalism which saw African literature as part of the "human" literary heritage which did not necessitate the adoption of fresh evaluative criteria. Since, as we saw in the last chapter, the logical index and reference point of universal humanism was the Western world, standards of performance and critical values from the Western tradition could freely be adopted for exegetizing and evaluating African literature. The excesses of colonialist criticism have more recently mellowed into a liberal absolute relativism which claims that there could be as many evaluations of an African literary work as there are critics provided we are sufficiently intelligent to distinguish between "good" and "bad" critics. Characteristically, Bernth Lindfors articulates the essence of this growing fashion: "A reasonable alternative . . . would be an approach which recognised the validity of various interpretations of the same work of art, a relative approach in matters of aesthetic discrimination."[5] Predictably, the response of African writers and critics to the underlying assumptions of this critical attitude has consisted of a series of defences of the authenticity, peculiarity and historical predication of African literature. Accordingly, the necessity for the adoption of African aesthetic criteria has come to be forcefully articulated while attention has duly been drawn to the existence, albeit latent, of a body of aesthetic values and artistic practices in pre-colonial African cultures which only need to be exhumed, refurbished and systematized to provide an alternative aesthetic of African literature and thus call the bluff of the Western literary establishment.

This position, once articulated, provided the basis for a new diversionary theology. In conference after conference on African literature and in the now familiar avalanche of amputated reviews and subjective exegeses that inundate journals in the field, it would appear that the bulk of intellectual energy in African literary discourse has been dissipated on the quest for an "African" aesthetic value system for our literature. The road to authentic African aesthetic values and artistic practices has led inexorably to pre-colonial and often destroyed or forgotten socio–cultural formations. Understandably, therefore, Africanist literary scholarship has had to fall back on those disciplines traditionally equipped to handle the past of societies. In this regard, history, anthropology and religious studies would ordinarily provide ready services. But here again, we come face to face with the ubiquitous West. Colonialist history of Africa of the sort associated with early Rowland Oliver and Eurocentric (primitivist) anthropology of the brand linked with Placide Temples, Levi-Bruhl and Jack Goody has had only stock European prejudices to offer.[6] Most scandalous perhaps, is the work of African professional religionists like Idowu and Mbiti whose sense of divinity and the sacred is so steeped in Judeo-Christian mythology that it cannot but see a hierarchy of Christian angels in African ethnic pantheons![7] We shall return to this point later.

Given the discordant tone and suspicious nature of information from these auxiliary disciplines, traditionalist aesthetics of African literature has tended to content itself with vague generalizations about the "African oral narrator", "the African world view", "the traditional poet" and so on. In some cases, the quest for an African aesthetic of African literature has been hijacked from African scholars by the Euro–American counterparts. I am referring specifically to the flurry of centres and institutes of African studies in North America in the last decade. These are programmes established with American blood-money and whose staple diet has been all manner of tape recordings, films, relics and allied exotica collected from some carefully chosen remote African village. The unrelenting collector (often in ragged denim outfit) soon returns from the African Tartarus to a well deserved professorial chair in the American Olympus as an Africanist or "specialist" on African culture. The readiest victims and consumers of the products of these programmes have understandably been Afro-Americans whose endless quest for roots has led them to invent all manner of interesting mythologies about Africa. Some of them have become so obsessed with the "golden past" that their sense of identity would be fatally damaged if they woke up one morning to find that the whole of Africa was swarming with jet planes, computerized assembly lines and bullet trains! Like the sympathizer who mourns more than the bereaved, American scholars of African literature have recently over-reached themselves in this quest for an African aesthetic of African literature. In a recent publication, *Toward Defining the African Aesthetic*,[8] the American-based African Literature Association displayed the most scandalous ignorance about the subject, for none of the series of unrelated essays in the collection defines or shows the faintest awareness of the ingredients or implications of the so-called African aesthetic. Such examples could be multiplied indefinitely in the works of the ever-increasing specialists on Africa in the West.

As a hegemonic intellectual preoccupation, the quest for an African aesthetic must be viewed as a prominent product of an intellectual climate in which African scholarship about Africa has been unconsciously performing a task assigned to it by the West. In the discharge of this task, there has emerged a body of pronouncements that fit our earlier definition of traditionalist aesthetics. The shortcomings of this intellectual formation will emerge more concretely if we examine the broad philosophical assumptions that underlie the pronouncements of some of its most glorified advocates.

An African World View: Illusion or Reality?

To the extent that aesthetic theories are almost always predicated on a philosophical premise, traditionalist aestheticians of African literature have relentlessly invoked a certain amorphously defined "African world view" as the informing metaphysical bedrock of their postulations. As it is popularized and bandied around by anthropologists, religionists and professional philosophers, *the* African world view refers to an absolute, fairly homogenous, immutable and eternal mode of perceiving reality and explaining phenomena by which Africa can be distinguished from the West in particular. As we had indicated earlier, the erection of this concept must be seen as a deliberate attempt to provide a rational mooring for the identity crisis which the Western imperialist assault has inflicted on Africans and peoples of African descent. As a result, in the pronouncements of this group of intellectuals, the African world view always has a past, pre-scientific, pre-colonial time reference. Kwasi Wiredu reinforces this explanation when he asserts that:

> African nationalists in search of an African identity, Afro-Americans in search of their African roots, and foreigners in search of exotic diversion – all demand an African philosophy fundamentally different from Western philosophy, even if it means the familiar witches' brew.[9]

In a bid to project the so-called African world view as a coherent philosphical proposition, every attempt is made to submerge the ethnic heterogeneity of the continent and put forward a set of beliefs, customs, taboos and practices as typically and uniformly African. One area in which this generalizing tendency is most evident is in the area of religious belief. The dominant tendency has been to posit animistic religion as the definitive mode of African religious practice. Consequently, the African sense of the real is presented as a conflation of the mundane world of working, waking and sleeping and a supra-mundane world of spirits, gods, and other numinous influences intricately matrixed in a complex cosmogonic design. As in Senghorian negritude, African man in the context of this world view intuitively grasps the essence of things and can change his material circumstances through an act of will mediated by supernatural collaboration. Says Kofi Awoonor in his book, *The Breast of the Earth*:

> The African established, from time immemorial, a spiritual hierarchy which reveals a cunning understanding of natural phenomena and a clever talent for manipulating them toward good for himself and evil for his enemies.[10]

Accordingly, advocates of this distinctive African metaphysics posit an interesting conception of deity. In establishing a certain hierarchical relationship among gods in whatever ethnic pantheon they choose to discuss, they have not quite played safe of stock Judaeo-Christian models. Kofi Awoonor, in the book in question, proffers a hierarchical ordering of gods in which there is a creator God somewhere spatially and metaphysically distanced from a chain of lesser gods:

> Beneath the Creator God is a host of minor deities. By the light of his own logic, the African assigns to the creator God a certain degree of distance and unapproachability, not because he considers Him unconcerned, but rather because he thinks of Him in his primal ancestral role as the supreme

paterfamilias who must not be bothered with the petty details of the universe. He, Himself, appoints lieutenants and assistants who become overseers and guardians of various natural phenomena and faculties.[11]

Other features of this world view include a certain cyclic conception of time, a belief in reincarnation and allied superstitions.

It is crucial to interject at this point that this conception of deity is Christian-based and largely a falsification of the reality of religious practice in most, if not all, African cultures. Pre-colonial Africa was essentially humanistic and, to that extent, the existence of human society was the precondition for the existence of religion and gods. As it were, people said: let there be gods and proceeded to create them! In turn, they were imbued with humanistic attributes (a point to which I shall return in my discussion of Achebe's *Arrow of God* in Chapter Six) and accordingly assigned them duties within the emergent concept of the social division of labour. The provinces (or "ministries") allocated to various gods corresponded to what, in the particular time and place, were conceived of as areas not totally within human control and competence – control of thunder, hail, earthquake, rainfall and so on. Thus, pre-scientific (or *traditional*) African gods were and have remained terrestrial, rather than celestial; they can be felt (through their moulded or sculpted symbolizations), touched, carved, cursed, reproached and dismantled or starved to death in response to material exigencies of social existence which formed the basis for the existence of gods in the first place. In most cases, the gods were essentially intensifications of existing personages who attain deification through a process of apotheosis by virtue of socially recognized acts of heroism and distinction. In conceptual terms, therefore, the abode of gods was a terrestrial but spatially intangible realm of spirituality which nevertheless mortal man could penetrate through acts of augury, invocation, and other magical feats. In objective terms, it was an imaginative extension of the real world furnished by human material necessity. That world did not exist as an objective reality. All in all, the relationship between people and their gods was essentially an instrumental one; they made the gods, who existed in human image to serve them. Belief in the gods in turn influenced social action in a dialectical process.

It is, in addition, illogical to use the metaphysics of a particular phase in the development of a society to generalize on and posit an immutable philosophical paradigm for the world view of members of that culture – dead, living and unborn. The religious practices and beliefs which have been used to characterize the African world view belong to an advanced neolithic phase in the development of human societies in general, a phase characterized by primitive communal social relations arising from a dependence on pastoral, subsistence, agricultural production. This stage of social evolution is the natural breeding ground of animism, totemism and their attendant profusion of ritualistic observances. Says Arnold Hauser:

> With the awareness of man's dependence on good and bad weather, on rain and

sunshine, lightning and hail, plague and famine, on the fertility or infertility of the earth and abundance or meagerness of litters, arises the conception of all kinds of demons and spirits – beneficent and malignant – distributing blessings and curses . . . The world is divided into two halves; man himself seems divided into two halves. This is the phase of animism, of spirit-worship, of belief in the survival of the soul and the cult of the dead.[12]

The similarities which Soyinka has noted between the rituals of Ogun worship and those of Dionysos are best grasped in such socio-economic terms. By positing these practices in a specific evolutionary context, however, one is not suggesting that animistic religion and the modes of perception attendant on it are things of the past in Africa. On the contrary, the reality of contemporary African experience is the active co-existence of a pre-scientific mode of perceiving reality with a modernizing tendency. This corresponds to the co-existence of pre-literate communal agricultural village societies with modern industrial urban centres; the former with its herbalists, shrines, hoes etc. and the latter complete with its computers, Mercedes cars and skyscrapers. And this is largely the case in most societies of the world, for at no point in time does a given national or transnational society attain a perfect uniformity in mode of production and world view. If this happens, such a society or culture is ready for a change into its antithesis. One must of course concede the preponderance of pre-scientific (traditional) modes of existence and experience with modern modes in contemporary Africa. According to Wiredu,

Contemporary African societies are still largely traditional in the anthropological sense. Nevertheless, it is important for the future that the significance of the current processes of modernisation in Africa should be realised not only in terms of material changes, but also in terms of intellectual development.[13]

From this perspective, it is undialectical to insist on an African world view as a static irreducible.

Against the foregoing background, therefore, it is my contention that the entire concept of an African world view – immutable, undifferentiated in time and space – is a mythical and illusory concept propagated and popularized to satisfy the hunger of African bourgeois intellectuals for an ideological sanctuary in the face of incessant harassments from a Western intelligentsia socialized by the exploits of their forefathers into thinking of other peoples, especially Africans, as inherently inferior.

The reality of the African situation must be rigorously confronted in its dynamic multivalence by a dialectical intelligence equipped with an acute sense of history. To drown oneself in a so-called African world view that thrives on romanticizations and complex rationalizations of bygone days is the height of a nihilistic narcissism which has nothing to do with defending one's African identity and dignity. It is, in addition, to lag behind the African masses themselves who, in their rural poverty and urban squalor and dispossession, are progressively losing confidence in gods, shrines and amulets that have no answers to rising costs of imported food, drugs, electricity and even the schnapps used in pouring libation to the gods. Fanon realized the limitation of an unrelenting obsession with a retrogressive conception of tradition and put the matter quite pointedly and analogically in the following quotes:

> All the proofs of a wonderful Songhai civilization will not change the fact that today the Songhais are underfed and illiterate, thrown between sky and water with empty heads and empty eyes.[14]

> It is not enough to try to get the people back to that past out of which they have already emerged, rather we must join them in that fluctuating movement which they are just giving a shape to.[15]

In spite of its myriad flaws, however, the notion of an African world view has informed an impressive body of aesthetic pronouncements on African literature which also embody the basic contradictions inherent in that philosophical proposition.

Pitfalls of Traditionalist Aesthetics

The indeterminacy and ambiguity inherent in the very concept of an African world view also bedevil attempts to distil an aesthetic from that world view. The resultant traditionalist aesthetics is from the outset, therefore, a prodigal proposition. The concept of *tradition* which informs our subsequent characterization of the aesthetics in question needs initial clarification. Traditionalist thought in Africa and elsewhere describes a pre-scientific mode of perceiving reality, explaining events and seeking to effect changes in the objective world through subjective (often magical) impulses uncorrected by rational enquiry. Thus, the term traditional in this context is not a temporal category but a modal one; it is a way of saying that traditionalist thought and perception, although a dominant mode in pre-colonial African societies, still features in post-colonial Africa and can be identified in specific formations even within advanced industrialized societies.

Against this background, the contradiction inherent in traditionalist aesthetics of African literature can be identified in three dominant tendencies:

1. a pseudo-universalist idealism which takes a pan-Africanist view of African literature and seeks to see that literature in terms of a universal world culture;

2. a narrow ethnocentric particularism which distils the aesthetic values of a particular ethnic culture and uses knowledge derived therefrom to pontificate on African literature and art;

3. a crusading neo-negritudist polemic that correctly identifies the need for the decolonization of African literature but conceives of that process in romantic idealist terms to the exclusion of the vital determinants of culture.

The first tendency is the product of an adulteration of the recognition of the specificity and peculiarity of African culture with a liberal universalist conception of literature and art. Stanley Macebuh, in his otherwise brilliant essay, "African Aesthetics in Traditional African Art",[16] typifies the main liabilities of this tendency. Probably because of a certain intellectual socialization into the best traditions of Western liberal idealist aesthetics, Macebuh attempts to define and situate the aesthetic referent of traditional African figurative and verbal arts in the realm of what amounts to Platonic ideals:

> What the artist seeks to represent in the sculpted figure is his direct apprehension of the ideal, mediated by an oppressive sense of the real, for the "real" is not merely phenomenological, but embraces . . . the mind of God.[17]

Which God (Stanley)? It is perhaps permissible to impose a rationalist–idealist order on the African world. But to proceed therefrom and impose the Christian God to preside over "order" in the African world, is, to say the least, a veritable abomination. There is no single God in whose image the African was sculpted (or moulded) nor is there a static monolithic conception of "the Ideal" or the real to which the African creative imagination aspires. What existed, and still exists, is the individual artist's active perception of reality defined in terms of the dialectics of social experience in his or her particular community. This perception was livened and given concrete artistic form as an expression of the artist's perennial commitment to the process of change and to the advancement of the consciousness of his or her society.

Macebuh's essay contains several other interesting off-hand generalizations about traditional literary art in particular which deserve quoting at some length:

> Traditional African narrative tends to be fluid, repetitious, incantatory, even "structureless", but far from being formless, it seeks indeed to recapture, through . . . direct mimesis, the oceanic infinitude and the interpenetration of things in the universe.[18]

> In traditional African literature, content, theme and subject matter had often to conform to the facts of immediate experience, structure, organisation, and meaning derived ultimately from a metaphysical consciousness.[19]

A much more disarming feature of this aspect of traditionalist aesthetics is its innocence of the inevitable socio-political implication of all artistic undertakings. In his essay, "An African Literary Aesthetic: A Prolegomena" (sic), Charles Nnolim contributes to the ongoing debate by arguing for an African literary renaissance sanitized of politics and political commitment, features which he sees as the source of the "trouble" with contemporary African literature. Hear Nnolim:

> African literature as it is written today is maggot-ridden to the core: it is flawed

by the very nature of its concerns, for it is, in the main, *littérature engagée*, and committed literature has a way of dying a natural death – certain to be dulled and dimmed by the fog of time when the issues it fought over are no longer current.[20]

Artistic nationalism should be a-political and should only be a nationalism that celebrates and revitalizes African oral tradition and its folkways. Such nationalism, therefore, should shun all the "isms" of modern political, economic, social and ideological struggles.[21]

Much as Nnolim's pronouncements speak for themselves, it would be necessary to ask whether in fact the age-long marriage between literature and politics has ever been dissolved. From the Homeric epics to the medieval morality play; from Elizabethan theatre to romantic poetry; from the literature of the Chinese cultural revolution to Russian socialist realism; from the literature of negritude to that of the Harlem renaissance; from African cultural nationalist literature to the most contemporary, anti-imperialist writings, has literature ever parted company with politics? Nationalism itself is a term that belongs squarely in the realm of politics. For an African professor of literature to speak of "artistic nationalism" without political content is anachronistic and tragic to say the least.

In this universalist idealist formation of the African aesthetic movement, a note of relief emerges in the writings of Isidore Okpewho. In his highly informative essay, "The Aesthetics of Old African Art",[22] Okpewho recognizes the compulsive social predication of traditional African art as well as the dynamic relationship between the artist and his society:

In view of . . . the traditional society's pressing sense of the real, the desire to have 'the inapprehensible world grasped', it seems logical to suggest that it has human experience as its fundamental frame of reference . . . The traditional African artist is then first and foremost a realist artist.[23]

I have chosen to see the traditional African artist as an active mind operating in a dynamic context.[24]

Perhaps Okpewho's most crucial contribution to the debate on traditional aesthetics consists in his recognition of the dialectical essence of tradition itself as "a pattern of growth rather than as a rigid invariable".

The second tendency in traditionalist aesthetics – that of elevating a particular ethnic mythology into a continental imperative – finds expression in Wole Soyinka's *Myth, Literature and the African World*. Soyinka's theoretical intervention in the question of Africa's position in world culture and civilization is partly a direct response to the romanticist and retrospective fixations of writers like Cheik Anta Diop who had relied almost solely on ethnological evidence to support their equally rigorous re-mythification of the African world and essence. Unlike Anta Diop, however, Soyinka insists on a process of racial apprehension rooted in myth. As Okpewho remarks, "[from] Soyinka's point of view this is the inward eye of mythic essence, which probes more deeply into the springs of a people's cultural life than anything we can derive from feeble archival resources".[25]

More specifically, Soyinka writes in response to promptings from two "hostile" and, in his view, equally insidious ideological camps: firstly, there are the "radicals" and "sophisticates" (African and non-African) – who maintain that traditionalist cultural reaffirmation is a reactionary diversion. Secondly and more immediately, he writes to address and confront that kind of racist arrogance which has continued to blind the English academic (especially at Oxford and Cambridge) to the specificity of the African world.

> This volume . . . is engaged in what should be the simultaneous act of eliciting from history, mythology and literature, for the benefit of both genuine aliens and alienated Africans, a continuing process of self-apprehension whose temporary dislocation appears to have persuaded many of its non-existence or its irrelevance . . . in contemporary world reality.[26]

The underlying assumption of the book, therefore, is the existence of an African world view, a homogeneous, immutable and eternal metaphysics by which Africa can be distinguished from the West in particular. This idealist construct is here elevated into a cultural mini-catechism which is adumbrated with relentless fervour and articulated in a characteristically turgid idiom.

Predictably, the notion of an African world view on which Soyinka predicates his aesthetic pronouncements in this book is a familiar landscape to those who are conversant with his obsession with the mythic realm. In *Myth, Literature and the African World*, a metasocial, transhistorical and mythic "reality" is juxtaposed with the phenomenological universe of everyday prosaic reality. A combination of both levels of "reality" is posited as the African sense of the real and the essence of the African world view. In the resultant world, man, nature and supernatural agencies are united in a complex cosmogonic design in which the laws of logic and causality peter out into irrelevance. Man is primarily a spiritual being and his social experience is submerged in ritual. Accordingly, conventional notions of space and time are dissolved in an oceanic continuum that denies periodicity and specificity to human experience and action. The lineal progression of events is replaced by a cyclic determinism: "Traditional thought operates, not a linear conception of time, but a cyclic reality".[27]

At the level of what remains of social reality, human existence is perpetually haunted by a plethora of ominous forebodings from the ever-present world of ancestors. Explanations for human action or for mishaps are to be sought from the great beyond through oracles. Most interestingly, human action is portrayed as in blind obedience to subliminal impulses radiating from the cosmic *will* of some god. Like in the world of the ancient Greeks as recreated by Nietzsche, human character is to be understood in terms of fixed *types* deducible from the peculiar attributes of different gods in the ethnic pantheon. For Soyinka, the metaphysical models for human action are furnished by the numerous deities in the Yoruba pantheon. This quality, the immanence of divine purpose in human essence, constitutes for him an invariable attribute of the African world which has been lost to modern Western man:

> In Asian and European antiquity . . . man did, like the African, exist within a cosmic totality, did possess a consciousness in which his own earth being, his gravity-bound apprehension of self, was inseparable from the entire cosmic phenomenon.[28]

In addition to the essentially Yoruba-centredness of Soyinka's "African World" and its resultant dramatic theory, there is a disturbingly paradoxical Eurocentrism about Soyinka's conceptualization of the metaphysical identity of Yoruba deities. This is in the sense that he delights in finding equivalents between key Yoruba gods and ancient Greek gods. It is this obsession with cross-cultural equivalents that informs his adaptation of Euripides' *The Bacchae*, an obsession which is theoretically illuminated and concretized in his essay, "The Fourth Stage": "Ogun . . . is best understood in Hellenic values as a totality of the Dionysian, Apollonian and Promethean virtues".[29] What is here being questioned is not Soyinka's right to perceive equivalents among cultures but the idea of legitimizing African deities by matching them with the gods of the ancestors of Europeans.

The crucial challenge for Soyinka, however, seems to be one of distinguishing a peculiarly African mode of perceiving and apprehending reality which will necessarily differ from what we have come to associate with the West (and here there are echoes of the ugly controversy: Is there anything like African philosophy?). In an attempt to see this quality in a certain "irrational" cast of mind, Soyinka falls into the familiar Senghorian trap of dismissing rational, philosophical and logical thinking as part of the reification and dehumanization of Western man. This rather unfortunate argument comes out when he tries to distinguish between Western and African dramatic traditions:

> The serious divergences between a traditional African approach to drama and the European . . . will be found more accurately in what is a recognisable Western cast of mind, a compartmentalising habit of thought which periodically selects aspects of human emotion, phenomenal observations, metaphysical intuitions and even scientific deductions and turns them into separatist myths (or "truths") sustained by a proliferating super-structure of presentation idioms, analogies and analytical modes.[30]

Implicit in this assertion is a certain romanticization of the African mind as non-rational but capable of "a cohesive understanding of irreducible truths". And here the wheel has come full cycle, for the neo-negritudist, neo-nationalist has begun to speak the language of Levi-Bruhl!

If one is sufficiently courageous to penetrate Soyinka's linguistic barrier, and resist the rhetorical seductiveness of his prose and the sheer eclectic expanse of his erudition, we come face to face with the pitfalls of his brand of traditionalist myth-making. We can safely itemize these shortcomings as contained in *Myth, Literature* as follows.

a) The excessive fixation on myth blurs the historical predication of myth itself.

b) History is almost totally excluded in the attempt to polarize mythic reality and prosaic reality.

c) There is a certain dissonance between the Yoruba-centredness of the ethnographic evidence and the Pan-Africanist reference of the book itself.

d) In the attempt to project an undifferentiated African cultural continuum, Soyinka dissolves the obvious contradictions in consciousness that we find in African literature in a general sea of apprehension. Consequently, obvious ideological and class divergences between writers are omitted or conveniently ignored in this fixation with continental/race retrieval.

Our quest for a definitive, coherent and systematic articulation of the aims and methods of traditionalist aesthetics leads to the doorstep of the third formation of the intellectual fashion itself – that represented by the troika of Chinweizu, Jemie and Madubuike. The now familiar book, *Toward the Decolonization of African Literature*, is the manifesto of this formation. The absence of history in the earlier formations is remedied here by situating the quest for an authentic African literary aesthetic in the context of decolonization, which is now posited as a cultural challenge in a purely superstructural sense:

> The cultural task in hand is to end all foreign domination of African culture, to systematically destroy all encrustations of colonial and slave mentality, to clear the bushes and stake out new foundations for a liberated African modernity.[31]

The warning shots of this thesis had earlier been fired in Chinweizu's deservedly controversial book, *The West and the Rest of Us*:

> A modern African culture, whatever else it might be, must be a continuation of old African culture. Whatever else it includes, it must include seminal and controlling elements from the African tradition, elements which determine its tone, hold it together, and give it a stamp of distinctness.[32]

This thesis is later adumbrated into the catechism of the troika in the later book.

It is important to preface our observations on the limitations of this "important" book with certain qualifications about its significance in African cultural scholarship. Firstly, it is the first systematic fairly incisive identification of the ills of modern African literary creativity and its criticism. In this regard, it punctures the naked under-belly of bourgeois criticism of African literature. More crucially, because of its intrinsic recognition of the fact that artistic values are often geo-politically and racially determined, it distinguishes between Afrocentric and Eurocentric values in matters of literary taste and thereby deflates the bogey of liberal humanist universalism. For an African audience, the crucial import of the book belongs in the psycho-affective domain of cultural perception and consumption in the sense that the authors earnestly, even if idealistically, ginger their African audience to shake off their Eurocentricity.

Beyond the foregoing admissions, however, the ideological and theoretical shortcomings of the book (which are legion) need to be highlighted if only for the purpose of advancing its ostensibly noble cause. The following critique of the positions in the book in question must be seen as an attempt to promote meta-criticism and the history of ideas in African scholarship. In short, *certain ideas come into being, enjoy prominence and fade out of fashion because of certain determinate socio-historical conditions. It is the responsibility of committed scholarship to identify these moments and conditions so that intellectual fashions and schools occupy their rightful historical positions. Reality can then be confronted with the tools of new ideas.*

Again, for purposes of clarity, we can itemize the pitfalls of the Chinweizu et al. contribution to traditionalist aesthetics as contained in *Toward the Decolonization of African Literature* in particular:

a) The pursuit of cultural (literary) decolonization rests on the false assumption that economic and political decolonization have been completed. It is common knowledge that the cultural domination of Africa by the West is only a symptom of a more fundamental domination. The interconnection between economic and cultural domination on one hand and liberation on the other is only hinted at but not articulated in clear structural terms. Cultural imperialism is only an outward superstructural manifestation of economic imperialism. The crucial task before Africa is economic liberation which will in turn encourage a liberated literary culture. Existence (economics) precedes essence (literature). This dialectic is apparently alien to the authors of this book.

b) The positing of Afrocentric values *vis-à-vis* Eurocentric values is undialectical. It negates the internal differences and putative heterogeneity of the two opposing geo-cultural zones. What is actually being juxtaposed and opposed are traditional (pre-colonial) African animistic values versus bourgeois Western values. Values in Africa and the West are group and class values and are in turn dynamic and historical.

c) There is a certain hypersensitivity to the Western hegemony that leads to a romanticization of the traditional African literary heritage. Negritude is smuggled back in through the back door under the guise of irreverent rhetoric.

d) In turn, tradition itself is conceived of in rather static terms. Again, it is obvious that the forces that are responsible for the shaping of a given tradition often lie outside the tradition itself. Similarly, whether modern African literature should be *traditionalist* in a pre-colonial sense is a function of a complex of factors primarily predicated on the nature of the social experiences that constitute the motivation and content of literature.

The kind of mechanical experimentation with tradition which the troika advocate will result in a simulated, synthetic art.

e) The conception of the political commitment of the writer which emerges from this book is extremely indeterminate and diffuse and smacks of familiar liberal equivocation:

> None can decide for the writer, as none can decide for the cook, the teacher, the soldier, doctor, merchant, lawyer . . . or politician. Each would have to decide which cause to serve by donation of his or her skill . . . [The writer] can defend or attack the state, if that is where his impulse leads him.[33]

Political commitment is one thing; artistic profundity is another. Political commitment is socio-historically determined. In certain social situations, some writers end up being irrelevant or plain traitors of their people.

f) In its pan-Africanist aspiration, the book does not give sufficient attention to the reality of individual national literatures which constitutes the most advanced stage in the evolution of African literature to date. Fanon had seen the danger signal implicit in this particular deficiency when he said that:

> [The] historical necessity in which the men of African culture find themselves to racialize their claims and to speak more of African culture than of national culture will tend to lead them up a blind alley.[34]

Nor do the troika give sufficient attention to regional and ethno-national contradictions and variations in African literary consciousness.

g) There is also the erroneous impression that cultural/literary renaissance is a self-generating phenomenon which can be pursued in its own terms and by itself. Whatever literary culture the Western Renaissance itself bred was the logical outcome of decisive alterations in the economic, social and political orientations of Europe. Elizabethan drama, for instance, was merely the cultural expression of the economic proposition symbolized by the Medicis or the increased secularization of political life represented by Queen Elizabeth I. Elsewhere in the world, where there has been a literary renaissance of the scope advocated by the troika, such a renaissance has always formed part of far-reaching changes at the political and economic levels. The literary harvest and the democratization of literary consumption that accompanied the Chinese revolution were organic outgrowths of the Chinese revolution. Similarly, movements like Russian formalism and socialist realism, respectively, were products of developments in the Russian revolution of 1917.

What are the ideological, socio-economic and political predicators of the traditionalist aesthetic renaissance being advocated by Chinweizu *et al.*? Is the task in hand strictly that of cultural decolonization? Can a dependent neo-colonial economy sustain a decolonized literary culture?

From the foregoing observations we can hazard certain tentative conclusions about the present hegemonic status of the kind of ideas expressed in *Toward the Decolonization of African Literature*. It would appear that the situation of complete cultural decolonization which it envisages would ordinarily flow from a situation of economic and political freedom, for it is not possible to achieve a decolonized literary culture in an atmosphere of imperialist tutelage.

It therefore needs to be said, and quite pointedly too, that for all its pseudo-radical posturing, its affected irreverence and its revisionist fervour, *Toward the Decolonization of African Literature* remains a fatally flawed book. Its cardinal premise is suspended on a precarious idealist proposition – that culture can be sequestered from its economic and political moorings. Its emotional appeal is founded on a dying anti-racist racism; its idea of tradition is static while its notion of society is undialectical. It is the kind of fundamentalist cultural nationalism which is capable of diverting the minds of the young and the young-at-heart from perceiving the integral nature of cultural struggles in the larger struggles for economic freedom and social justice which currently stare Africa in the face.

Most dangerously, there is a certain intellectual and theoretical superficiality and philistinism about this book which is deliberately submerged in pugilistic phraseology and an unnecessarily quarrelsome tone. Ultimately, the book is in fact a very *colonial* book in the sense that it defines the African world in decadent animistic terms, thus advocating for Africa an image based on backward integration, which is the staple diet of European racist mythology. It is no wonder then that Chinweizu *et al.* have had only a nuisance value in African cultural scholarship. Nor could they be said to have influenced any writers or critics of note. Their book is ultimately mythic and its brand of myth-making is good only for the Black Power-mongering, fist-clenching adolescent and for the lazy intellectual unwilling to apply himself rigorously to the real challenge of an intellectual calling.

All the foregoing formations of traditionalist aesthetics are united by a common fundamental historical and ideational dislocation. They fail to recognize that in all traditional societies, theorizing about aesthetics was not a distinct social undertaking divorced from the consumption and creation of art. Says Terry Eagleton of the rise of aesthetics as a discipline:

> Previously, men and women had written poems, staged plays or painted pictures for a variety of purposes, while others had read, watched or viewed them in a variety of ways. Now these concrete, historically variable practices were being subsumed into some special mysterious faculty known as the "aesthetic".

> Art was extricated from the material practices, social relations and ideological meanings in which it is always caught up, and raised to the status of a solitary fetish.[35]

The rise of traditionalist aesthetics in African literary discourse must also be seen as part of a general process of reification which has little to do with faithfulness to traditional artistic practice in its original manifestation.

The abiding significance of traditionalist aesthetics however resides in its contribution to the necessary task of imparting more knowledge about African artistic traditions, ethno-philosophies and extant aesthetic value systems to an indifferent world while imbuing the ignorant and miseducated African with greater confidence to understand both himself and the position of his mortally injured race in the world. But the crucial task of compelling the world, especially the West, to recognize Africa through its practical achievements demands more than self-definition and rhetorical reaffirmation. Accordingly, in the area of culture, it calls for a theoretical framework in which the absolutist separation between idea and praxis is finally banished. We need a theoretical framework which would seek to integrate cultural liberation into the larger struggle for economic and political liberation. In this regard, a dialectical theory of African literature, corrected by an anti-imperialist ideological stance, seems most suited for consolidating the gains of traditionalist aesthetics and transcending its particular limitations to a greater understanding of the African reality. The three subsequent chapters pursue this line of thought in greater detail.

Notes

1. Ngugi Wa Thiong'o, *Writers in Politics* (London: Heinemann, 1982) p. 25.
2. Odia Ofeimun, *The Poet Lied* (London: Longman, 1982) p. 35.
3. Chinweizu et al., *Toward the Decolonization of African Literature* (Enugu: Fourth Dimension, 1980).
4. Wole Soyinka, *Myth, Literature and the African World* (Cambridge: Cambridge University Press, 1976).
5. Bernth Lindfors, "The Blind Men and the Elephant", *African Literature Today*, no. 7, 1974, p. 63.
6. See, for instance Levi-Bruhl's *The Primitive Mentality* and also, with some modifications, Robin Horton's essay, "African Traditional Thought and Western Science" in B. R. Wilson (ed.) *Rationality* (Oxford: Basil Blackwell, 1970).
7. John Mbiti, *African Religions and Philosophy* (London: Heinemann, 1969).
8. Lemuel Johnson et al. (eds.) *Toward Defining the African Aesthetic* (Washington, DC: Three Continents Press, 1982).
9. Kwasi Wiredu, *Philosophy and African Culture* (Cambridge: Cambridge University Press, 1980) p. 30.
10. Kofi Awoonor, *The Breast of the Earth* (New York/Enugu: NOK, 1975) p. 51.
11. Ibid.
12. Arnold Hauser, *The Social History of Art*, vol. I, trans. Stanley Godman (London: Routledge & Kegan Paul, 1977) p. 11.
13. Wiredu, *Philosophy and African Culture*, p. 38.
14. Frantz Fanon, *The Wretched of the Earth* (Harmondsworth: Penguin, 1967) p. 168.
15. Ibid., p. 183.

16. Stanley Macebuh, "African Aesthetics in Traditional African Art", *Okike*, no. 5, 1974, pp. 13–25.

17. Ibid., p. 15.

18. Ibid., p. 20.

19. Ibid.

20. Charles E. Nnolim, "An African Literary Aesthetic: A Prolegomena", *Ba Shiru*, vol. 17, 1976, p. 71.

21. Ibid., pp. 61–2.

22. Isidore Okpewho, "The Aesthetics of Old African Art", *Okike*, no. 8, 1975, pp. 38–55.

23. Isidore Okpewho, "The Principles of Traditional African Art", *The Journal of Aesthetics & Art Criticism*, vol. 35, no. 3, 1977, p. 305.

24. Ibid., p. 311.

25. Isidore Okpewho, *Myth in Africa* (Cambridge: Cambridge University Press, 1985) p. 242.

26. Soyinka, *Myth, Literature and the African World*, p. xi.

27. Ibid., p. 10.

28. Ibid., p. 3.

29. Ibid., p. 41.

30. Ibid., p. 37.

31. Chinweizu et al., *Toward the Decolonization of African Literature*, p. 1.

32. Chinweizu, *The West and the Rest of Us* (Lagos: NOK, 1978) p. 298.

33. Chinweizu et al., *Toward the Decolonization of African Literature*, p. 254.

34. Fanon, *The Wretched of the Earth*, p. 172.

35. Terry Eagleton, *Literary Theory: An Introduction* (Oxford: Blackwell, 1983) p. 21.

3 Marxism and African Literature

Marxism is the symbolism of dialectical conflict, of drama, of the unity of opposites, of revolutionary change, of matter and man in motion, constantly transcending the moment, pointing into the future.   **Maynard Solomon**[1]

When I . . . used to write plays and novels that were only critical of the racism in the colonial system, I was praised. I was awarded prizes, and my novels were in the syllabus. But when toward the seventies I started writing in a language understood by peasants, and in an idiom understood by them and I started questioning the very foundations of imperialism and of foreign domination of Kenya economy and culture, I was sent to Kamiti Maximum Security Prison.   **Ngugi Wa Thiong'o**[2]

Marxist Aesthetics: An Open-ended Legacy

To seek to transcend the limitations of the various formations of bourgeois criticism of African literature is to quest for a politically engaged, ideologically progressive and dialectical theory of that literature. In this quest, Marxism has been palpably and critically implicated not only because it represents the finest crystallization of dialectical thought into a social and political proposition but also because it encapsulates an ideological proposition in the context of which progressive forces in Africa are engaged in the struggle for negating the legacy of neo-colonialism and frustrating the designs of imperialism. Somewhat paradoxically, however, the Marxist theory of literature or the body of postulations that have come to be consecrated into a Marxist aesthetics is an area fraught with conflicting and often contradictory positions. Part of the problem arises from the familiar fact that Marx and Engels never had enough time to develop their aesthetic perceptions and observations into a coherent aesthetic. This was a task which Marx in particular continued to procrastinate on until his death, as evidenced in his numerous correspondences on the matter. In a letter to Engels in July, 1865, he wrote:

As for my work, I want to tell you the unvarnished truth. Three chapters have still to be written to finish the theoretical part . . . Then the fourth book, the historical and literary part, remains to be written.[3]

Consequently, what successive generations of Marxist theoreticians have come to consecrate into Marxist aesthetics is derived largely from a combination of the random jottings/observations of Marx and Engels on specific aspects of artistic creativity and extrapolations of thoughts from their key philosophical writings into matters of literature and art.

It is important to note, however, that even if Marx/Engels were able to devote a volume to matters of aesthetics, such a work would have borne the marks of inconclusiveness and open-endedness which inhere in the very essence of dialectical thinking itself. In effect, Marxist aesthetics could not and can never be a closed system in the sense of Aristotle's *Poetics* for instance, for Marx's work was essentially a rebellion against the constrictive systematization of knowledge implicit in most idealist philosophies before him. Observes Maynard Solomon:

> Marx's work arose in part as a reaction against the grandiose attempts at the systematization of knowledge by his metaphysical predecessors. His intellectual labours can be regarded as a perpetual tension between the desire to enclose knowledge in form and the equally powerful desire to reveal the explosive form-destroying power of knowledge.[4]

On the strength of this rather sensitive observation, Solomon concludes further that Marx's writings on aesthetic and artistic matters "are aphorisms pregnant with an aesthetics – an unsystematized aesthetics open to endless analogical and metaphorical development".[5]

To make this vital admission, however, is not to imply that Marxist aesthetics cannot be identified in terms of certain determinate tasks, goals and assumptions which mark it out from bourgeois aesthetics in general. To the extent that Marx recognized artistic production as a form of labour and the work of art as an embodiment of cognitions and values which could be deployed in the service of freedom, he also saw the artist as a vital agent (among other collaborating agents in the social totality) in the shaping of social consciousness through the creation of artifacts which reveal the dynamics of social life and shatter the veils and complacencies of false consciousness. The elaboration of this central perception yields the following broad features as the primary characteristics of Marxist aesthetics:

a) a definite relationship (even if ambiguous) between literature/art and the material base defined in terms of the totality of the relations of production;

b) the class basis of art and the progressive nature of proletarian art;

c) a dialectical relationship between content and form;

d) a glorification of realism as the most progressive form of artistic representation.

In turn, specific problems in the sociology of literature and art arise from the application of Marxist dialectics to literature and art. Some of these include

    a) the relationship between literature and history,
    b) the nature of creativity,
    c) the dialectics of form itself,
    d) the nature of the aesthetic experience,
    e) the etiology of art forms,
    f) the evolving relationship between the writer and his audience.

Most of these areas, it needs to be pointed out, have as yet remained relatively unexplored by successive generations of Marxist literary theoreticians and critics.

From Plekhanov to Adorno and Althusser, from Trotsky and Mao to Eagleton, Ngugi and Gramsci, the precise manner and relative prominence which individual theoreticians have given to the above features and problems has been historically determined. As with Marxism itself, Marxist aesthetics and its applications to literary criticism contains what Raymond Williams calls a "variety of selective and alternative traditions within it" which are defined in terms of differing national and epochal imperatives.[6] This historical variability of Marxist aesthetics is in turn conditioned by the stage in the evolution of historical and productive forces in a given society which in turn define the conflicts and contradictions of social life which art, through mediation, seeks to resolve. Consequently, while for instance, contemporary Western Marxist literary theory as articulated by Fredric Jameson, Terry Eagleton and others has been concerned mainly with defining the precise relationship between advanced capitalism and art in the form of post-modernism,[7] radical Marxist literary theory in Africa and parts of the Third World is preoccupied with the responsibility of literature and art in the task of national liberation, anti-imperialism and the redressing of social inequities within individual national societies.

To a certain extent, it can further be argued that the great diversity of perspectives and approaches in Marxist aesthetics and criticism is contingent on the nature of art itself. A true work of art presents a dialectical image, at once specific and universal, immediate and transcendental, tangible and intangible, structured and yet exploding all attempts at rigid structuration; even defying at times the original formative intention. "Art has both a *here* and *now* and a certain universality. This is what enables specific works of art to survive beyond the particular eras that generated them".[8] When, therefore, the dialectical essence of art is matched with the very historical nature of dialectical thinking itself, Marxist aesthetics emerges as an internally differentiated open system, defying a monolithic perspective of both art and reality. Adolfo Vazquez summarizes this point with characteristic pungency:

Art is a phenomenon that constantly defies vacuous and hasty generalizations that result from a one-dimensional point of view. Within the Marxist camp today we can see profound differences in the emphasis given a particular aspect or function of artistic creation. These emphases derive from a shared conception of humanity and society and should not be considered exclusive as long as no one of them walls itself in and closes its door to a different basic approach to art.[9]

To restate the above fact is to call into question the very credentials of mechanical materialists whose insistence on a one-to-one correspondence between art and ideology has given Marxist aesthetics the reputation of unrelieved dogmatism. Both Marx/Engels and Lenin recognized the relative autonomy of literature and art and relentlessly emphasized the problematic relationship between literature and art on one hand and ideological and historical development on the other.[10] Obviously angered by the excesses of those of his "disciples" who tended to constrict and subvert the *spirit* of his own thoughts, Marx protested: "I am not a Marxist". Trotsky was later to react in the same vein by somewhat overstating the autonomy of art in *Literature and Revolution*. No better resolution can be found for the danger posed by the mechanical materialist usurpation of Marxist aesthetics than to restate that art is one (only one) of the spheres in which social men and women wage the historical struggle for the positive alteration of their circumstances and themselves. As a sphere of practical and constitutive social activity, literature and art possess an autonomy in the form of internal laws of performance and evaluation which are nevertheless subject to socio-historical conditioning. Again, Vazquez has the last word on this matter: "Art is an autonomous sphere, but its autonomy exists only *by*, *in* and *through* its social conditioning."[11] Given the rather young history of Marxist theorizing in Africa, the fledgling tradition of Marxist criticism of African literature (whose manifestations we shall presently discuss) can be protected against the pitfalls of the earlier Marxists, especially the neo-Hegelians. Such protection is best offered in the form of disclaimers emphasizing what Marxist theory of literature *is not*. Briefly, these warnings are as follows

1. Literature and art cannot be mechanically equated with ideology: ("class ideologies come and go, but true art persists").

2. There is no parallel relationship between class interest and artistic/literary expression although literary works cannot but bear the stamp of their class origins and orientation.

3. Literary/artistic achievement does not stand in direct relationship with social development but literature appropriates and testifies to its socio-historical determination.

4. The social and historical conditioning of literature and art is not reducible to economic determinism but economic factors cannot be ignored in the production and understanding of literature.

Again, these disclaimers do not amount to an acquiescence to the indeterminancy and absolute relativism which are the hallmarks of liberal bourgeois poetics. On the contrary, they amount to an admission that within Marxist literary theory and criticism, there are gradations in terms of level of approximation to the dialectical paradigm. But the crucial discrimination which needs to be made within literary theory in general is between Marxist and non-Marxist positions.

Marxist aesthetics, therefore, is ultimately an open-ended legacy, a fact which inheres in its dialectical heritage. In the African context, we can identify specific challenges which have provided the locus for the engagement of Marxism in literary creativity, theory and criticism. Prominent among these is the centrality of politics and ideology in African literature, the implication of literature in the struggle for national liberation and definition and the use of literature and culture to objectify and illuminate the national and class contradictions within individual African national societies to date.

Politics and Ideology in African Literature

The African politician is a blind man: he moves only in one direction – towards himself.   **Nuruddin Farah**[12]

Politics and issues of a fundamentally political nature have always occupied a central position in African literature. The griots and bards of ancient Africa who used their art to uphold or subvert the feudal status quo: Olaudah Equiano and his fellow freed slaves who deployed their nascent literary skills in the service of the anti-slavery cause; anti-colonial writers like Caseley Hayford, David Diop, Leopold Senghor and Chinua Achebe who used literature to challenge the supremacist mythology of colonialism; post-colonial writers like Armah, Serumaga, Aidoo and Ba using their art to pierce the hypocrisy and flatulence of the black elite, or the black and coloured South African writer using his skill to expose one of the world's most inhuman systems: all these varied practitioners of African literature are united by the basic political sensibility which has nurtured their creativity. What distinguishes each generation from the other is the nature and intensity of the political challenges which it has had to grapple with and recreate in its art.

If, however, the political involvement of African literature can be taken for granted, its ideological complexion calls for greater qualification. Although ideology is implicit in the very nature of all literature as a socio-linguistic institution, the emergence of ideology, in a serious aligned sense, as an issue in the literature of any society is always traceable to determinate circumstances and socio-historical conditions. In the African instance, the emergence of overt ideological considerations and polarizations in African literary creativity and discourse is fairly recent especially in West Africa and parts of East Africa. In the ex-Portuguese territories of Southern Africa, namely Mozambique and Angola, the liberation struggle was waged in the context of a clear anti-imperialist ideological standpoint which in turn necessitated a mass mobilization of culture and literature in the service of the struggle for freedom. The writings of Agostinho Neto, Pepetela and other Angolan writers as well as Cabral's polemical statements on culture (on which we elaborate in the next chapter) provide ample evidence of the integral nature of ideology in the literary culture of the areas in question.

In most countries of East and West Africa, especially Kenya and Nigeria, the emergence of the ideological question in literature can roughly be traced to developments between the late 1960s and the present. The decisive development consists in the rise of a tradition of radical thinking in general and whose strongest ideological alignment is generally Marxism. At the level of general theory, the development in question is a vindication of Lukacs' generalization that "in class society, literary movements are the inevitable, if not automatic, outgrowth of class struggles, of conflicts among social and political directions".

In the Nigerian instance, Marxist thinking in literature, as an orchestrated and concerted effort gradually building up into an alternative tradition, became significant in the mid- and late-1970s. It is my contention that the overall radicalization of consciousness in Nigerian literature along ideological lines is the logical outcome of the post-war period of unexpected oil wealth and its accompanying social, economic and political dislocations. The realities of Nigerian national life in the decade of the 1970s took the form of a frightening disparity between the scandalous affluence of the few and the abject penury of the majority; a total neglect of public infrastructure and a near breakdown of all recognizable codes of ethical conduct. The resultant literature has largely been preoccupied with objectifying this reality with an underlying revolutionary aspiration. The purveyors of this new literary sensibility have, understandably, been a younger generation of writers who came into maturation in the post-colonial era with its attendant hopes, which were dashed in the Civil War of 1966–70 and further squandered in the 1970s. The literary testimonies to this new consciousness include Femi Osofisan's plays: *Once Upon Four Robbers, Who is Afraid of Tai Solarin?* and *The Chattering and the Song*, Festus Iyayi's novels: *Violence* and *The Contract*; the poetry of Odia Ofeimun: *The Poet Lied*; Niyi Osundare: *Songs of the Market Place* and a host of others. The underlying perspective in these works emphasizes a certain projection of the masses as the real makers of history, a clamour for a revolutionary transformation of society and the abandonment of the capitalist economic framework. Consequently, one can now conveniently talk of two ideologically polarized traditions in contemporary Nigerian literature: the older, more conservative, ethnic-based tradition with an essentially liberal outlook, and with a no less acute political awareness represented by Achebe, Soyinka and Clark and the younger, more leftist and ideologically committed tradition that we have just spotlighted. Polemical exchanges between these two traditions have been characterized by a certain vitriol which cannot be explained by "literature" as an enclosed system. The upshot of this observation is that in contemporary Africa, writers and their works are implicated in the larger struggles which define political life in the wider society. Even among writers of the same nationality, of the same class alignment and even the same generation, it will not be uncommon to find great divergences in world view and ideological alignment.

In Kenya, we encounter more or less the same picture. After the initial euphoria of Uhuru and solidarity under Kenyatta, the 1970s witnessed a growing realization on the part of the more nationalistic arm of the national elite that the relationship between the KANU government and European commercial interests was closer than that between that government and the broad masses of Kenyans. In effect, the post-colonial period in Kenya has witnessed a gradual but progressive betrayal of the aspirations for which the peasants waged the Mau Mau guerilla struggle against British colonialism. The present situation in which the bulk of Kenya's economy and culture are controlled by foreign interests and in which the United States and other Western countries maintain military bases in that country provides a veritable ambience for the flowering of revolutionary thought and literature.[13] Ngugi wa Thiong'o is one writer who can be said, without fear of contradiction, to represent the conscience of patriotic and progressive forces in Kenya. Both artistically and polemically, Ngugi has sharply focused the anti-imperialist struggle in Kenya, Africa and the Third World in general into a consistent ideological proposition that is ultimately informed by Marxian dialectics. "The fundamental opposition in Africa today is between imperialism and capitalism on the one hand, and national liberation and socialism on the other".[14] Accordingly, around Ngugi is developing an alternative tradition in Kenyan literature which is ideologically partisan in a progressive revolutionary sense. Ngugi's own more recent works: *Petals of Blood*, *Devil on the Cross*, *Detained* as well as those he has undertaken in collaboration with other patriotic Kenyan writers: *The Trial of Dedan Kimathi* (with Micere Mugo); *I Will Marry When I Want*, and *Mother, Cry for Me* (both with Ngugi wa Mirii) all testify to this new temper. It is important to note that Ngugi has in fact moved further than his Nigerian counterparts in the direction of evolving a truly people's literature. Prompted by the crude immediacy of imperialist presence in Kenya, Ngugi has had to dismount from the ivory tower to lose his elitist identity by immersing himself in struggle with the people thereby creating with them an authentic literary culture. In this direction, he has had to work in the medium of indigenous languages, especially Gikuyu in which he wrote and produced *I Will Marry When I Want* (as *Ndeenda Ngaahika*) and *Devil on the Cross* (as *Caitaani Mutharaba-ini*). In contrast, Nigerian radical writers have remained largely theoretical, aloof and relatively more timid for obvious historical reasons. A non-combatant nationalist movement coupled with a high degree of indigenous participation in the post-colonial economy has disguised the dependency status of the Nigerian economy. There is also the absence of a tradition of systematized cultural repression coupled with the existence of interminable languages which make it nearly impossible for literature to aspire to appeal to a nation-wide audience in any single local language. *In effect, the nature and intensity of the ideological struggle in African literature is contingent on local circumstances and will vary from nation-state to nation-state.*

These developments in literary creativity resonate at the level of criticism with no less intensity. The emergence of Marxist criticism of African literature is predicated on precisely the same factors that have informed radical creativity in African literature. Understandably, the emergence of Marxist criticism of African literature has been greeted with greater noise than the literature itself. This is precisely as a result of the relative entrenchment and dominance of two traditions of criticism: the Western-inspired bourgeois tradition and the unmediated traditionalist formation. I have elsewhere pointed out the incoherence and theoretical hollowness of these two traditions. It is still germane to note that the series of confrontations between bourgeois critics and Marxist critics is a reflection of the struggle between the two *interests* they represent in real life. In class society (which is what all contemporary African societies are), as Lukacs correctly observes, "there is no less intensity in [literary] struggles and no less vehemence in the antagonisms in literature than in politics itself". To the extent that bourgeois criticism is an extension, to the cultural realm, of imperialist ideology, its precarious fortunes will be adequately neutralized by an anti-imperialist perspective.

Traditionalist reservations against Marxism belong in a different category. The major charge has been that Marxism is an alien doctrine and that radical change in Africa can be pursued without necessarily recruiting an alien philosophical system. The most reasoned articulation of this position is contained in a recent essay by the brilliant Ghanaian novelist, Ayi Kwei Armah. The main thrust of Armah's argument is essentially that Marxism, like other Western intellectual and cultural value systems, assumes a patronizing, even condescending, attitude towards Africa and that revolutionary theory is not the private property of some 19th Century European. Pre-colonial Africa and, indeed, other human societies have had cause in the process of their historical development to experience revolutionary changes and where such changes have been coupled with an organizational blueprint, a communist society has always resulted. "Revolution and communism are phenomena and concepts of universal occurrence. They have been known and experienced in different parts of the world during different periods of history".[15] Armah correctly identifies some of the acknowledged pitfalls of Marxism and arrives at the Afrocentric conclusion that Marxism is part of the neo-colonialist African vogue of worshipping Western products.

While no apologia is here being entered for some of Marxism's more scandalous oversights, it needs to be pointed out that Armah is flogging a dead horse. Marxism arose when and where it did as a result of determinate conditions primary among which was the ascendancy of capitalism, the alienation of labour, and the galvanization of working-class consciousness.

Consequently, as a system of ideas, it was bound to reflect, even in its avowed "scientific" aspirations, the major weaknesses (including racial arrogance) in the world view of the period. What is crucial in Marxism, therefore, is not the nationality of Marx and Engels but the practical content of their ideas especially in terms of positing, in hypothetical form, an antithesis to the capitalist alienation of labour. In this regard, Marxism still offers the most consistent and systematic theoretical framework for mobilizing against capitalism. And to the extent that most of the problems of contemporary Africa, which also form the essential preoccupations of African literature, can be traced to capitalist imperialism, the instrumentality of Marxism for dealing with that literature falls into place. No doubt revolutionary theory and communism are of an ancient and universal lineage. But to insist, as Armah does, on a resuscitation and systematization of revolutionary theory and practice wherever in pre-colonial Africa such theories may have existed is akin to the argument of those who insist that Africa should re-invent the wheel in order to overcome her present technological stultification. Marxism, like the products of modern technology (Eastern or Western), is a universal tool which can be put to the service of freedom. Above all, historical materialism, which constitutes the core of Marxist theory, recognizes the specificity and relativity of the historical conditions of divergent societies.

The implications of challenges such as Armah's for the application of Marxist categories to the criticism of African literature are by now obvious. A great sense of discrimination and rigour is called for. Thus, the real problem that has confronted the nascent tradition of Marxist criticism of African literature is that of domesticating the classical axioms of Marxist cultural theory to the specific demands of the literatures of historically related Third World countries. In this regard, two dominant modes of Marxist criticism of African literature are becoming increasingly obvious: first, we have an extremely prescriptive and reductionistic criticism which insists on the reflection theory of art and society. Critics in this school are quick to regurgitate the more doctrinaire axioms of Marx and Engels and proceed therefrom to castigate and hector specific writers for not reflecting all the topical events of the day in specific works or for not objectifying a given experience from the point of view of "the class struggle".[16] This brand of criticism issues from a vulgar, adolescent and orthodox Marxism whose negative implications have been restated by Roland Barthes in the following terms:

> We know how sterile orthodox Marxism has proved to be in criticism, proposing a purely mechanical explanation of works or promulgating slogans rather than criteria of values.[17]

On the contrary, the responsibility of genuine and profound Marxist criticism is to provide analytical insight into and "explain" the social resonance and aesthetic integrity of literary works as art objects which contain (or do not contain) certain experiences, assume specific forms and articulate specific viewpoints of man and woman in society by virtue of their objective socio-historical determination. Healthy signs in this direction are to be located in the works of such critics as Emmanuel Ngara (*Art and Ideology in the African Novel*), Biodun Jeyifo (*The Truthful Lie* and *The Yoruba Travelling Theatre of Nigeria*), Omafume Onoge, Ngugi in his critical essays (especially in *Homecoming*) and the critical and theoretical works of Femi Osofisan among others. These critics are distinguishable by their realization that literary criticism, like the literature which forms its subject, is a constitutive social practice with a definite history. It is, therefore, socially determined. Thus conceived, genuine Marxist criticism must explode the bourgeois lie that only certain kinds of texts lend themselves to Marxist sociological analysis. Thus equipped with a dialectical scalpel, Marxist criticism can competently handle literary events from the oral tale to science fiction.

The readiest and, I believe, the most puerile charge which bourgeois intellectuals have levelled against African Marxist critics is that of a certain hypocrisy. Why be a university-based, privileged Marxist?, they ask.[18] While the African Marxist intellectuals, in terms of the source of their livelihood, belong to the petty bourgeois class, they have a singular advantage over their liberal bourgeois counterparts: they carry out their critical practice within a conceptual and ideological framework in which criticism transcends the limited confines of a narrow academicism and becomes integral to social praxis. Thus perceived, the African Marxist critic is not just a mere "literary" technician in a purely culturological sense. On the contrary, s/he is a concerned, involved and socially committed patriot with a sense of pedagogical responsibility. The new breed of African Marxist critics, in their clear-headed manifestation, are not red-eyed Zdanovian thugs brandishing copies of the Communist Manifesto and intent on executing writers who do not *conform*.

The present stage in the evolution of socio-cultural consciousness in Africa defines two vital areas for Marxist theory of African literature, namely, the relationship between literature on the one hand and the national and class questions on the other.

African Literature and the National Question

The native intellectual who wishes to create an authentic work of art must realise that the truths of a nation are in the first place its realities.   **Frantz Fanon**[19]

After the elimination of white rule shall have been completed the single most important fact in Africa in the second half of the twentieth century will appear to be the rise of individual nation states. I believe that African literature will follow the same pattern.   **Chinua Achebe**[20]

Perhaps the most remarkable political phenomenon in Africa in the 20th Century is the progressive dismantling of colonialism and the emergence of individual nation-states. The peculiarity of this ongoing process inheres in the very nature of the colonial heritage of the emergent states which brought together diverse ethno-nationalities into unified political entities. Lenin had given due prominence to the national question in the form of individual nation-state identity.[21] However, the colonial heritage of the African continent coupled with the near absolute absence of an industrial capitalist class in Africa by the late 1950s and early 1960s creates a context in which national liberation, redefinition and assertion take precedence over the class question. A conspicuous implication of nation-state formation in Africa, therefore, is the conflict between primordial ethnic values and loyalties on one hand and the imperatives of a wider nationalism which demands that members of diverse ethnic groups should submit themselves to the dictates of a common judicial system, police, army, as well as common economic and political institutions. The contradictions inherent in this development are manifested in the emergent national cultures of Africa, especially in the area of literature. While insisting on the increasingly nationalist character of African literature, however, one must, from the outset, underline the historical fact that the growth of consciousness in African literature began from a racial foundation, progressed to a continental framework before assuming its present nationalist character. This qualification is made more crucial because of the hegemonistic tendency among bourgeois scholars to overemphasize and absolutize the continental imperative in their discourse.

The reality of the national question in contemporary African literature, therefore, is predicated on the specificities of social experience within individual nation-states which also provide the creative locus for the writings and performances of individual artists. The insistence of imperialist scholars like Bernth Lindfors that there are as yet no national literatures in sub-Saharan Africa amounts to ignoring the vital relationship between literary art and the historical process in individual African nation-states.[22] If we adopt the view that a national literature is nothing more than the total body of literature(s) created by members of a given national society, it becomes clear that the difference between African national literatures and their Western counterparts is one of emphasis, relative age and degree of consolidation.

The crucial challenge which the national question in Africa raises for a Marxist conception of literature has to do with the general relationship between history and literature. In the exploration of the possibilities made available by this relationship in the instance of African literature, it is important to keep in view Marx's qualification on the contradictory nature of the relationship:

> It is well known that certain periods of highest development of art stand in no direct connection with the general development of society, nor with the material basis and the skeleton structure of its organization.[23]

Yet it is indisputable that national history and national social experience furnish a thematic quarry and an ideological imperative in the context of which African writers have been working, especially in the post-colonial period. Individual African writers have consistently testified to this fact in both their polemical utterances and literary creativity.

Writing from his experiences in the national liberation struggle in South Africa, the late Alex La Guma insisted that "the anti-imperialist struggle involves that of national liberation, a struggle for the consolidation of a cultural community, for a national economy".[24] While reaffirming La Guma's conception of the problem, it is crucial to note that in the post-colonial period, the African writer's conception of national culture (within which national literature forms only a sub-category) often runs counter to that of the politician. This divergence is the result of an intra-class cleavage within the ranks of most African national elites. It is a cleavage resulting from the writer's moral outrage at the excesses of the politician. Nigeria's Wole Soyinka, for instance, confronted the power elite of his country in the Civil War years and earned himself detention without trial for articulating the idea of a class-ridden Nigerian nation with a partisan clarity that exposed the ideological bankruptcy of the power elite who insisted on such vacuous notions as "national unity" and "territorial integrity" as the basic issues at stake in the war over and above class contradictions. In place of the indeterminacy of the spokesmen of the system, Soyinka resolutely asserted in *The Man Died*, his prison memoirs: "I think, after all, there is only one common definition for . . . a nation – a unit of humanity bound together by a common ideology".[25] In similar vein, the exiled Somalian writer, Nuruddin Farah, testifies to the ideological and political chasm that has since existed between him and the ruling class of his country on the national question. He articulates his position with venomous insistence:

> The problems of Somalia are poverty, ignorance and tribalism; the problem is . . . does the politician ever accept this? . . . the problem is "himself" not "Africa", is not "Somalia" in Siyad Barre's case: for he, Siyad Barre is the problem. A country ruled by a collective of bandits whose names are shuffled every now and then, with X being minister of this today and Y minister of that the following day; a country ruled by a collective of nearly the same bandits for the past fourteen years.[26]

If the foregoing evidence reveals that that the African writer has reaffirmed the national question through polemical outpourings largely defined by negation, the evidence in the creative literature presents a much more complex elaboration of this basic attitude, a point to which we shall return presently.

For their part, the ruling classes in different African countries have responded to this oppositional stance of the writers and other cultural workers by enthroning an alternative, more "convenient" notion of national culture. This has taken the form of an unbridled obsession with revivalisms of decadent myths, sensuous gyrations and other cultural practices from selected precolonial societies. This "official" notion of national culture which has become the norm in most African countries is usually popularized through state-sponsored festivals, jamborees and airport reception dances and recitations organized to thrill the endless retinues of dignitaries. This view of African culture was given a continental outing during the lavish FESTAC '77 hosted by Nigeria during her oil boom days. The dysfunctionality and reactionary essence of this view of culture lies of course in its a-historical and non-dynamic perspective. It is also vital, in the context of this essay, to draw attention to the fact that this attitude to national culture has been reflected in the kind of writers to whom individual African ruling classes have come to accord recognition. In the Nigerian instance, the state has come to adopt and reward such relatively "harmless" writers as the soldier-poet, Mamman Vatsa (a copious producer of juvenile verse), Chinua Achebe (a liberal reformist neo-traditionalist pioneer writer) and Cyprian Ekwensi (a chronicler without any discernible political commitment).

The emergent national literatures of Africa so far testify to the complexity of the experience of nation-state formation itself. The basic constituents of the literary mediation of these "realities" can, for theoretical convenience, be reduced to (a) deployment of continuities of consciousness and technique from the oral cultures of the various ethnic groups, (b) recreations of aspects of national history, and (c) depictions of experiences from contemporary society in its structural manifestations.

The presence of aspects of ethno-philosophy and oral literary techniques in contemporary African literature testifies to the original ethnic-based structure of pre-colonial African societies. Most of what may be described as "first generation" African writers (Achebe, Senghor, Soyinka etc.) are people whose childhood experiences are deeply rooted in ethnic cultures and consciousness. Their literary articulation of national experiences is bound to reflect this background. Thus, after the initial articulation of Pan-Negro consciousness that we witness in such works as Caseley Hayford's *Ethiopia Unbound*, Senghor's *Ethiopiques*, David Diop's *Hammer Blows*, and Wole Soyinka's "Two in London" and "Telephone Conversation", we encounter an attempt by writers in the immediate post-colonial period to use specific ethnic myths to come to terms with the imperatives of the nation-state. A practical illustration of this genre of African literature is provided by Wole Soyinka's *A Dance of the Forests*. This is a play which premiered as part of Nigeria's independence celebrations in 1960 and in which the playwright explores the prospects of independent nationhood through a dense mass of mythic strands from Yoruba ethno-philosophy. A plethora of ancestral deities are invoked in what amounts to a historic stock-taking on the eve of a great communal event and in an obvious attempt to negate the romantic image of the African past that is dominant in Senghorian Negritude. The verdict that emerges in this play about the African (Nigerian) past is simple: guilty. The various human characters wear this badge of guilt as a historic burden which fills them and the atmosphere of the play with cosmic apprehension.

Therefore, the prognostications which issue from the various godlings who are invited by Forest Head to preview the future amount to a gigantic apocalyptic image. Ultimately, the vision of national independence which emerges from this play is that of an invitation to the various ethnic groups to absolve themselves, through purposive communal living, of a heritage of sin and false expectations. Even in this otherwise predominantly ethnocentric and highly mythic play, Soyinka emerges with an essentially materialist view of history, for the burden of guilt in the past is laid squarely on the shoulders of kings (Mata Kharibu) and their attendants (Court Poet, Court Historian), councillors and exploitative transporters. What emerges is a typically dialectical image in which aspects of ethnic mythology yield vital insights into the emergent structural models and socio-economic potentials of the newly independent state. To a great extent, the same utilization of ethnic myth for the complex exploration of national experiences and possibilities can be located in the works of Kofi Awoonor (*This Earth, My Brother; Night of My Blood*), Masizi Kunene and J. P. Clark (*Ozidi*). *This feature of African literature is a way of reaffirming the fact that when historically changed conditions necessitate a new level of consciousness, the literary imagination usually invokes beliefs, symbols and values from a preceding level of consciousness and ethos in order to authenticate and validate new realities.*

African literature has grappled with the national question in yet another way: by constituting specific events, experiences and personages in national history into objects of fictive elaboration. Where this has happened, the resultant literature has mainly assumed the form of a painful historical reconstruction for the purpose of redressing the misrepresentations and deliberate lies which constitute the hallmarks of colonialist history of Africa. Readers of Mofolo's *Chaka* and Ola Rotimi's *Ovonramwen Nogbaisi* cannot but be familiar with this feature. On the other hand, historical reconstruction sometimes becomes a means of "correcting" received versions of national history through new aesthetic possibilities for the purpose of positing fresh ideological options in a national context. Ngugi's *The Trial of Dedan Kimathi* and Ousmane's *God's Bits of Wood* provide ample illustrations of this alternative in the context of colonial and contemporary Kenyan and Senegalese national histories respectively. In the context of these works, history is recycled in the mill of the revolutionary imagination and the result is a new truth transcending the original propositions and conflicts in actual history and reaching out for a new humanized history. In *God's Bits of Wood*, the idealist notion of history as the rise and fall of kings is discredited while an essentially materialist proposition is aesthetically enthroned through a "democratic" approach to characterization. At other times, literary depiction of specific events in national history becomes a means of celebrating a certain acceptance, no matter how bitter, of the fact of nationhood. Abundant evidence of this manifestation is to be found in the rich body of literature that has been generated by the Nigerian Civil War (1967–70). In various ways, Ike's

Sunset at Dawn, Soyinka's *Madmen and Specialists*, Okpewho's *The Last Duty*, Iroh's *Forty-eight Guns for the General* and *Toads of War*, Emecheta's *Destination Biafra*, Achebe's *Beware Soul Brother* and a host of others testify to the *acceptance*, by the Nigerian writer, of the fact of his nation. Through these various works, the writers in question are engaged in a painful process of national self-interrogation. But the contextual framework is consistently the Nigerian nation as an objective reality. Even the most rabid imperialist critic cannot deny the *national* stamp of this body of literature, for it portrays situations and characters that testify to a complete awareness of the fullest implications of creating a nation-state.

The engagement of African literature with the vicissitudes of national history finds its most profound and trenchant manifestation in the literatures of those African nations that achieved political independence through the barrel of the gun. Here again, the ex-Portuguese territories provide the best illustrations. In Angolan literature, there is hardly any need to separate national literature from the nationalist armed struggle, for both constitute an organic unity. The chanted word, the written story, the dramatized experience, each emanates from *actual* involvement in the struggle and each in turn attains aesthetic profundity in the process, for the highest creativity is the involvement of men and women in the actual process of changing their historical circumstances and themselves in the process of struggle. In addition to the fine poetry of Angolan combatants anthologized by Michael Wolfers under the title *Angolan Poetry*, it would appear that the poetry of Agostinho Neto represents the finest crystallization so far of the organic relationship between literature and national history in the Angolan instance. In her introduction to the collection of Neto's poems, *Sacred Hope*, Marga Holness aptly summarizes the essential spirit of Neto's verse:

> The poems in this volume tell the epic story of the growth of consciousness of a people in the era of the modern form of the liberation movement. Here the pressing need is not to preserve elements of the past which are being shattered by the present but to release the future imprisoned in the present, overcoming everything which prevents history from being realised, whether it be fear, ignorance, passivity, erosion or the whole arsenal of armed tyranny.

The national question in African literature becomes even more pronounced in those works which are created well into the post-colonial period and in which settings, characters and situations bear an unmistakably national stamp. In such works, the social totality as it is mediated in literature wears a recognizably local stamp to the extent that the African reader can, through imaginative involvement, recognize familiar places, events and people in his real national world. Allegory becomes too weak a device to camouflage the national specificity of the writer's referent. In Armah's *The Beautyful Ones Are Not Yet Born*, references to contemporary Ghana are hardly disguised – the Osagyefo, the

Flagstaff House, the streets of Accra etc. – reveal Armah's sense of moral outrage as emanating from a fervent concern with the atrophy of vision and widespread corruption in Ghana's body politic in the dying days of the Nkrumah regime. In similar fashion, there is a disturbing historicism about Nigerian Civil War literature which almost threatens the ontological essence of most of the works as aesthetic entities. Specific battles, historical events, dates and theatres of war provide the skeleton structure for the plot and artistry of Iroh's *Forty-eight Guns for the General* and Ike's *Sunset at Dawn*. In Meja Mwangi's and Ngugi's works, real places (River Road, Nairobi, Eldoret, Nakuru, Uhuru Avenue) and people (Kenyatta, Kimathi, Kariuki) betray the unmistakably Kenyan identity and consciousness of the writers in question.

In these works, it is not merely the mimetic representation of people, places and events as epiphenomena that confers a national identity but a certain cognitive and affective disposition (in short, consciousness) which inheres in the ideologies of the individual texts. There is in these works and among these writers a sense in which socio-political commitment can primarily be defined in a nationalistic sense.

To give prominence to the increasing nationalist identity of African literature, however, is not to diminish the ultimately Pan-Africanist aspiration of African national cultures. There is a sense in which Africa's subjection to the same broad historical forces (colonialist brigandage, imperialist capitalism and East–West ideological polarization) can be said to forge a unity in diversity among African national cultures. The relationship between the national and continental imperatives in African literatures re-echoes the theoretical relationship between the specific and the general in the identity of individual works of literature. Each work of African literature created from a national perspective approaches the continental *truth* through a rigorous objectification of its specific national realities, for both realms of experience are dialectically and historically interconnected.

Furthermore, to underline the growing nationalist consciousness in African literature is not to deny the fact that there are still at the moment important works of African literature which are created purely within the framework of a Pan-African, even Pan-Negro consciousness. Such relatively recent works as Armah's *Two Thousand Seasons* and Soyinka's *A Play of Giants* and *Ogun Abibiman* testify to this lingering nostalgia for continental and black solidarity. The co-existence of these two levels of consciousness (the nationalistic and the continental Pan-Negro) further testifies to the problematic relationship between literature and history which Marx had hinted at.

Beneath the national consciousness in much of recent African literary creativity and discourse is a much more discriminating consciousness which has begun to see the emergent African national societies and the literary works predicated on them in clearer structural terms. This vital level of discrimination which is compelled by the pseudo-capitalist political economies of most African countries is that which perceives African literature in terms of the emergent class structures of contemporary African national societies.

The Class Question: African Literature or Literature of the African People?

> I sit on a man's back choking him and making him carry me, and yet assure myself and others that I am very sorry for him and wish to ease his lot by any means possible except getting off his back.   **Tolstoy**[27]

> We can only talk meaningfully of class love, class joy, class marriage, class families, class culture.   **Ngugi wa Thiong'o**[28]

The relevance of Marxism for the understanding of African literature acquires greater stridency if we examine the relationship between that literature and contemporary African society from insights made available by class analysis. In this regard, the reality of the African situation is the co-existence of both relative affluence and abject poverty in both the rural and urban areas. Contrary to the main thrust in some reductionist types of "radical" analysis, the vital discrimination is not in terms of an urban-rural divide *per se*. In both the urban and rural areas, we encounter obvious class stratifications in terms of relative access to power, privilege and material contentment.

In the urban milieu, there are the powerful and rich bourgeoisie – middlemen, army officers, industrial barons, ministers, clergymen, contractors, bureaucrats, technocrats, etc., etc., who inhabit the exclusive reservations and suburbs. This is the class that *decides* on behalf of its collaborators in New York, Paris, London and Tokyo. There is of course a middle social and economic stratum: the middle-class army of small executives, young engineers, confused university teachers, apprentice attorneys, technicians, doctors, police officers etc. who *execute* the orders of their black masters without a clear knowledge of where the original orders emanate from. Like bats in the social spectrum, they are what Ake calls "exploiters by class" but are equally "exploited" in the wider sense that their skills and proficiencies are sapped in return for creature comforts (cars, apartments, colour television sets etc.).[29] These are, in Soyinka's words, the "privileged slaves who prop up the marble palaces of today's tyrants".[30] These inhabit the multiple apartment blocks, semi-detached bungalows in the not-so-reserved residential areas of Dakar, Nairobi, Lagos and Abidjan.

At the bottom of the social ladder in urban Africa, we encounter the intimidating face of a vast army of humanity existing in spite of a variety of deprivations. There are the unemployed youth, prostitutes, pimps, beggars, swindlers, barmaids, bicycle repairers, small-time thieves and roadside hawkers of assortments of inconsequential merchandise. They are the inhabitants of the slums and hovels that have become part of the unofficial plan of every African city. They and the rural poor *sweat* for the leisure enjoyed by those who *decide* and *execute* from air-conditioned offices.

Against the widespread notion that rural Africa is the abode of unrelieved penury and toil, we can discern relative inequalities fostered by the primordial or emergent class structures/character of the rural areas as well. In feudal and pseudo-monarchical societies, we encounter the relative affluence of the feudal lords and their proxies *vis-à-vis* the tattered poverty of the majority of the peasantry. The urban political elite constantly recruits its "leaders of thought" and mobilizes its "grass-roots support" from amongst these feudal appendages, councillors and "traditional rulers", thus enshrining class antagonism in the rural areas as well.

The foregoing spectacle cannot but find reflection at the level of literature and culture, for, as is common knowledge, there is a strong class character to all culture. The literary artist, a member of a recognizable social class, creates out of the experiences made available by the material circumstances and the resultant world view of the class to which he belongs. The audience which he anticipates, even where he cognitively and ideologically *leaps* out of his social class, is always that which is conditioned by the class out of which his consciousness and communicative competence derives. Accordingly, different classes crave different kinds of literature because of the very experiences to which they are subject and the very conditions which shape their aesthetic responses. The ruling classes and the bourgeoisie in Africa are hardly men of culture in any patriotic sense of that word. Their cultural indulgences range from polo and casino in five-star hotels to the latest exotica from Hollywood. They may remember a few passages from Shakespeare with which they garnish their numerous speeches and anecdotes at state functions and boardroom sessions. For most of them, books (often in the form of sets of encyclopaedia with titles embossed in gold) constitute part of the penthouse décor. For the urban middle class, literature begins from the pulp and juvenilia of Western popular culture – Harold Robbins, Hadley Chase, Denise Robbins – freely hawked in hotels, supermarkets and rail cars. The members of this class do have a familiarity with African written literature to the extent that they may have been compelled to "study" these as part of the syllabus of a liberal arts education in an African university.

For the urban poor, on the other hand, literary taste assumes the form of songs in defiance of their oppressors, photo magazines about the courage, love, adventure and leisure which their marginalized existence often denies them. In the rural areas, however, the oral literary culture of Africa is still alive in the form of festival theatre, folk songs, moonlight narratives and riddles. But these oral forms do not exist in a static form. They are constantly changing, in both content and form, in accordance with the changing realities of life and the dynamics of the struggle for subsistence.

There is in fact a great solidarity between the literature and culture of the rural peasantry and that of the urban poor. Says Ngugi:

> In these towns and cities, new cultures are emerging out of [the] struggle for total liberation from imperialism. This can be seen in the poetry and songs and theatre among workers in the urban areas of the developing world. It is a fighting culture, and though fusing different elements, it is in basic harmony with the resistance culture of the countryside. The urban and the rural struggles are actually in basic harmony in their opposition to exploitation and domination by an alliance of a servile native ruling class and imperialism.[31]

This solidarity and complementarity between the urban poor and rural peasant literary cultures is reinforced by the demographic dominance of these groups which relegates bourgeois culture to a minority status. In reference to the Nigerian situation, Emmanuel Obiechina observes in a related context:

> The élite constitute an inconsequential, if disproportionately powerful segment of the Nigerian society. By far the largest number of Nigerians are . . . agricultural peasants that inhabit Nigeria's countless villages, the multitudes of tradesmen and women that throng the towns and villages, the army of petty traders, artisans, skilled and unskilled men and women who people the townships, the slums and the shantytowns.[32]

Against this background, a rigorous investigation of the class question in African literature and culture takes us back to the national question. The crucial question, then, is whether we can talk of a truly national literature in an atmosphere riven by class and ethnic antagonisms. In this regard, two conclusions compete for primacy: either that African national literatures and cultures are to be defined in the pluralistic terms revealed by the sheer class and ethnic diversity of the national societies themselves; or that national literature and culture in Africa is to be defined by a nationalist socialist ideal in which the social class that enjoys demographic dominance and produces the bulk of the wealth of the nation is also the custodian and repository of authentic national literature and culture. We reject the former proposition and accept the latter, for it is not only just and logical but also theoretically consistent with the spirit of this essay. Arguing in this vein, Obiechina argues for the Nigerian masses when he proposes that the "logic of numbers is on their side. Their culture and not the culture of the élite represents the authentic culture of the Nigerian people".[33] But the enthronement of the culture of the masses as *the* national culture in any African state is not and cannot be a given. It is a proposition which can only be actualized in the context of the larger struggle against imperialism. Ngugi, whose recent creative praxis has been informed by this conviction, articulates this view quite pointedly.

> My thesis, when we come to today's Africa, is then very simple: a completely socialized economy, collectively owned and controlled by the people, through

the elimination of all exploitative forces, is necessary for a national culture. A stratified society, even in pre-colonial Africa, produces a stratified culture or sub-cultures, sometimes to the total exclusion from the central hub of national life of the *ahois*, the *ndungatas*, the *osus*, the *mbaras*, the slaves and serfs in such pre-colonial societies, and of the peasantry and working people in modern neo-colonial states.[34]

Our insistence on a socialist democratic conception of national literary culture in Africa seriously calls to question the hegemony hitherto enjoyed by African literature written in the European languages by members of the *executive* arm of the various national elites as defined previously. The literature of Soyinka, Achebe, Ngugi, Armah, Farah, La Guma, Lenrie Peters, Aidoo etc., etc., which bourgeois criticism and imperialist media have come to consecrate into African literature constitutes, alas, a fragmentary minority literary culture! This shocking realization does not, however, diminish the African identity of these writers but instead puts them in their rightful position. A basic preoccupation with experiences emanating from Africa and the fact of being African by birth are the essential entry qualifications into the broad category of *African literature* even in the limited minority sense of African literature written in Western European languages. It is an umbrella term which is becoming increasingly dysfunctional if we must come to terms with the *use value* of African literature (even in this limited bourgeois sense) in the anti-imperialist struggle. While historically acknowledging the contribution of various African *writers* to the various struggles that have brought Africa to its present stage, the anti-imperialist imperative compels that we begin to discriminate among our writers, even as members of the elite, in terms of their ideological and class partisanship. This is perhaps one way in which the present polarization between bourgeois culture and the culture of the African masses can be bridged in the service of continental liberation. In this regard, we can make a tentative distinction between *African literature* in general and *literature of the African people*. The former will appear to correspond to what imperialist myth-making and scholarship has popularized and advertised as "African literature". The latter, on the other hand, consists of the literatures of the African masses in addition to the literature created by those members of the elite who, through ideological commitment, have *lost* and *found* themselves amongst the people. In whatever language these elite writers may be creating, their works contain the bitter *truths* about the conditions of the African people in their struggle against imperialism. Such literature is essentially antagonistic to the values that sustain exploitative structures in Africa.

The most recent, most refined crystallization of consciousness in African literature is therefore necessarily class partisan. In Ngugi's *Petals of Blood*, *Devil on the Cross* and *I Will Marry When I Want*; in Osofisan's *Once Upon Four Robbers* and *Morountodun*; in Ousmane's *Xala*; in Iyayi's *Violence* and a host of other new works, man is no longer just "the African" but the exploiter and the exploited, the rich and the poor, the literate and illiterate, the hungry and the overfed. The objectification of these polarizations in literature and the unambiguous articulation of the writer's alignment spells a fundamental rupture in the fold of African literature. These latter works, along with the anti-exploitative, anti-imperialist songs, dances and other performances of the urban poor and rural peasantry constitute, for this writer, the literature of the African people, for it adopts the people as its point of departure, centralizes them in its content and edifies them in its form while simultaneously espousing their cause as the definitive alternative to the present hegemony of enlightened slaves.

Beyond Orthodox Marxism: The Framework for a Post-Marxist Theory of African Literature and Culture

The foregoing discussion reveals, even in its essentially literary fixation, certain features of contemporary African society which suggest possibilities far too trying for the categories of orthodox Marxist social historical theory. Much as the major conjunctural tragedies of present day Africa can be traced ultimately to Western imperialism, itself an aspect of the deformation of capitalism, this contact has unleashed a plethora of socio-historical manifestations which the largely linear logic of Marxism may not quite have anticipated. In Africa today isolated urban-based pockets of industrial capital coexist with stubborn survivals of decadent feudalism often in the same urban setting. There is also an identity of material circumstances between the urban poor and the rural peasantry which cannot yet be said to have galvanized into a class consciousness and a recent high incidence of maniacal dictators (Mobutu, Nguema, Bokassa, Idi Amin etc.) whose psychological make-up would have baffled Marx's most imaginative application of the theory of class struggle. Similarly in today's Africa, the attempts at revolutionary transformation of society have been carried out mainly by military regimes (Ethiopia, Burkina Faso, Libya, Ghana) rebelling against the legacy of colonialist military traditions while the vanguards of the African revolution have been drawn, not from an industrial working class but from an odd mixture of peasants, students, women's groups and the urban poor, with workers in industry often constituting an incoherent minority. These features, which are also manifest in other parts of the world, have tended to problematize human history in a manner that has compelled a reassessment of Marxism and the socialist project.

While the contradictions in question have tempted bourgeois intellectuals to celebrate the apocalypse of Marxism, Marxist and progressive intellectuals have been challenged to undertake a more thorough and rigorous understanding of what Marx really *said* about the course of human history and the socio-cultural consequences of the process of history.

Among Western Marxists, the main sources of doubt have come from such developments as the welfare state, the cold war, nuclearism, ethnic-racial conflicts, nationalism and feminism within post-industrial Western societies, developments which tend to dull the centrality of the class struggle almost to extinction. The extent of this crisis is so deep that the New Left in Europe has of recent years been forced (from its academic and polemical exchanges on the matter) to admit that like capitalism, Marxism, and in fact the leftist alternative is caught in a deep crisis. Part of the editorial of the silver jubilee issue of *New Left Review* ran thus:

> Today the political scenery of the 80's is a much harsher one than anything the left has known since the 30's. A new imperialist cycle of the Cold War is pushing the nuclear arms race beyond the limits of the earth itself. A global recession is steadily increasing unemployment in the upper side of the capitalist world, and spreading debt and famine in its underside. The world communist movement has passed away: the post-revolutionary states of the East which once formed its magnetic pole have lost their force of attraction. The labour movement in the West has been unable to resist the consolidation of regimes of the Anglo-American Right, or the emulation of their policies by governments of the Eurosocialist Left.[35]

The most far-reaching implication of this admission resounds fundamentally at the level of Marxism as the theoretical bedrock of the left itself. Writes Ronald Aronson:

> In spite of its sheer appeal as a system and in spite of its claims to be comprehensive, Marxism becomes increasingly reductive and sterile in trying to account for [the] decisive concerns of our world.[36]

The sources of these increasing reservations are contained in the theoretical limitations of Marxism itself. The principal limitation is in the implication of the linear emphasis of Marxist philosophy of history, which does not seem to have sufficient elasticity to accommodate the dizzying developments in today's world. Allied to this is the fact that the development of productive forces in world societies has tended to challenge the predictive validity of Marx's philosophy of history.

On the part of committed African intellectuals, the source of worry about the appropriateness of Marxism as a theoretical framework for prosecuting the African revolution inheres in the very limitations imposed by the historical determination of Marxism itself and which are manifest in its very world view and conceptual categories. Marxism developed as a philosophical response to capitalism and the liberal idealism of the bourgeoisie. Its theoretical inspiration and conceptual categories were formulated in the context of industrial capitalism in its infant stages. This historical determination and theoretical orientation renders Marxism impotent when it comes to the elaboration of societies, cultural manifestations and historical developments that did not form part of the cognitive universe of Marx and Engels. Consequently, the works of Hegel and Marx/Engels after him contain blatant ignorances and even outright uncomplimentary remarks about Africans and other non-Western peoples. Ayi Kwei Armah has provided the most rigorous and "Afrocentric" articulation of these aberrations. These include Marxism's patronizing and Eurocentric silence about Africa, its implicit belief in the stupidity of the peasantry and the wisdom of the industrial proletariat, the notion of autotelic technology as well as the linear conception of history which places Western man at the helm and forefront of human history and progress.[37]

Given these limitations and to the extent that African literature is essentially an artistic mediation of the main features of contemporary African society, a progressive anti-imperialist theory of that literature, in order to approach a *total* picture of its historical conditioning, must of necessity transcend the limitations of orthodox Marxism. For the progressive African intelligentsia enamoured of the revolutionary potential of Marxism and yet sufficiently alert to its contextual limitations and theoretical blindspots, the way out seems to lie in a recourse to the philosophical breakthrough which Marxism represents, namely, historical materialism. As the application of the principles of dialectical materialist thought to the understanding of human societies and their process of development, historical materialism transcends Marxism and embodies a certain general theoretical *elasticity* that could salvage Marxism from its present crisis and imminent obsolescence. Ronald Aronson illuminates this option further:

> If Marxism as we know it is inadequate, . . . historical materialism provides a path out of the crisis.
>
> I am distinguishing historical materialism *from* Marxism: it alone allows us to pursue a layered analysis of the complex evolution of bourgeois society, following its displacements and repressions of original conflict *and* its generation of new conflicts, to the point it has reached today . . .[38]

The revolutionary implication of historical materialism inheres in the fact that it makes possible "a radical, structured, layered analysis of contemporary society" in general. In its dialectical sweep, therefore, historical materialism can incorporate "classical Marxism and the systemic changes since its heyday". The new vista of revolutionary change that emerges is essentially a collaborative one, what Aronson calls a *radical pluralism* in which workers as a *conscious* minority align with other groups *created* by capitalism in its negating logic. In Africa, the alliance would include the urban proletariat, urban poor students, progressive intellectuals, the peasantry, progressive army cadres, progressive women's organizations etc. Taken together, this group constitutes, in a demographic and political sense, the "vital majority" who are carrying the burden of imperialist hegemony and capitalist exploitation in Africa.

The challenge of this proposition for literary theory inheres in a totalizing, dialectical (in place of a metaphysical) perspective anchored on the specific experiences in the context of which literary creativity is taking place and which also provide the subject of and social necessity of literature.

Notes

1. Maynard Solomon (ed.) *Marxism and Art: Essays Classic and Contemporary* (New York: Vintage Books, 1973) p. 17.
2. Ngugi Wa Thiong'o, *Barrel of a Pen* (London/Port of Spain: New Beacon, 1985) p. 65.
3. Karl Marx and Friedrich Engels, *On Literature and Art* (Moscow: Progress Publishers, 1976) p. 111.
4. Solomon, *Marxism and Art*, p. 8.
5. Ibid., p. 9.
6. Raymond Williams, *Marxism and Literature* (Oxford: O.U.P., 1977) p. 3.
7. See, for instance, the following recent essays: Fredric Jameson, "Post Modernism, or the Cultural Logic of Late Capitalism", *New Left Review*, no. 146, 1985, pp. 53–92; Terry Eagleton, "Capitalism, Modernism and Post-Modernism", *New Left Review*, no. 152, 1985, pp. 60–73.
8. Adolfo Sanchez Vazquez, *Art and Society: Essays in Marxist Aesthetics* (New York: Monthly Review Press, 1973) p. 25.
9. Ibid., p. 23.
10. See Marx and Engels: *On Literature and Art*, p. 88. This refers specifically to Engels' letter to Minna Kautsky, 26 November 1885.
11. Vazquez, *Art and Society*, p. 98.
12. Nuruddin Farah, "The Creative Writer and the African Politician", *The Guardian*, Lagos, 9 September 1983, p. 11.
13. Ngugi Wa Thiong'o's recent writings, namely, *Writers in Politics* (London: Heinemann, 1981) and *Barrel of a Pen* come into focus here.
14. Ngugi, *Writers in Politics*, pp.78–9.
15. Ayi Kwei Armah, "Masks and Marx: The Marxist Ethos *vis-à-vis* African Revolutionary Theory and Praxis", *Présence Africaine*, no. 131, 1984, p. 37.
16. This tendency is most likely to be encountered in the essays of African critics who are making an initial contact with Marxism.
17. Roland Barthes, *Critical Essays*, trans. and ed. Richard Howard, (Evanston: Northwestern University Press, 1972) p. 255.
18. This charge is a recurrent feature of the rebuttals of bourgeois writers and intellectuals to some of the most trenchant critiques of their works from the Marxist camp. See, for instance, Soyinka's inaugural lecture, "The Critic and Society: Barthes, Leftocracy and other Mythologies", University of Ife, 1980; the preface to J. P. Clark Bekederemo's *State of the Union* (Essex: Longman, 1985).
19. Frantz Fanon, *The Wretched of the Earth* (Harmondsworth: Penguin, 1967) p. 180.
20. Chinua Achebe, *Morning Yet on Creation Day* (London: Heinemann, 1975) p. 56.
21. See V. I. Lenin, *Critical Remarks on the National Question* (Moscow: Progress, 1976) p. 25.

22. Bernth Lindfors, "Are There Any National Literatures in Sub-Saharan Black Africa Yet?", *English in Africa*, vol. 2, no. 2 (1975), pp. 1–9.

23. From Marx's Introduction to *A Contribution to the Critique of Political Economy* in Maynard Solomon (ed.) *Marxism and Art*, p. 61.

24. Alex La Guma, "Culture and Liberation", *World Literature Written in English*, vol. 18, no. 1, 1979, p. 30.

25. Wole Soyinka, *The Man Died* (Harmondsworth: Penguin, 1975) p. 183.

26. Farah, "The Creative Writer and the African Politician", p. 11.

27. Quoted in Ngugi, *Barrel of a Pen*, p. 83.

28. Ibid.

29. Claude Ake, *Revolutionary Pressures in Africa* (London: Zed Press, 1978) p. 62.

30. Soyinka, *The Man Died*, p. 15.

31. Ngugi, *Barrel of a Pen*, p. 80.

32. Emmanuel Obiechina, "Television and the Challenge of Culture", *The Guardian*, Lagos, 17 January 1985, p. 7.

33. Ibid.

34. Ngugi Wa Thiong'o, *Homecoming: Essays* (London: Heinemann), p. 13.

35. *New Left Review*, no. 150, 1985, p. 1.

36. Ronald Aronson, "Historical Materialism, Answer to Marxism's Crisis", *New Left Review*, no. 152, 1985, p. 87.

37. Armah, "Marx and Masks" p. 54 ff.

38. Aronson, "Historical Materialism" p. 88.

4 A Dialectical Theory of African Literature: Categories and Springboards

> Literary theory is less an object of intellectual enquiry in its own right than a particular perspective in which to view the history of our times. Nor should this be in the least cause for surprise. For any body of theory concerned with human meaning, value, language, feeling and experience will inevitably engage with broader, deeper beliefs about the nature of human individuals and societies, problems of power and sexuality, interpretations of past history, versions of the present and hopes for the future. **Terry Eagleton**[1]

Dialectics and Cultural Theory

If the strongest handicap of traditionalist and formalistic theories of literature is their polarization of literature away from socio-historical processes, the greatest attraction of a dialectical alternative is that it dissolves the apparent dissonance between literature and society, between literary theory and creative practice and re-establishes the indissoluble linkage between the two realms. Thus conceived, literary theory becomes not an estranged body of abstractions about an equally abstract "enclave" but an aspect of the all-embracing area of social discourse.

In the African instance, the attraction of a dialectical alternative becomes even stronger because of the incontrovertible socio-historical determination of African literature in general. From the oral chants and narratives of ancient Africa to the most contemporary literary expressions of our modern writers, the challenges and artistic limits of African literature have almost always been set by experiences and problems of a fundamentally socio-historical nature. Accordingly, the precise nature of these challenges and problems has equally been historical and dynamic.

In this chapter, therefore, we attempt a theoretical confrontation with this challenge by drawing attention to the cultural implications of dialectical thought, its potentials for African literary theory at the level of epistemological and hermeneutical categories. We also highlight three instances in Africanist socio-political thought (Fanon, Cabral and Ngugi) from which an anti-imperialist poetics of African literature could ultimately be derived.

The nature and fortunes of a dialectical theory of literature and culture are inextricably matrixed with the very history of dialectical thought itself. In the familiar Western tradition, the various revisions of Aristotelian idealist poetics suffered a devastating deformation with the emergence of Hegel and his dialectic of consciousness, for he restated the organic link between history, in its practical social meaning, and literary art in unambiguous terms:

> Every work belongs to its *age*, to its *nation*, and to its environment, and depends upon particular historical and other ideas and aims. For this reason art scholarship further requires a vast wealth of historical information of a very special kind.[2]

But Hegelian dialectics was bedevilled by its obsession with negation, self-actualization and with consciousness aspiring towards the pure spirit and constantly in a state of becoming.

If we try to transcend the limitations of Hegelian dialectics, we come face to face with two familiar bearded ghosts: those of Marx and Engels. Here, the dialectics acquires not only a materialist basis but also becomes systematized into a philosophy of history, a scientific political theory and a sociological aesthetic. We have already considered the aesthetic implications and possible limitations of Marxian dialectics in the last chapter.

The essential ingredients of the dialectic are contradiction, inter-relationships, and qualitative change. Says Engels: "dialectics . . . grasps things and their images, ideas, essentially in their interconnection, in their sequence, their movement, their birth and death".[3] Lenin subsequently dwelt on the nature of the dialectic and enunciated it in terms of the natural and social sciences as follows:

> In mathematics: + and –. Differential and integral
> In mechanics: action and reaction
> In physics: positive and negative === electricity
> In chemistry: the combination and dissociation of atoms
> In social science: the class struggle.[4]

Beyond these binary oppositions, however, the dialectic is essentially an epistemological proposition, a way of knowing reality. It offers in this respect a multi-faceted knowledge of nature and reality. It reveals, as Lenin further observed, "the transformation of the individual into the universal, of the contingent into the necessary, transitions, modulations, and the reciprocal connection of opposites".[5]

Applied to society and its products, the most striking aspect of dialectical theory is its holistic and totalizing nature, a quality which makes it comprehensive and rigorous. As Fredric Jameson observes:

> The peculiar difficulty of dialectical writing lies indeed in its holistic, "totalizing" character: as though you could not say any one thing until you had first said everything; as though with each new idea you were bound to recapitulate the entire system.[6]

In purely socio-political terms, the crucial implication of dialectical thinking lies in its "subversive" essence. As Onoge has observed,

> [The] dialectical paradigm underscores conflict rather than harmony; stresses forces tending to disrupt and transform the *status quo* rather than equilibrating ones; and affirms qualitative discontinuity rather than gradualism. The upshot of this is that social systems are accorded only temporary legitimacy.[7]

Because culture is the crystallization of social consciousness in different areas of historically conditioned material and ideational practices, a dialectical theory of culture must have society as its starting point. In effect, to command relevance, any body of theories on the cultural productions of a society or an epoch must be organically rooted in the historical circumstances and forces which provide the conditionalities of human consciousness in that setting. In essence, then, a dialectical theory of culture must be sociological in a radical sense. It would provide insight not only into the relationship between society and its cultural productions but more crucially into the series of relationships that provide the ontological integrity of the cultural productions themselves. In the area of art, the series of relationships in question can be reformulated as follows: the artist is a member of society and incarnates its structural and ideological inflections; the artist's individuality and the society's values are mediated in the work of art; the work of art recreates both the artist and the society and in itself is not a passive object but a restless concourse of images, actions, movements, experiences, statements. The end result is a new higher reality in which both artist and society assume both a particular and universal identity. This proposition can be extended to the area of literature with only minor modifications.

Properly defined, then, a dialectical theory of literature primarily underlines the inexorable socio-historical predication of literature. In being a product of social experience, literature is in turn an active producer of meanings, values and aesthetic effects which have great implications for the historical development of society. As a refraction of social experience through the prism of the human imagination, the ontological essence of literature is to be located in terms of the extent to which it recycles social experience and transforms it into an aesthetic proposition. The values, criteria and standards by which literature is measured are in themselves matrixed in the system of values of a given society. But society manifests itself in terms of definite classes, groups and formations in the process of the production and reproduction of the means and ends for the sustenance of life. Therefore, literary values are not after all very *literary* but derive from the class configuration of social values in general. Nor does the literary enterprise operate to the exclusion of other dimensions of the social totality. For instance, the writer must be fed, must be free to write, must have the means and education to write; his work will need publishers who in turn will weigh its profitability and so on. In this simple sequence of events, agriculture, politics, education, commerce and industry have entered into what began as a literary proposition. Nor would an exclusivist consideration of these determinants, no matter how rigorous and exhaustive it may be, provide a comprehensive understanding of the phenomenon of literature, for the literary event possesses an ontological integrity which is contingent on but not directly derivable from its determinants. The existence of the literary work with its essential self-containment and autonomy is one of the problem areas for a dialectical theory of literature.

> [The] initial problem which a dialectical theory of literature has to face is that of the unity of the literary work itself, its existence as a complete thing, as an autonomous whole, which, indeed, resists assimilation to the totality of the historical here and now.[8]

Yet this autonomy is only apparent if we insist that the literary work is the product of a definite form of social practice at the material level. It is in the nature of a literary work to appropriate its determinants in the form of concrete experiences while refusing to be appropriated by them, hence retaining its fictive essence.

Categories for a Dialectical Theory of African Literature

We can approach a dialectical understanding of a given body of literature first through an identification of specific categories which encapsulate the ramified interrelationships between works in that literature and their determinants.

In the African instance, the acute challenge and proper responsibility of a dialectical theory of modern African literature is to insist on the rootedness of literary art, as a constitutive social practice, in the very processes and social experiences which constitute African history and from which we can correctly characterize the African *reality*. But the precise nature of the relationship between history and this literature is problematic and needs to be confronted at the level of rigorous theoretical practice.

In quest of a specific module for a dialectical theory of African literature (and literature in general), I have arrived at the following three tentative *primary* categories; namely, *history*, *a mediating subject* and *the literary event*. In the subsequent discussion of these items, categories are understood as ultimate concepts (not in the Kantian idealist sense), each embracing an enormous number of narrower concepts, while all categories combine to embrace all concepts at the command of human thought in a given field of enquiry.

History
History is conceived in its materialist sense as the complex of material forces and objective conditions which shape social experience and therefore furnish the raw material for literature. Because it consists of the

activities of real people in active roles in equally real situations, history is not only knowable but also a process resulting from human activity.

African history is the primary condition for the existence and understanding of modern African literature especially since the contact with the West. In this respect, it is possible to plot a trajectory in the development of African literature either in terms of definite stages in the historical transformation of Africa or in terms of the local variations of the historical challenges which African literature has had to grapple with. In other words, we can approach the primacy of history in African literature in terms of the evolution of consciousness from the anti-slavery, anti-colonialism, to the contemporary neo-colonial stages. We can also approach the problem in terms of situational or geo-political variations – South Africa, North Africa, East Africa, West Africa with emphasis on the specific experiences that distinguish each of these areas. Either way, the critical intelligence cannot avoid the inevitable conclusion that modern African literature is a historically determined and complex admixture of art forms marked by a *reactive* stance towards major historical experiences (or misfortunes) such as slavery, colonialism, cultural emasculation, political corruption, apartheid, class antagonism and imperialism.

To see this heavy historical predication as a negative quality in African literature, as many bourgeois critics have suggested, is the height of theoretical myopia. Literature and art have a primary commitment to freedom and can only thrive in a free state. In a situation bedevilled with unfreedom, the primary responsibility of art is to enlist in the service of freedom and aspire to profundity within the context of this active process. To brush aside this primary responsibility and go in search of artistic excellence in spite of the struggle for freedom is to indulge in theoretical prodigality and abstract formalism.

The Mediating Subject
The category of the mediating subject, as the approximation of the artist/writer, is predicated on the rejection of a mimetic conception of the relationship between the world of art and that of reality. The process by which socio-historical experiences enter a work of art is essentially one of *mediation*, the active and purposive transposition of the empirically real into a fictive reality. Accordingly, the human agency by means of which this process is realized is the author, the narrator, chanter or performer depending on the stage in the development of the mode of literary production. In the case of written literature, the author is the mediating subject and his mode of representing socio-historical experience is a function of objective factors such as facts of biography, class orientation, ideology and political alignment. He is engaged in an active process of mediation, i.e. recycling socio-historical experience according to the laws of imaginative projection.

The African writer can therefore be located as a producer within a specific socio-economic context. He or she is more likely to be found in the petty bourgeois echelon of a society in which formal education is still a privileged means to power and wealth.

The importance of the mediating subject as a category in a dialectical theory inheres in the very materiality and constitutive nature of literary creativity. It is essentially human practice at the level of consciousness and through which the writer as a subject in the historical process tries to change reality by compelling an *imaginative* understanding of it.

For the mediating subject, literary creativity is an act of praxis, a historical act. To insist on a theory of literature that treats the literary work as an epiphenomenon which can be understood in spite of the centrality of its producer is to dehumanize literature and to succumb to the reification theories of art which capitalist alienation compels. On the contrary, to emphasize the crucial role of the writer as an active subject is to underline the centrality of the human factor in literature.

The Literary Event

The literary event is the product of the attempt by the mediating subject to derive form from socio-historical experience. It manifests itself variously as text (novel, play text, poem etc.) or event (performance, recitation, chant). Its ontological essence is formal and aesthetic in the sense that it differs from most other linguistic events by appealing to our sense of beauty/ugliness. If we correctly participate in its formal essence, we are able to retrieve the prime condition of its existence, which is history. In short, history informs the literary artifact and is revealed *in* and *through* it.

The relationship among these three categories is dialectical and mutually reinforcing and can be schematically represented as follows:

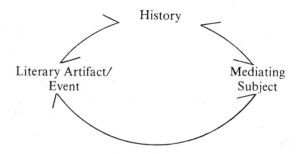

History

Literary Artifact/
Event

Mediating
Subject

The logic of this scheme runs thus: the individual as mediating subject derives experience from history and is in turn making history through creativity; by imaginatively mediating experiences into a given artistic form, s/he changes her- or himself and others; the artistic form which s/he creates is not passive, it is an active producer of meanings, values and aesthetic effects from which we can *know* both history and the mediating subject's participation in it.

This schema has universal applicability as an epistemological proposition, i.e. as a way of knowing the relationship between history and literature. But the precise content of the relationship in different societies would be historically variable. This is in the sense that different historical experiences will produce different formations of writers/performers who will in turn produce different kinds of literary artifacts. It becomes possible to designate a group of works or writers according to periods, milieux or regions. *The historical challenges of a specific epoch and locality find expression in the literature of the period. This is the basis of literary history.*

The foregoing categories are however appropriate for understanding the phenomenon of literature in general as a social institution. In terms of understanding the ontological essence of specific literary works as autonomous entities, however, the value of the distinctions made above is circumscribed by the fact that the autonomy of a literary work is contextual, a conditioned autonomy.

Contrary to the main thrust of theoretical opinion in much of Marxist literary theory and criticism to date, therefore, the possibilities open to a dialectical theory of literature are not exhausted by a consideration of the dialectical relationship between *content* and *form* alone.[9] Both categories are intrinsic to and circumscribed by the existence of the literary work or event as an entity and to insist stubbornly on them to the exclusion of the *context* within which the work derives meaning amounts to a "dialectical" acceptance of an "enclave" notion of literature. Even the most intense perception of the congruence or dissonance between form and content in a work of art evokes a whole series of questions such as *who* crafted the masterpiece, for *what* purpose, *when* and *why* and so on. As I encounter a bronze head in the Ife Museum, I cannot resist its expressionistic aura: the vision in the parted eyelid, the serenity in the relaxed facial contours, or the dignity in the silence of the sealed lips. In each case, there is an unspoken concord between form and content which in the first place made my visit to the museum necessary or even necessitated the building of a museum to begin with. Yet the aesthetic profundity of the bronze head evokes further questions which the art object as a silent museum piece suggests but cannot *in itself* answer. These are questions about the *context* of art; and which need to be answered by the critical intelligence if it is to approach a total understanding of the work.

Consequently, a dialectical theory of literature (and art) cannot ignore the relationship between *context* (the realm of determinations) on the one hand and the *content* and *form* (the realm of the ontology of the art work) on the other. I insist, in this book, therefore, that the essence of a dialectical theory of literature is to explore the range of relationships among these two realms.

Context, *content* and *form* thus emerge as secondary categories for a total understanding of specific literary works and therefore require further elaboration.

Context

The context of a literary work involves the totality of its historical ambience. It includes such factors as the level or development of productive forces which in turn determine the mode of literary production and the amount of leisure available to members of society for the creation and consumption of literature.

More importantly, it involves such elements as the philosophical and aesthetic traditions within which the work is created as well as its paradigmatic relationship with other works in the same tradition or in preceding traditions. For instance, when I encounter a new work of African literature like Pepetela's *Mayombe*, the information that it is set in the context of the liberation war in Angola provides a launching pad for my understanding of it which in turn sets me thinking about its relationship to the tradition of *neo-realismo* which is the Portuguese African equivalent of socialist realism. I am also eager to establish the new work *vis-à-vis* such other works deriving from the same historical experience as Antonio Vieira's *The Real Life of Domingo Xavier*.

Furthermore, the context of a work of literature in the African instance will include its situation within the political and ideological framework of Africa's colonial and neo-colonial experiences.

A contextual perception of a literary work therefore discourages a monolithic and monographic interpretation of the work or the individual writer, for in the dialectical framework, no literary work is "born alone": "the monographic study of an individual writer – no matter how adroitly pursued – imposes an inevitable falsification through its very structure, an optical illusion of totality projected by what is in reality only an artificial isolation".[10] Thus, to read Achebe in *Things Fall Apart* is to be intensely aware of the broad range of works, even of diverse genres and nationalities, that belong in the anti-colonial tradition of cultural nationalism, a mode of perception which makes it impossible for *Things Fall Apart* to "exist" alone without inviting to itself such other related works as Ngugi's *The River Between*, p'Bitek's *Song of Lawino*, Soyinka's *The Lion and the Jewel*, or Kane's *Ambiguous Adventure*. In short, to insist on the importance of *context* in a dialectical theory of literature is to insist actively that critical practice, especially in relation to African literature, must abandon its current predominantly isolationist approach – the study of individual works and writers – and move towards a wider perception in which criticism is informed by issues in the history of society. Only by so doing can our criticism shed its prodigal Western modernist heritage and re-integrate with political discourse, which is where it rightly belongs.

In neo-colonial Africa, for instance, what furnishes the decisive *context* of all cultural practice is capitalist imperialism. And by virtue of the extent of its economic motivation and institutional entrenchment, it is inextricably implicated in both the politics and the culture of its client societies. In the neo-colonial period, imperialism permeates every facet of life in Africa even if in more subtle ways than in the colonial era. In place of outright denigration and patronizing stereotypes, it offers endless doses of cinema mainly from Hollywood in which Western supremacist attitudes towards Africa are elevated to the status of cosmic truths – *The Exorcist*. In place of the iconoclastic missionary who burnt down the shrines of ancestral Africa, we now have a moral and spiritual justification of capitalism perfumed and packaged as Christian theology and disseminated via sponsored television slots (Billy Graham, Christian Broadcasting Network etc.). In place of Shakespeare and Milton, we now have millions of Hadley Chase, Harold Robbins, Nick Carter and allied pulp and juvenilia to sharpen the appetite of tomorrow's consumers of Western goods. In place of the slave-trading factors and middlemen, imperialism has created a scandalously uncreative comprador bourgeoisie (local directors of multinationals, politician–businessmen, distributors, manu-facturers' representatives, papal delegates, liberal professors). It is precisely these prodigious features of the contemporary African reality that define the context not only of African literature but also of other areas of cultural and intellectual activity.

In concrete terms, the implications of this spectacle are that the contexts of works in contemporary African literature are varied and sometimes contradictory. Essentially the situation is one of conflicts and polarizations, of options and choices between two sets of antagonistic propositions: between imperialism and the forces of anti-imperialism. In terms of aesthetic traditions, the choice is between an art-for-art's sake conception of literature and a utilitarian realistic and engaged poetics. In terms of ideology – both textual and authorial – the option is between liberal bourgeois individualism and an anti-imperialist consciousness with its attendant solidarity with the masses of African peasants and workers. For this writer, while the theoretical challenge in contemporary African literature logically suggests the dialectical option, the ideological imperative of the moment is an unambiguous, anti-imperialist and leftist commitment. I have elsewhere articulated the basic outlines of this ideological position in the following terms:

> The anti-imperialist consciousness is characterised by a vehement rejection of political independence vacuously defined in terms of the freedom of African nations to erect their own flags and sing their own anthems. It also rejects and seeks avenues for repudiating the leadership of African . . . nations by the comprador bourgeoisie. Its main thrust is economic and cultural independence defined in terms of the total transfer of the means of production and distribution of resources and cultural communication into the hands of the masses of Africans. Its envisaged political economy is socialism . . . Necessarily, its ideological slant is leftist, defined in broad democratic socialist terms.[11]

This ideological imperative defines for African literature an essentially socio-political challenge in the context of which specific contents and forms can take root and be evaluated.

Content and Form

The notion of literary art as a harmonious integration of content and form has been at the core of literary theory from Aristotle. But the dialectical paradigm underscores the relationship between the two categories in a manner that accords precedence (not superiority or pre-eminence) to content over form. This departure strikes us most conspicuously in Marxist literary theory where the dominant position holds that although there is a dialectical relationship between content and form, the former determines the latter.

From the outset, it needs to be understood that while *context* caters for the external relationship of a literary work to its informing socio-historical totality, a consideration of the dialectics of *content* and *form* is concerned with a more intensive entity.

In this regard, a dialectical conception of the relationship between the two categories must be rooted in the fundamental relationship which historical materialism makes between base and superstructure. Literature is an aspect of superstructure. Yet within the internal materialism of a given literary object it is possible that content, as an approximation of social experience or the reflection of the conflicts and contradictions in social experience, finds correspondence in the concept of base, while form as the totality of images, symbols, structures or other significations constitutes an attempt to provide this base (content) with a legitimizing *superstructure*. Thus, content determines form as base determines superstructure not on a unidirectional axis but along a line of reversible determinations and over-determinations: in short, as base is to superstructure in the realm of socio-economic reality, so is content to form in the realm of fictional *reality*:

Form
(Superstructure)

Content
(Base)

It needs to be pointed out that the conscious separation of *content* and *form* into two disparate areas of intellectual contemplation is not a natural aspect of the process of poetic composition in its realistic or naturalistic meaning. Nor does the literary work as an autonomous approximation of reality in its appearance permit such conscious polarization. The *content* and *form* discrimination is a product of the contemplative and analytical gaze of the critic and theorist. "We begin to distinguish between *what* a work of art tells us and *how* it does this. We see both the psychology and philosophy of a work, and the devices, means and techniques used in creating an image."[12] Thus conceived, the *form* and *content* dichotomy is an epistemological proposition, a way of approaching knowledge of the ontology of art works.

Therefore, to insist on a dialectical relationship between the two categories is to restate their inseparability while recognizing them as separate areas of rationalization at the level of critical inquiry and within the context of aesthetics as a self-accounting profession. It is only in these contradictory but mutually reinforcing terms that we can approach a better understanding of the categories in question.

Content in literature, then, is a semantic appropriation of a slice of the external reality furnished by *context* (as history) into the microcosmic totality of the literary work, an attempt by the creative imagination as a mediating subject to intensify the social experiences that constitute the conditionalities of literature into a sensually graspable reality. To that extent, the content of a work of art is in itself an artistic proposition because it derives meaning only in an artistic context. It is not reducible to the *context* of the work of art in the sense that we understand that category in the foregoing discussion. Observes V. V. Vanslov:

> The content of art is not an illustration of the general ideas of a world outlook or class ideology. It is itself a special artistic, or figurative, idea, independently reflecting life in all its fullness and essential features.[13]

Contrary to the popular belief in bourgeois circles, the content of literature is not reducible to its themes either, for the themes represent crystallizations of experiences into issues and subjects that are either particular or universal or both.

But the concrete realization of the art object consists in content assuming a precise form which we can perceive through our senses. By its very nature, the content as a figurative entity already embodies a certain form.

> Content must reveal itself externally, or take form, in order to become accessible to those who perceive art. Form . . . is reflexive, turned not only outward but also on itself, it is transparent and inspired. Content is visible through it. Thanks to this, form is not empty but saturated, not superficial but significant; it is something more than a purely external, tangible phenomenon. It is the content's form and means of existence, the aspect through which it appears to us. Without this dialectic there is no art. *When we perceive art we constantly move from form to content and "vice versa", comprehending the whole fullness of the work.*[14] (my emphasis)

In the context of the foregoing line of thought, therefore, there can be no content devoid of form or vice versa. To insist on content at the expense of form is to succumb to a narrow sociologism which belongs in the realm of adolescent Marxism of the most vulgarized variety. On the contrary, to project an absolutized form devoid of content is the bane of all ideologists of different formalist schools who try "to erect a theoretical basis under diverse means of destroying art".

Nor should we be tempted by the trend of the above discussion into seeing either *content* or *form* as undifferentiated entities in themselves. On the contrary, the socio-historical reality (or even the world of nature) which is appropriated in the content is a structured whole with parts – experiences, incidents, people as individuals and in groups relating with one another in definable ways. Consequently, its realization in form will bear the stamp of its inherent structuration. Therefore, the dialectics of content and form is in addition a systemic dialectics, one based on a whole complex of interrelationships between two sets of variables. It is precisely this quality that tends to cancel out the possibility of separating content from form.

Throughout the foregoing exposition, what has constantly been stressed is the precedence (not primacy or superiority) of content over form. It is important to underline this in the light of the propensity among bourgeois scholars and peripheral Marxists and dialecticians to insist on the contrary. As a dialectical theory of literature, Marxist literary theory also insists on this order of precedence just as it does in the case of the dialectical relationship between base and superstructure. It is, therefore, utterly wrong-headed and erroneous for Emmanuel Ngara to insist that:

> While Marxist criticism is very rich in what it can reveal about content and ideology in literature, it has serious shortcomings in respect of its handling of the aesthetic component of a work of art. It is a *content-based* theory which, in its present state, cannot adequately account for the formal aspects of fiction.[15]

All the foregoing three categories – *context*, *content* and *form* – are relevant at the level of critical analysis for an understanding of the literary work as an object or event with an apparent autonomy. In the dialectical relationship among them, context is to be seen as the ever-present halo around the literary work as a self-contained entity, which, as the epiphany of history, constantly enters the literary work in rays of inspirational illumination but resists total appropriation by the literary work. The context thus retains its integrity as the repository of referential values in terms of which the literary work reaffirms or subverts, advances or betrays the challenges of its specific historical inspiration.

On the other hand, *content* and *form* as two sides to a common truth play themselves out in a dialectical puzzle which cannot be unravelled except by destroying the art work. A proper grasp of their interplay reveals that profound art is essentially content–become–form. To perceive that profundity is to reach out for the historical substratum of the work and to seek an understanding of the work not only in relation to history but also in relation to other works in its time and place as well as its place in the overall ideological struggle in which literature *qua* literature is inexorably engaged.

The relationship among these three categories can be schematically represented in the following terms:

$$\text{Literary work} = \text{Context} \rightleftharpoons \text{Content} + \text{Form}$$

In short, a literary work is the mediation of context into content and form. In turn, the context is derivable from an analytical perception of the dialectics of content and form.

Springboards for a Dialectical Theory of African Literature and Culture

The foregoing discussion reveals that the cornerstone of a dialectical theory of African literature is the need to historicize that literature, to re-establish that organic link between literature and its informing and sustaining historical milieu which bourgeois criticism in its purely formalistic manifestations constantly obfuscates. In the African instance, the ambience for a dialectical theory from which one can begin to aspire towards specific hermeneutical categories is the challenge of the imperialist assault on Africa and the reality of neo-colonialism. Awareness of the impact of colonialism and the contradictions of neo-colonialism and a commitment to their negation has informed the utterances of key African nationalists and men of culture over the years. Consequently, where key African and Africanist nationalists have dwelt on the cultural implications of imperialism, we can perceive the vague outlines of what, in the context of this volume, we may regard as a "poetics of the oppressed".

For illustration, we shall dwell principally on the theoretical implications for African literature of the statements of Fanon, Cabral and Ngugi on the relationship between African culture in general and colonialism and neo-colonialism respectively.

In making this choice, one is merely entering the obvious contention that a truly de-colonized and anti-imperialist theory of African literature can only be derived from an anti-imperialist ideological framework, not from a perennial feeling of nostalgia about forgotten pasts and romantic re-creations of village life.[16] The ancient beauty of the African flower has been mortally corrupted by the smoke of the maxim gun of colonialism and the sins of the exploiting classes in the neo-colonial state. Fanon, Cabral and Ngugi demonstrate this truism with disturbing frequency in their writings on culture and national liberation in the context of Africa's long-standing tradition of resistance to alien (mainly Western) domination.

Fanon: The Aesthetics of National Liberation

Fanon's position on national culture as contained in *The Wretched of the Earth* represents his most orchestrated articulation of the cultural (especially literary) implications of colonialism and its antithesis, the anti-colonial struggle. As is characteristic of other aspects of his writings on the colonial question, Fanon's position on culture is predicated on his essentially materialist recognition of the exploitative economic motive of colonialism as the decisive determinant of all aspects of the life of the colonized. Yet his grasp of the intricacy of culture transcends such mechanical materialism and perceives certain inner dynamics within the development of culture among the colonized. In this respect, the most enduring value of Fanon's views on the cultural question is to be located in the evolutionary paradigm which he established as well as in his emphasis on the *national* dimension of the anti-colonial consciousness in contrast to the racial emphasis of his contemporaries.

Proceeding from the familiar premise that cultural emasculation of the subjugated group is the necessary correlate of colonialist entrenchment, Fanon projected the pattern of cultural evolution among the colonized both during and even after the colonial era. Briefly, Fanon's evolutionary schema advances three distinct phases as follows:

1. The assimilationist phase in which "the native intellectual gives proof that he has assimilated the culture of the occupying power". Characteristically, the literary productions of the native at this stage bear resemblance to those in the literary tradition of the colonizing country.

2. The *cultural nationalist* phase in which the native intellectual remembers his authentic identity and kicks against attempts to assimilate him. But owing to his own cultural alienation, the native intellectual's attempts at cultural reaffirmation stop at romanticizations of bygone days corrected by philosophical traditions and aesthetic conventions borrowed from the world of the colonizer.

3. The nationalist phase which is also the fighting phase in which the native man of culture "after having tried to lose himself in the people and with the people, will on the contrary shake the people". This is the revolutionary and nationalist phase in the literature of the colonized in which the exposure of more natives to the realities of colonialist oppression also contributes to a democratization of the drive for literary expression.[17]

In the context of this schema, then, the relevant response of the colonized intellectual is contained in the second phase, that of cultural reaffirmation characterized by unbridled traditionalism and even ancestor-worship. This recourse to the resuscitation of past glories in literature is only a defence mechanism by native intellectuals "to shrink away from that Western culture in which they all risk being swamped". Fanon was however intensely aware of the limitations of this retrospective fixation in terms of altering the present material conditions of life among the colonized: "all the proofs of a wonderful Songhai civilization will not change the fact that today the Songhais are underfed and illiterate".[18]

Cultural nationalism, because it is predicated on a negation of racially-inflicted insults and psychological injuries, has political significance mainly at a racial or at best a continental level: "The native intellectual who decides to give battle to colonial lies fights on the field of the whole continent". Fanon was sufficiently realistic to admit the legitimacy and historical necessity of this phase in the consciousness of the native. But he equally cautioned that it must constitute only a transient phase, for to adopt continental cultural reaffirmation and nostalgic romanticism as a permanent stance would amount to a false consciousness totally dysfunctional in the task of national liberation.

> The historical necessity in which the men of African culture find themselves to racialize their claims and to speak more of African culture than of national culture will tend to lead them up a blind alley.[19]

In this respect, Fanon's articulation of the basic requirements of a national culture was sufficiently rigorous to have anticipated some of the most radical positions of our contemporary criticism. He emphasized the need for the writer to see and understand clearly the people who constitute the object of his poetry through a process of self-immersion that literally approximates class suicide. Rightly regarded, therefore, cultural action cannot be divorced from the larger struggle for the liberation of the nation. In effect, there ought to be a reciprocal relationship between national culture and the fight for freedom, a relationship in which national culture subserves national liberation.

In spite of his emphasis on the present and immediate, Fanon never totally discountenanced the insight which the past could provide in the process of national liberation. For him, the nationalist writer's preoccupation with the past must be "with the intention of opening the future, as an invitation to action and a basis for hope". This recognition contains a tacit warning with far-reaching implications for the relationship between the writer and his people. It is the responsibility of the writer not to immerse the people in a past they have left behind but to join and inspire them to confront the present as a historic moment. This is perhaps Fanon's most trenchant articulation of the challenge confronting culture, especially literature, in the process of national liberation:

> It is not enough to try to get back to the people in that past out of which they have already emerged; rather we must join them in that fluctuating movement which they are just giving a shape to, and which, as soon as it has started, will be the signal for everything to be called in question. Let there be no mistake about it; it is to this zone of occult instability where the people dwell that we must come; and it is there that our souls are crystallized and that our perceptions and our lives are transfused with light.[20]

It is in this revolutionary, nationalist sense that Fanon proffers his radical definition of national culture;

A national culture is not a folklore, nor an abstract populism that believes it can discover the people's true nature. It is not made up of the inert dregs of gratuitous actions, that is to say actions which are less and less attached to the everpresent reality of the people. A national culture is the whole body of efforts made by a people in the sphere of thought to describe, justify and praise the action through which that people has created itself and keeps itself in existence.[21]

National liberation, national survival and national assertion are, therefore, the preconditions for national culture: "culture is the expression of a nation".

Against the background of this pragmatic and materialist understanding of national culture, Fanon proceeded to sketch in the outlines of national literature in the context of the liberation struggle. For brevity and convenience, the essential features of his submissions in this area can be itemized under two broad categories: *written* and *oral* literatures respectively:

Written Literature

1. Features and clarifies themes which are typically nationalistic, deriving from national experiences.

2. Assumes a combative stance and tone by calling on the people to fight and defend their existence as a nation and thereby widening their political horizon and intensifying their consciousness.

3. Literature creates a new style and generates a new home-grown audience; the writer turns his back on the oppressor and addresses his own people.

4. The writer is committed in a manifest, overt sense. This literature is "the will to liberty expressed in terms of time and space".

Oral Literature

1. The nationalist struggle leads to an invigoration of previously inert themes and a modernization of the struggles and conflicts enacted in the oral fables.

2. The remoteness of the experiences in oral tradition is imbued with greater immediacy.

3. Methods of delivery and rendition acquire greater stridency, immediacy and innovativeness.

4. Characters become contemporaneous and are drawn from among "the wretched of the earth" – highway robbers, anti-social vagabonds etc. – converting them into subjects (rather than objects) of history.

5. Comedy and farce lose their appeal or disappear completely, for the grim historical struggle for liberation is not a laughing matter.

6. Drama loses a sense of the tragic and of despair and assumes a revolutionary optimistic dimension. The aesthetic implications of Fanon's position on national culture can thus be summarized in terms of a dialectical relationship between literary culture and the national liberation

struggle in which the specific demands of the struggle at every stage necessitate fresh expressive possibilities and compel the person of culture to obey the law implicit in his classic injunction that: "Each generation must, out of relative obscurity, discover its mission, fulfil it, or betray it".

Cabral: National Liberation as an Act of Culture

> Come with me, old Mama, come,
> gather your strength to reach the gate.
> The friendly rain has already come to greet you
> and is beating within my heart.[22]

This verse from Cabral's youthful writings is an apt summation of his subsequent conception of the instrumental and reciprocal relationship between culture and national liberation. Cabral's views on this vital relationship acquire stridency and significance mainly on account of the fact that he was writing from a position of direct active involvement in the liberation struggle within the context of the African Party for the Independence of Guinea and Cape Verde (PAIGC) which he led. Most importantly, Cabral's convictions and political actions were solidly predicated on a clear perception of the true meaning of both imperialism and national liberation as its logical antithesis:

> Imperialism may be defined as the world-wide expression of the profit motive and the ever-increasing accumulation of *surplus values* by monopoly financial capital. [It] is piracy transplanted from the seas to dry land, piracy reorganised, consolidated and adapted to the aim of plundering the natural and human resources of our peoples.[23]

As a stage in the evolution of productive forces, Cabral recognized the "necessity" of imperialism only to the extent that it equally enlists the antithetical necessity "of the national liberation of peoples, the destruction of capitalism and the advent of socialism". To the extent that he translated these convictions into armed struggle and political organization, Cabral represents one of the highest manifestations of anti-imperialist theory and praxis in African history to date.

His position on culture, it needs to be pointed out, is broad-based, taking in its stride all aspects of culture, but its basic outlines can be extrapolated into the specific domain of literature.

Like Fanon, Cabral was operating within an essentially materialist and libertarian notion of culture. In re-stating the classic pattern of colonialist denigration and subjugation of the cultural life of the colonized, he redefined the relationship between *history* (which exposes contradictions and conflicts in the life of society) and *culture* (which provides insights into the dynamic syntheses to resolve these conflicts) in very dialectical reciprocal terms:

> Whatever may be the ideology or idealist characteristics of cultural expression,

culture is an essential element of the history of a people. Culture is, perhaps, the product of this history just as the flower is the product of a plant. Like history, or because it is history, culture has as its material base the level of the productive forces and the mode of production.[24]

The main thrust of Cabral's argument was to intensify the reciprocal relationship between history and culture to a point that both categories become hardly distinguishable. Thus, the national liberation struggle as a historical act also becomes an act of cultural resistance to the extent that it is recognized that the object of national liberation is the freedom of a society and its values from foreign domination:

> At any moment, depending on internal and external factors determining the evolution of the society in question, cultural resistance (indestructible) may take on new forms (political, economic, armed) in order to fully contest foreign domination.[25]

The great force of culture as an instrument of nationalist resistance derives from its ideological appeal in terms of its ability to reflect history. Its political force is enhanced because it has great influence in determining relationships between people and nature, between one person and another, among groups in society and among societies in the international community.

Yet Cabral did not succumb to the liberal tendency to view culture as an undifferentiated continuum, unrelated to the structural manifestations of its informing society. In this regard, he made a distinction not only between the culture of the colonizers and that of the colonized but also in terms of the different levels of cultural expression among the colonized peoples. This recognition was equally predicated on his realization of the sectoral and class character of the socio-economic determinants of culture: "while . . . culture has a mass character, it is not uniform, it is not equally developed in all sectors of society". Thus, among the colonized, we can identify the culture of the urban Western-educated elite, of the religious leaders and "traditional" rulers on one hand and the indigenous cultural expressions of the rural peasantry, untramelled by the encrustations of foreign impositions and appropriations.

Given Cabral's belief in the instrumentality of culture in the national liberation struggle, it is only the culture of the rural peasantry, because it represents the authentic culture of African peoples and embraces the interests of the great majority of Africans, that can inform genuine natural liberation. It is therefore on the culture of the peasantry that the heavy accent in Cabral's position falls. Even at that, he was alive to the divergences and differences within authentic indigenous cultures arising from the intrinsic organic structures of those societies themselves. In this respect, he identified two types of pre-colonial African social structure, with their attendant cultural imperatives: the *horizontal* and *vertical* patterns.

In societies with a horizontal structure, class differentiation is minimized and cultural expression is relatively uniform with variations only along individual or age-group lines. On the other hand, in societies with a vertical structure, cultural expression varies from top to bottom in broad conformity to the class character of the society. It is in the latter societies that colonialist culture grips the upper classes and converts them into caricatures of Western man, producing the psychological condition of mental colonization. Cabral's cultural theory was sufficiently informed by political wisdom to realize the inevitability of elite leadership in the national liberation struggle. Hence he advocated a process of re-Africanization, a reconversion of the minds of the colonized African elite. This could only be achieved through a process of reintegration with the culture of the masses: "Such reconversion – re-Africanization . . . is completed only during the course of the struggle, through daily contact with the popular masses in the communion of sacrifice required by the struggle".[26]

Consequently, the liberation struggle must be based on the popular culture of the masses of the rural areas and the urban working class "including the nationalist (revolutionary) 'petite bourgeoisie' who have been re-Africanized or who are ready for cultural reconversion".[27]

It is important to note that Cabral's insistence on "a return to source" cannot be reduced to an advocacy of that kind of unbridled Pan-Negro romanticism which we have come to associate with traditionalist aestheticians in general. His recourse to the culture of the rural masses was informed by the recognition that rural Africa remains the repository of the authentic consciousness of African peoples in the context of which the battle for genuine anti-colonial values can be waged. Thus, Cabral's cultural theory contains overt warnings against an indiscriminate valorization of the African past. He warned against indiscriminate compliments, the systematic exaltation of virtues without a corresponding condemnation of faults as well as blind acceptance of the positive values in African culture without considering its regressive elements. In short, Cabral frowned on a narrow cultic "professional" approach to African culture:

> Thus, the important thing is not to lose time in more or less idle discussion of the specific or unspecific characteristics of African cultural values, but rather to look upon these values as a conquest of a small piece of humanity for the common heritage of humanity, achieved in one or several phases of its evolution.[28]

Nor did Cabral come to see Africa as an undifferentiated cultural universe. On the contrary, he was keenly alert to the ethnic complexity and cultural heterogeneity of the African world.

> The fact of recognising the existence of common and particular features in the cultures of African peoples, independent of the color of their skin, does not

necessarily imply that one and only one culture exists on the continent. In the same way that from an economic and political viewpoint we can recognise the existence of several Africas, so also there are many African cultures.[29]

A broad summation of Cabral's position on the cultural question in the anti-imperialist struggle, then, reveals the following central ideas: (a) an emphasis on popular culture with a high indigenous content, (b) the development of a national culture based on the historic achievements of the liberation struggle, (c) the use of culture in the service of patriotic political goals and in the creation of moral awareness, and (d) the development of a scientific and technological culture.

Ngugi: Literature and the Anti-imperialist Struggle

To be familiar with Ngugi's reputation as an African writer is to come into acquaintance with his intense sense of progressive social commitment which has quickened over the years into a clear-cut anti-imperialist consciousness predicated on a socialist ideological leaning. Ngugi's commitment has, however, not been confined to his creative writing but has found polemical and theoretical outlet in a series of brilliant essays, addresses, and anecdotes published in various anthologies and journals. More crucially, there is a sense in which Ngugi's polemical and theoretical statements can be seen as elaborations of the fictional worlds of his creative writing. Such volumes of essays as *Homecoming*, *Writers in Politics*, *Barrel of a Pen* and, recently, *Decolonizing the Mind* can, therefore, be said to exist to provide theoretical anchorage to his fictional works, for instance *The River Between*; *Weep Not, Child*; *A Grain of Wheat*, and *Petals of Blood*. It is on the theoretical works that we shall dwell in this section.

There is an unmistakably anti-imperialist thrust that runs through Ngugi's social philosophy which betrays the influence on his thought of both Fanon and Cabral on the one hand and the classics of Marxism/Leninism on the other. There is in fact a sense in which Ngugi's view on African literature and art can be said to place the more generalized cultural theories of Fanon and Cabral in a more specialized literary context without however underplaying the dialectical relationship between African literature and the historical determinants of modern African society. It would not be an overstatement to say that while articulating views that are fast building up into an anti-imperialist aesthetics of African literature, Ngugi has simultaneously been creating works that practically illustrate the main features of his emergent aesthetics.

For ease of handling, we can discuss Ngugi's artistic and social philosophy in terms of specific areas of concern which cut across his major polemical and theoretical writings to date.

Literature, National History and National Culture

While recognizing the continental relevance of Ngugi's art, it can be said that a certain consciousness of and attachment to the history of the Kenyan nation constitutes the single most important object of his commitment and inspiration. (I deal with his fictional mediations of aspects of Kenyan history later in this volume.) In this respect, Ngugi's historical consciousness understandably assumes the dimensions of an obsession given the fact that he grew up in the midst of the turbulence of the anti-colonial struggle.[30]

The central experience which informs his historical consciousness is the Mau Mau armed struggle which Kenyan peasants and nationalists had to wage against British colonialism. The period of national emergency revealed not only the physical violence with which colonialism sought to entrench itself but also the cultural violence which it inflicted on the consciousness of the colonized. It was against this background that Ngugi may have derived the prominence which he has continued to give to the cultural aspects of the Mau Mau struggle.

> They (the freedom fighters) rediscovered the old songs – they had never completely lost touch with them – and reshaped them to meet the new needs of their struggle. They also created new songs and dances with new rhythms where the old ones were found inadequate.[31]

More importantly, Ngugi's conviction about the crucial role of literature in creating a truly historical consciousness is born of his recognition of the instrumentality of colonialist writers in the denigration of Kenyan national identity. In this regard, Ngugi has relentlessly drawn attention to the condescending and uncomplimentary depictions of the Kenyan (and African) reality by such imperialist writers as Elspeth Huxley, Robert Ruark, Karen Blixen, Rider Haggard and Rudyard Kipling, among others.

It is perhaps within the larger context of national culture that the peculiar challenges of Kenyan national history assume particular stridency in Ngugi's scheme. Here, it is important to note that Ngugi's articulation of the concept and responsibilities of national culture echo Fanon and Cabral respectively in many respects. This identity of viewpoint is forged by the very nature of the colonial experience which provides the locus for the work of the three writers. Equally founded on the familiar axioms of the materialist view of culture, Ngugi's views have been articulated against the background of the obvious domination of the vital sectors of contemporary Kenyan national life by foreign interests and institutions. In the area of culture, the domination is in the form of (a) the preponderance of works by foreign (mainly English) authors in the literature syllabi of schools and colleges, (b) domination of the film industry by American influence, (c) domination of the mass media and publishing outfits by Western interests as well as the high foreign content of performances at the national theatre. These aberrations pose a double challenge for patriotic Kenyans: "A central fact of Kenyan life today is the fierce struggle between the cultural forces representing foreign interests and those representing patriotic national interests".[32]

Firstly, it entails a radical reformulation of the idea of national culture in a manner that calls to question foreign domination and its informing values. Secondly, and more crucially, nationalist cultural assertion must form an integral part of an overall revolutionary project that confronts and seeks to banish the economic domination which is the precondition for cultural domination in the first place. "Political and economic liberation are the essential condition for cultural liberation, for the true release of a people's creative spirit and imagination."[33]

Like Fanon and Cabral before him, Ngugi has consistently valorized the fidelity of the culture of the countryside without however equating culture with blind traditionalism.

> It is surely not possible to lift traditional structures and cultures intact into modern Africa. A meaningful culture is the one born out of the present hopes and especially the hopes of an impoverished peasantry, and that of the growing body of urban workers.[34]

In other words, authentic national culture is only realizable in the context of the struggle among the contending classes in society.

Literature, Class and Politics

The emphasis which Ngugi has consistently placed on the class question in African literature derives logically from a greater crystallization of his ideological perspective in recent years. In both his recent creative writing (*Devil on the Cross*, *I Will Marry When I Want*) and his active involvement in the struggle for the exposure of the hypocrisy of the bourgeois-led KANU government in Kenya, Ngugi has emerged with an unambiguous class partisanship.

This partisanship is predicated on a clear and keen perception of the structural dynamics and polarizations in contemporary Kenyan society:

> The fundamental opposition in Africa today is between imperialism and capitalism on the one hand, and national liberation and socialism on the other: between a small class of native 'haves' which is tied to international monopoly capital and the masses of the people.[35]

Ngugi's response to this antagonistic polarization has taken the form of an active alignment with the broad masses of peasants and the urban working class in the company of whom he has created his most recent works: "A writer needs people around him. He needs live struggles of active life".[36]

This need for partisanship has obvious political implications for Ngugi in particular and the African writer in general. In terms of political and ideological alignment, Ngugi has identified two broad formations of writers: firstly, idealist writers who insist on a static image of society, seeing no class differentiation and no possibility of change, and secondly, materialist writers who reflect the historicity and dynamism of human action in their works. In the context of this polarization, it is no longer adequate just to perceive African writers in ideologically neutral terms. And for the writer, the problem of choosing between these two options is often the source of cynicism and disillusionment in African literature especially in the post-colonial period.

Pedagogy and Cultural Imperialism

To the extent that the educational and other cultural institutions have been the major conduits for the propagation and perpetuation of imperialist values in Africa, Ngugi has articulated the necessity for the anti-imperialist struggle to be waged at a pedagogical level as well. This implies the use of culture in the educational system for the propagation of progressive Afrocentric values, attitudes and a revolutionary world view.

> The aim is to devise an education system that not only gives people a true knowledge of their relations to nature and to other men, but which imparts a culture that embodies a consciousness, an ideological world outlook and value system that is a complete negation of imperialist culture, value systems, and world outlook.[37]

In the specific area of literature and art, there is a clear recognition of their cognitive value and hence their crucial role in the shaping of social consciousness:

> The arts . . . are a form of knowledge about reality acquired through a pile of images. But these images are not neutral. The images given us by the arts try to make us not only see and understand the world of man and nature, apprehend it, but to see and understand it in a certain way . . .[38]

Consequently, the literature syllabus in African schools and universities should de-emphasize the imperialist cultures of the West and concentrate emphasis on African literature (oral and written), literatures of the African diaspora, the anti-imperialist literatures of Asia, Latin America and the socialist countries. More crucially, the teaching and analysis (in short, pedagogy) of literature should be pursued from the point of view of the masses, a point which re-echoes Ngugi's radical ideological stance.

Linguistic Indigenization in Literature

A very conspicuous aspect of Ngugi's emergent aesthetics of African literature to date is his position on the language question. (We return to a broader treatment of this problem in Chapter Five.) The main emphasis in Ngugi's utterances on the matter hinge around linguistic indigenization: the insistence that African literature, properly defined, can only be written (or expressed) in African languages. Coupled with this is the logical deduction that African literature expressed in the European languages to date constitutes only insignificant tributaries to the major current of literary creativity in the metropolitan countries in question. Re-echoing the position popularized earlier in the century by Obi Wali of Nigeria, Ngugi asserts, somewhat romantically,

> African literature can only be written in the African languages of the peasantry

and working class, the major alliance of classes in each of our nationalities and the agency for the coming revolutionary break with neo-colonialism.

Afro-European literature can be defined as literature written by Africans in European languages in the era of imperialism.[39]

The argument for the use of African languages is predicated on the reality that the majority of Africans live in the rural areas and speak mainly African languages. This is a position which flows only logically from Ngugi's class partisan position.

However, it is not enough to write in African languages. Ngugi realizes the vital place of technique in the ontology of the literary work as an artistic entity. More significantly, he displays a keen awareness of the need for literary style to conform to the various levels of aesthetic socialization within the class configuration of society: "You cannot possibly write for a peasant–worker audience . . . the same things in the same way as you would for the parasitic jet set in Africa."[40]

If Ngugi's position on the language question seems a little too extreme and romanticized, it needs to be conceded that he has been fully cognizant of the limitations, in the context of contemporary realities, of an excessive emphasis on linguistic indigenization. This recognition can be located in his admission that linguistic indigenization cannot in and of itself guarantee the cultural revolution which his ideological predilection anticipates.

But writing in our languages . . . will not in itself bring about the renaissance in African cultures if that literature does not carry the content of our peoples' anti-imperialist struggles to liberate their productive forces from foreign control.[41]

Taken together, the views of Fanon, Cabral and Ngugi outlined in the foregoing discussion contain what, in the context of this volume, we consider the kernel and essential ingredients of a dialectical theory of African literature and culture. This is a theoretical perspective enriched by the history of the anti-imperialist endeavours of African peoples which is also the ultimate source of modern African literature.

The adoption of this perspective can be further strengthened if we consider the possibilities it opens for a redefinition of the major issues and questions which have crystallized in critical and theoretical discourse on African literature to date.

Notes

1. Terry Eagleton, *Literary Theory: An Introduction* (Oxford: Basil Blackwell, 1983) pp. 194–5.

2. G. W. F. Hegel, *On Art, Religion, Philosophy*, ed. J. Glenn Grey (New York/Evanston: Harper and Row, 1970) p. 38.

3. Excerpt from Engels' *Anti-Dühring*, quoted in Maynard Solomon (ed.) *Marxism and Art* (New York: Vintage Books, 1974) p. 28.

4. V. I. Lenin, *Philosophical Notebooks*, excerpt quoted in Maynard Solomon (ed.) *Marxism and Art*, p. 183.

5. Ibid., p. 185.

6. Fredric Jameson, *Marxism and Form* (Princeton: Princeton University Press, 1974) p. 306.

7. Omafume Onoge, "The Possibilities of a Radical Sociology of African Literature" in D. I. Nwoga (ed.) *Literature and Modern West African Culture* (Benin: Ethiope, 1978) pp. 93–4.

8. Fredric Jameson, *Marxism and Form* p. 313.

9. The mainstream of Marxist theorizing on aesthetics to date has come to consecrate the dialectics of content and form into a kind of idealism which tends to elevate the literary work as an entity to the status of a given.

10. Fredric Jameson, *Marxism and Form* p. 315.

11. Chidi Amuta, "The African Writer and the Anti-Imperialist Struggle", *Journal of African Marxism*, no. 6, 1984, p. 107.

12. V. V. Vanslov, "On Content and Form in Art as a Reflection of Life" in *Marxist Leninist Aesthetics and the Arts* (Moscow: Progress, 1980) p. 271.

13. Ibid., p. 279.

14. Ibid.

15. Emmanuel Ngara, *Art and Ideology in the African Novel* (London: Heinemann, 1985) pp. 2–6.

16. I have entered a full critique of this dysfunctional intellectual tradition in Chapter Two of this volume.

17. Frantz Fanon, *The Wretched of the Earth* (Harmondsworth: Penguin, 1967) pp. 178–9.

18. Ibid., p. 168.

19. Ibid., p. 172.

20. Ibid., pp. 182–3.

21. Ibid., p. 188.

22. Amilcar Cabral, *Unity and Struggle*, trans. Michael Wolfers (London: Heinemann, 1980) p. 3.

23. Ibid., p. 127.

24. Amilcar Cabral, *Return to the Source: Selected Speeches* (New York/London: Monthly Review Press, 1973) p. 42.

25. Ibid., p. 40.

26. Ibid., p. 45.

27. Ibid.

28. Ibid., p. 51.

29. Ibid.

30. Ngugi was a schoolboy in the days of the Mau Mau struggle and the traumatic and turbulent experiences must have left a permanent imprint on his psychology. This, coupled with his historical consciousness has made the Mau Mau emergency a permanent feature of his art and polemics.

31. Ngugi Wa Thiong'o, *Homecoming: Essays* (London: Heinemann, 1972) p. 30.

32. Ngugi Wa Thiong'o, *Writers in Politics* (London: Heinemann, 1981) p. 42.

33. Ngugi, *Homecoming*, p. 11.

34. Ibid., p. 12.

35. Ngugi, *Writers in Politics*, pp. 78–9.

36. Ngugi Wa Thiong'o, *Detained: A Writer's Prison Diary* (London: Heinemann, 1985) p. 30.

37. Ngugi Wa Thiong'o, *Barrel of a Pen* (London/Port of Spain: New Beacon, 1986) p. 98.

38. Ibid., p. 57.

39. Ngugi Wa Thiong'o, "The Language of African Literature", *New Left Review*, no. 125, 1985, p. 125.

40. Ngugi, *Writers in Politics*, p. 54.

41. Ngugi, "The Language of African Literature", p. 127.

5 Issues and Problems in African Literature: A Dialectical Revision

> What we demand is the unity of politics and art, the unity of content and form, the unity of revolutionary political content and the highest possible perfection of artistic form.   **Mao Tse-Tung**[1]

A modulation of the fundamental assumptions of dialectical theory of culture by the imperatives of the anti-imperialism struggle is bound to yield a radical aesthetic of African literature with an intrinsically compelling logic. The outlines of such an aesthetic are bound to be further clarified if we relate its general categories (as outlined in the last chapter) to the various conceptual issues and problems which have come into prominence in the overall discussion of African literature to date. In approaching the latter task, I adopt in this chapter a method of discourse akin to what obtains in Raymond Williams' informative book, *Marxism and Literature*: each issue or problem is examined as a conceptual category in its evolution and applications (or misapplications) over time. In each case, a dialectical reconsideration is entered as a dynamic synthesis of the warring concourse of conflictual meanings and values.

The overall premise that underlies our treatment of the various issues raised here is that concepts, questions and issues in a given literary culture are raised and equally become problematic in concrete historical situations. In turn, the definitions, meanings and values which are ascribed to them are in themselves contingent on the very historical circumstances as they crystallize into the major ideational contradictions among the members of the social class(es) whose responsibility in society it is to deal with culture and cultural values at the level of theory. As we have pointed out in Chapter One, the conflict and indeterminacy which have become the dominant characteristics of the criticism of modern African literature constitute reverberations, at an ideological level, of the crisis of consciousness and theoretical-philosophical insight among major formations of the cultural intelligentsia. A much more concrete manifestation of this crisis emerges in the handling of concepts and issues such as: what constitutes African literature? What is the social position of the African writer? What should constitute the object of the writer's commitment? Prior to any application of theory to practical exegetical problems and situations, there is an urgent need to reconsider these larger issues in the context of a consistent theoretical outlook informed by a clear historical perspective. Such dialectical revision of broader conceptual issues as is attempted here becomes of *strategic* importance in view of the urgent need to free African literary discourse from the prison house of unrelieved traditionalism and false decolonization. It is additionally crucial to enter these theoretical disclaimers in order that literary discourse can abandon the realm of abstractions and mythologizing and rejoin other aspects of social discourse and thus become preoccupied with larger concrete issues in the life of the contemporary African society.

African Literature: Beyond Definition

The initial shock which a first year (African) undergraduate student of African literature is bound to experience will arise from the fact that the identity of his subject of study is presented as an object of controversy. Our student's shock is bound to be aggravated by the fact that although his basic identity as an African is not in doubt, an aspect of his cultural heritage and identity is subjected to such a wide variety of interpretations – all aspiring towards a rigid all-inclusive definition. The abiding question which should haunt a perceptive student of our subject is that of whether a whole body of a people's literary culture is reducible to the status of a biological specimen to be identified, defined, categorized, labelled and displayed for posterity to behold with unquestioning horror! Or whether, in fact, literature (any literature) lends itself to such rigidity in the first place.

The problematization of the identity of African literature is historical. The quest for a definition is in itself an aspect of the 'quest' for the black man's identity that was inaugurated in the wake of the slave trade and colonialism with their attendant dehumanization and denigration. Because colonialist ideology called to question the basic humanity of the black man, the major features of the tradition of anti-colonial intellection in general have been heated reaffirmations, definitions and redefinitions of aspects of black culture and civilization. The literature on these matters is quite copious and familiar.[2]

The most fundamental problem which scholarship on African literature has had to grapple with, in this respect, is that of identifying the "African-ness" of a body of literary productions consisting of both oral expressions (in African languages) and written texts in both African and European languages. Because of the appropriating greed of imperialist intellectual culture, it is only African literature written in the colonial languages that seems to have necessitated a definition.

The dominant contending positions on this latter aspect have variously emphasized factors such as nationality (whether a writer is an African by birth or naturalization or not), consciousness, language of expression, locale of the action fictionalized, the primary or target audience of the work and so on. The crisis of consciousness that is at the root of the entire "definition" project itself is evident in the pervasive indeterminancy in the conception of these various factorial considerations. Chinweizu et al., for instance, insist that the question of nationality is one "that a passport can decide".[3] In other words, if a Joyce Cary, a Karen Blixen, a Rider Haggard or an Elspeth Huxley, all European writers united by their uncomplimentary racist depictions of Africa, decided for naturalization in an African country of their choice – say Bokassa's Central African Republic or Nguema's Equatorial Guinea – and such a choice is granted through the issue of a new (African) passport, the writer in question, whose work, mind you, is already set in Africa, becomes an African writer and his/her work African literature!

Other critics/intellectuals like Obi Wali and Ngugi insist that African literature consists of those works which are "written" in African languages. Here again, two controversial and historically variable functions – mode of transmission and language of expression – are imposed as conditionalities for a sacrosanct definition of African literature. Nor can we reasonably insist on such other factors as target audience and consciousness without running into the same problems. It is perhaps Chinua Achebe who has struck the necessary note of caution when he observed that "[any] attempt to define African literature in terms which overlook the complexities of the African scene at the material time is doomed to failure".[4] If a definition were to exhaust the epistemological issue at stake in coming to terms with the reality of African literature, Achebe's dynamic pluralist definition would seem to offer a fairly durable solace. He says, *inter alia*,

> You cannot cram African literature into a small, neat definition. I do not see African literature as one unit but as a group of associated units – in fact the sum total of all the *national* and *ethnic* literatures of Africa.[5]

As in most of the other attempts, Achebe's definition places undue emphasis on literature as essentially *written*.

Legitimate and historically necessary as the above attempts at a definition may appear, they embody contradictions which negate and betray their very socio-historical predication. At the centre of these contradictions is the social position of the various "authorities" on the issue. As members of the neo-colonial bourgeoisie, the various scholars and writers of African literature are inheritors of a bourgeois Western-inspired 18th Century aesthetic tradition in which the creation and consumption of literature has been polarized away from social life and consecrated into a narrow specialization known as *aesthetics*. In the context of this aesthetic socialization, literature is reduced from the status of an all-encompassing social institution to a series of texts. This accounts for the reluctance with which the African cultural intelligentsia came to recognize that oral literature is also *literature*. Caught in the textbound conception of literature, they coined the convenient term *orature* in order to accommodate the reality of the oral mode of transmitting the literary.

The trouble with African literature is not that of a definition. It has to do with the larger task of freeing knowledge about African literature from the constrictive embrace of bourgeois intellectual mystifications. In this respect, if we take a closer look at the phenomenon which bourgeois aesthetics has come to call "literature", we will discover that it invokes a broad spectrum of meanings outside the suggestions made available by the etymology of the word itself. Here we need to make a clear distinction between the essence of the *literary* on one hand and the system of inclusion (or exclusion), codification and valuation of literary works which is what aesthetics is all about, on the other.

The essence of the social practice which we have come to popularize as "literature" consists in the creative exploitation of the social properties of human language for the mediation of social experience in a manner that approximates an apparent resolution of the contradictions of daily life, positing this resolution as an alternative world. These fundamental properties derive meaning in the context of man's primordial social and psychological needs. Mao Tse-Tung articulates these needs, which Ernst Fischer calls "the social necessity of art", in the following succinct terms:

> Although man's social life is the only source of literature and art and is incomparably livelier and richer in content, the people are not satisfied with life alone and demand literature and art as well. Why? Because, while both are beautiful, life as reflected in works of literature and art can and ought to be on a higher plane, more intense, more concentrated, more typical, nearer the ideal, and therefore more universal than actual everyday life.[6]

This primordial thirst to experience the ideal lies at the root of the longing for and patronage of fictionality, from the folk narratives of animistic villagers to the epics of Homer and the most modern written fiction. It also accounts for the relative popularity of the cinema as a cultural form worldwide. The concrete manifestations of this general quest for fictionality is what aesthetics has come to reduce to "literature". It is this aspect that is transcendental. What has been changing across time is the mode of transmission, the content in terms of specific experiences as well as the system and standards of evaluation, not the fundamental fact of linguistically communicated fiction and its rootedness in social experience and psychology.

In terms of the system of valuation, there is no sacrosanctity about the precise conception of literature as a cultural category. Its precise definition, associations, inclusions and exclusions are in themselves historical, contingent on the system and criteria of values in a given society. In turn, these aspects cannot be dissociated from changes in the means of production of material life, meanings and values in a given society. Says Eagleton:

> Literature does not exist in the sense that insects do, and . . . the value-

judgements by which it is constituted are historically variable. [These] value-judgements themselves have a close relation to social ideologies. They refer in the end not simply to private taste, but to the assumptions by which certain social groups exercise and maintain power over others.[7]

Therefore, aesthetics as a set of legitimating rules proposing criteria for distinguishing between the "literary" and the "non-literary" is an aspect of the contest of ideologies in class society. In these terms, what has been bandied around as "African literature" must be seen as what bourgeois African aesthetics, in its Euro-modernist and traditionalist formations, have come to define as such. The popular definitions of African literature so far constitute an aspect of the hegemonistic ideology of the cultural intelligentsia.

In terms of the modes and media of transmitting the literary, changes and variations represent changes in the modes of production. If we look beyond the 18th–20th Centuries' script-bound European conception of "literature", we can perceive African literature as manifesting itself in a variety of modes of production ranging from the oral to the written and electronically transmitted. If any of these modes can be described as hegemonic in the African instance, it must be the oral form, for it constitutes the most widespread form among the majority African peoples who inhabit the rural areas and urban slums.

The relationship among these co-existent modes of literary production is a dynamic one corresponding to the precise patterns in which segments of society undergo transitions from one mode of production of meanings and effects to another. As more people get educated, the oral mode will shed its dominance to the written mode. In turn, the necessity for a wider audience among the educated, mainly urban, populace, will create a necessity for literature to partake in mass for a reduction in the amount of time available for reading communication. Raymond Williams summarizes this phenomenon in the following terms:

> What can . . . be seen as happening, in each transition, is a historical development of social language itself: finding new means, and new forms and then new definitions of a changing practical consciousness.[8]

In effect, the present hegemonic conception of literature in terms of "print" is bound to be modified and modulated in the light of changing necessities and modes of production.

It is perhaps in these dynamic terms that African literature is best understood at the present time.

African Literature and its Audience

A conspicuous aspect of discourse on African literature in its written expression to date has had to do with the relationship between the writer and literature on one hand and the audience on the other. In the formulation of this question into a problematic, the writer is usually presented as synonymous with literature, the phenomenon and social institution. We know of course that the writer as a socially conditioned producer of artefacts does speak through his works but is by no means synonymous with them. His relationship with the society he inhabits is similarly not identical with the relationship between his work and its audience. The writer, in the African instance and up to the present time, is a member of a minority elite whose preparation for the social practice of writing is furnished by a relatively high level of formal Western education. Accordingly, his precise relationship with the society is definable in terms of his mode of insertion into the class and ideological formations of a neo-colonial society. In most cases, the African writer (especially in European languages) is a member of the petty bourgeois class, those we had previously referred to as "exploiters by class position". Most often, the moral and ideological commitment of his writing therefore stands in ironic and contradictory relationship to his position within the socio-economic structure of contemporary African society.

Accordingly, the relationship between the writer as a person and his audience needs clarification in theoretical terms. Once written and published, a literary work enters the domain of public discourse and the international market place. The audience of the work becomes universal. It is possible however to distinguish between audience in this general sense and a more restricted sense in which an African writer may want to see his "target audience" as an African one. Even at that, such an African audience is drawn from among those members of African societies who possess the necessary literacy to partake of the literary experience. In such a context, a discussion of the relationship between the writer and his audience will amount to an exploration of intra-class communication. Ironically, previous discussions of this relationship, even by practising writers themselves, have assumed that the totality of Africa constitutes an automatic audience for African literature.

Whether we conceive of audience in terms of the universal or the specific (target), the point remains that writing the published text is an economic undertaking which stands the writer (as a producer) in a definite relationship to the publisher and the market. Thus, the African writer is no different from writers in other open market economies. The profit motive of the publishers and booksellers is important in understanding his socio-economic standing and hence his relationship with the members of his immediate society. Vazquez illuminates this point in the following terms:

> [The] artist is a member of a particular society, and he must create and subsist within the range of possibilities offered by that society.
>
> The material living conditions of artists reveal both the nature of their relationship to the consumer (the public) and the position of the work of art within the given hierarchy of social relations. This in turn is determined by the stage of . . . material production.[9]

Perhaps a more appropriate formulation of the problematic should emphasize the relationship between African literature as a social institution consisting of a series of ontologically related cultural practices and its audience in general. Thus posited, we can confront some of the positions on the matter with greater clarity. The most popular positions have presumed the idea of an African community, an undifferentiated and aesthetically homogeneous community in which literary works will appeal to and enlist identical responses from all and sundry. The argument adduced in support of this reductionism is a certain romantic traditionalism in which the close and spontaneously informal relationship that existed between the oral performer in village communities and his audience is advanced as a definitive and immutable paradigm for communication relationships in all of African culture. The irrepressible Chinweizu et al. parade this view as part of their manifesto poetics: "They [African writers] should . . . work from the standpoint of the African community, not the Euro–American, not that of some abstract *Civilization de l'Universel*."[10] In the same spirit, Emmanuel Ngara, in his ambitiously titled book, *Art and Ideology in the African Novel*, correctly distinguishes between literature and writers but lapses into the familiar prescriptive clichés about what the relationship between African literature and its audience *should* be.

> The broad masses are estranged from African literature by the writers' choice of a foreign language . . . To fulfil its social function adequately, literature must be able to speak to the widest spectrum of society possible. It must be truly popular. It must be at once national and universal.[11]

This parade of idealities must now be interrupted in order to stem the tide of confusion in African literary scholarship. If we see African literature as a complex set of practices involving several modes of producing literary effects, we can identify several layers of literary expression each entailing a specific relationship between literature and its audience. In short, there is a dialectical relationship between aspects of a given literary culture and their audience which finds reflection in the adaptation of literary production techniques to suit the specific demands of given audiences. Even within a given historical milieu, there will be different audiences and different *literatures* in consonance with the class configuration of society.

In the contemporary African situation, oral literature, written literature, and electronic or print media-disseminated literature coexist side by side. And in fact, each of these modes of literary production has its internal gradations in terms of relative sophistication. In turn, each necessitates a different kind of relationship between literature and its audience.

Oral literature in a village setting presupposes a spontaneous, live audience in which there is physical proximity between the artist and his audience. He creates and modulates his art in response to the determinate needs and whims of his audience. Except in cases where poets are hired to perform to a royal audience, there is a fairly perceptible identity of material circumstances between artist and audience which enhances the pedagogical power of literature to its audience. Cultic esotericism and "high" literature does exist here mainly in societies where the division of labour has yielded specialization into cults, castes and so on. But the spontaneity and physical proximity between literature and audience can still be regarded as a given.

In the era of electronic communication, oral literature loses this immediate relationship with its audience. Literary experience rides the air waves as the faceless performer speaks to an equally faceless audience that may be thousands of miles away. Both artist and audience lose the benefit of mutual reinforcement and aesthetic cross-fertilization on which the oral form depended in its communal village habitat. Once oral literature is taken out of its pastoral village setting, the concept of the audience as a community dies a natural death.

In the case of written literature, we encounter an equally complex picture. There is always an impersonal relationship between the writer and his audience. Both reading and writing are acts of desperate anguish. The social and economic environment in which writing functions as a dominant mode of communicating literature is one in which communication has broken down. To sit down in one's study to communicate experiences, feelings and emotions artistically is a veritable act of anguish, a desperate reaching out for the warmth of fellow men. Similarly, to sit down and read a work of literature is frustrating in the sense that the enjoyment of literature which should ordinarily be a shared experience is personalized and privatized. Both writing and reading (except in reading aloud!) take place in the context of graveyard silence. This is a central attribute of the relationship between writer and audience.

> [The writer] is a material agent, an intermediary inserted in a particular place, under conditions he has not created, in submission to contradictions which by definition he cannot control, through a particular social division of labour, characteristic of the ideological superstructure of bourgeois society, which individuates him.[12]

Nor is written literature a monolithic entity. It is written from varying class positions and aesthetic perspectives and thus exists in a fairly complex and often hierarchical formation. This accounts for varying levels of difficulty and the distinction between "high" and "popular" literature which is constantly made in literary discourse. Thus, the complaint and charge of wilful obscurantism made against the early writings of some African writers may not be based on sound judgement after all. In this respect, the early poetry of Soyinka, Okigbo and Clark has been cited as an instance to demonstrate the estrangement of African writers from their "community".[13] The truth, however, is that there is no community of taste or interest to be found between the writers in question and the rest of their countrymen and -women most of whom are illiterate and underfed. Obscurantism in their works must be seen in the context of their Euro-modernist aesthetic socialization as well as their aspiration to convince the metropolitan bourgeois audience that they can effectively compete with their counterparts in Europe. Nor did they envisage the kind of communal popular audience which their detractors have come to use as a benchmark for judging their achievement as artists. These writers were writing for a literate, sophisticated, Western-educated bourgeois audience to which they also belong.

Within the written tradition in African literature, therefore, we can plot a gradation in terms of relative popularity ranging from Onitsha Market Literature to Ekwensi's chronicles and up to the most esoteric verbal gymnastics of Soyinka, Awoonor and Dumbudzo Marechera. To state this is in effect to further underline the truism that in every literary culture, there will exist literary works whose differing levels of accessibility also serve as active indicators of the class structure and differing world views in the society in question. Even in situations of revolutionary change, when literature and art are called upon to assume widespread popularity in the service of a specific cause, there is always a provision for the literary tastes of different strata engaged in the struggle usually with the proviso that there must be an ideological solidarity among the works of artists representing the different classes. Mao conceded this much in his famous Yenan essay: "Whether more advanced or elementary, all our literature and art are for the masses of the people."[14]

In effect, what is being advocated here is that the relationship between aspects of a given literature and its audience is historical and problematic, defying a monolithic conception. The factors which account for the popularity of certain works in certain periods must be seen as peculiar. For instance, the works of Maxim Gorky and Charles Dickens respectively were popular for different reasons and those reasons cannot justifiably be extrapolated into the African situation.

While recognizing the great diversity of expressions and audiences in African literature at present, progressive cultural policy must aim at submerging these divergences under a broad historical challenge. The crucial question ought to be: literature for whom? And for what? Mao answered this question in the context of the Chinese revolution by identifying the masses, peasants, armed workers and urban petty-bourgeois intellectuals as the strategic audience of the Chinese literature of the time. The African situation necessitates more or less the same answer, namely the need for popularization. But those who have advocated popularization have done so outside the context of a definite political and ideological programme.

In the context of a cultural policy geared towards revolutionary anti-imperialist ends, African literature should constitute a shared experience, not a one-way traffic in which the bourgeois writer assumes the condescending mien of a "teacher" whose godgiven responsibility it is to teach an inherently stupid audience of fellow Africans. Ideally, our writers should have the humility to commit class suicide, ready to learn from peasants and workers and in turn trying to inspire, inform and correct them from the benefit of their (the writers') better formal education and exposure. The purpose of literature in such a context would be to expand the scope of cultural communication for the purpose of uplifting the consciousness of the broad masses to a level where they too can make history.

The Language Question

Perhaps the most enduring symptom of the colonialist fixation of discourse on African literature is the problematization of the language question. The issue, which has been articulated mainly at an emotional level, has also managed to attract to itself the most heated controversies. Two dominant positions have emerged, each drawing advocates from writers and critics alike. There are those like Achebe and Soyinka who insist that African literature written in European languages is historically legitimate and that the use of these languages to communicate African experiences enriches both the languages in question and the literature itself. These writers also recognize the legitimacy of literature in African languages. Squarely opposed to this accommodationist/assimilationist position are others like Ngugi and Obi Wali who insist on linguistic indigenization as a minimum condition for the existence of African literature. Ngugi has driven this position to its logical conclusion by advancing the controversial view that African literature in the European languages in fact constitutes Afro-European literature.[15] In other words, genuine African literature can only be written in African languages. This side of the argument has tried to find ideological mooring in the fact that the European languages were a crucial part of the arsenal of colonialism while African languages still hold the reservoir of values and institutions that stand in antithetical opposition to imperialism.

It is instructive to note that most of the advocates of these positions have consistently been preoccupied with the written tradition to the near exclusion of the other modes which we have already identified. This is an indication of the elite character of the entire debate in the first place.

If, however, we relate the language controversy to the realities of the language situation in today's Africa and the possibilities open in literary practice, the redundancy of the controversy becomes obvious.

For historical reasons, the linguistic profile of each African country today is one in which there is an active coexistence of at least one European language and a plethora of African languages. In most cases, the European language functions as the dominant medium of official instruction and communication in education and government while the various African languages continue to play the politically subordinate role of social communication among members of the same or related ethnic groups. Owing to the ethnic heterogeneity of all African nation-states, European languages – as official languages – have been instrumental to the realization of national cohesion among members of erstwhile disparate nationalities. It is crucial to acknowledge here that the instruments that created African countries in the heyday of colonialism were fashioned in European languages. To that extent, these languages, by helping to sustain these nation-states as homogenous political entities have thus negated their originally negative historical "mission". At the level of social experience, the use of English in a country like Nigeria, for instance, makes it possible to sustain interaction among members of the nearly 350 ethnic groups. Inter-ethnic marriages have become rampant and the offspring of these marriages in fact speak English as a first language in the absence of mutual intelligibility between both parents in their respective ethnic languages. This analogy can be extended to other areas of social experience.

Literary creativity and consumption in each African country is simultaneously taking place in both the European and African languages. While the bulk of oral literary creativity is being carried out in African languages in the rural areas, much of written literature is done in European languages. African literature written in English, French and Portuguese exists alongside a growing tradition of written literature in Yoruba, Igbo, Gikuyu and Xosa. Given this spectacle, to insist that African literature be created exclusively in either of these sets of languages is to ignore the social and historical predication of the language situation itself. Even if all of African literature were suddenly to be created in African languages without due attention to the ideological content of the literature and its relationship with its audience, the revolutionary dreams of the advocates of linguistic indigenization would be thwarted.

If literature *qua* literature is to play its sectoral role as a cultural force in the transformation of society, then the language question needs to be redefined in more pragmatic terms. The problem, to my mind, is not that of language in the sense of verbal signification – that is, European vs. African – but rather that of strategies for cultural communication in a neo-colonial situation. In effect, language needs to be reconceptualized to mean the totality of the *means* available for communicating a cultural form to the greatest majority in a manner that will achieve a clearly defined cognitive–ideological effect in the consciousness of the audience so defined. In the context of this perspective, to insist on literature as either solely oral or solely written and packaged in the form of books is to remain nostalgic to a very archaic notion of literature.

The bulk of intellectual energy currently being dissipated in controversial exchanges on the language question should be directed to strategic thinking on alternative cultural policies for African countries in the context of which literature can play its rightful role in the reformulation of social relationships. In effect, no meaningful popular literary culture can be achieved outside the context of a social and political organization that recognizes the masses as the decisive force in history.

Language *qua* language is therefore not the issue in African literature. The problem of communication in our literature is directly related to the forces that prevent human communication at the economic and social levels. As part of the struggle to correct this anomaly, all the avenues of cultural communication should be explored to get the benefit of progressive revolutionary literature across to the greatest possible majority of our peoples. In this respect, European languages, African languages, oral performance, written expression, radio broadcasts, etc. are implicated.

Commitment and Alignment

> The writer may not want to concern himself with society, but society concerns itself with him.   **Harry Slochower**[16]

Parallel to the euphoric celebration of the "arrival" of modern African literature was the inauguration of a controversy around the question of social commitment. Given the historical predication of the literature in question, especially in its written expression, its social and political implications were bound to be as contentious as the racial identity of the African himself. More importantly, because the Euro-modernist criticism that had to "announce" the "arrival" of African literature was deeply rooted in the liberal bourgeois tradition, with its emphasis on value-free culture and art for its own sake, literature's social relevance was made an object of intellectual dispute. Actively conterpoised to this has been the insistence on the part of the majority of the writers that the totality of their art is a mode of apprehending and coming to terms with the reality of Africa's historical experiences from the slave trade to the contemporary neo-colonial era. Consequently, the initial line of contention in the commitment controversy emerged in the early and mid-1960s as essentially that between an "art-for-art's sake" school of critics and writers and those who insisted that literature must be concerned with forces in its social ambience. Says Kyalo Mativo about this polarization:

> The ideological struggle in literature congeals finally . . . into two schools of African writers: those who are answerable only to themselves and consider their 'creative process' as private property, and those who use their craft for a social purpose.[17]

While the "art-for-art" school has diminished into an incoherent minority voice, those who insist on an engaged and committed African literature have come to articulate the parameters and manifestations of commitment in several ways. Achebe, for instance, has articulated the responsibility of the writer as an essentially pedagogical one in which the writer in addition to writing about the issues of his day also has to assume the role of "teacher" and guardian of his society. In similar vein, the Chinweizu formation has reaffirmed the necessity for the African writer to be concerned with public issues;

> The function of the artist in Africa, in keeping with our traditions and needs, demands that the writer, as a public voice, assume a responsibility to reflect public concerns in his writings, and not preoccupy himself with his puny ego.[18]

It needs to be said, however, that a reaffirmation of the need for commitment is not in itself innovative, for commitment in one sense or the other is intrinsic to the nature of all art especially literature. Commitment in the liberal sense of a preoccupation with issues of socio-political contemporaneity can in fact be taken for granted in any valid discussion of African literature and art. The crucial questions ought to be: commitment to what and to whom? In effect, commitment in order to command relevance and strike a socio-political significance must be aligned, for the socio-political world which the writer inhabits and which the literary work mediates is a function of structural contradictions and conflicts among identifiable social forces which in themselves compel choices and options. As Raymond Williams rightly observes, "commitment . . . is surely conscious, active, and open: a *choice* of position".[19] Therefore, the oft quoted critique of "tendency literature" by Marx and Engels is a strong case for serious, purposive commitment, not a repudiation of it. What needs to be underlined is the fact that commitment in literature is *essentially* artistic; the commitment in a literary work of art strikes us through the laws of artistic composition. When artistic commitment appeals according to the laws of mundane social rhetoric, art yields to propaganda.

To underline the intricate connection between commitment and alignment is not, however, to posit them as immutable and given. They operate in a strictly historical and therefore dynamic terrain. *The positions which the literary works of an epoch assume are in themselves contingent on the socio-historical challenges which literature as an aspect of culture is compelled to face in that time and place.*

> Commitment, strictly, is conscious alignment, or conscious change of alignment . . . In any specific society, in a specific phase, writers can discover in their writing the realities of their social relations, and in this sense their alignment. If they determine to change these, the reality of the whole social process is at once in question, and the writer within a revolution is necessarily in a different position from the writer under fascism or inside capitalism or in exile.[20]

This dynamic nature of commitment and alignment cuts across the various modes of literary expression. The commitment of the oral performer in pre-colonial Africa was circumscribed by local conditions in his village community and the limited economic and political options it made available. In the colonial era, the question of conscious alignment came into greater focus as song, drama, and narrative were challenged to grapple with the aberrations of colonialism. Among the Mau Mau freedom fighters, among the Aba Women's Patriotic Movement (1929), among the country folk of pre-independence Mozambique and Angola, the object of oral literature's commitment was defined by the challenges of the nationalist struggle. Even in the era of electronic transmission, the oral performer who has to "produce" for a recording company or entertain dignitaries at an airport reception knows the limits of creative freedom and creates in line with the laws of patronage in a capitalist society. Similarly when a Sembene Ousmane or a Soyinka decides that the written text is inadequate for communicating the social message in his work and opts for the film medium he is expressing a conscious commitment and change of alignment dictated by an acute awareness of the changing nature of his audience and the ambience for the reception of literary experiences. Their recourse to the film as a medium for transmitting their works is an indicator of a fundamental change of commitment and alignment.

Beyond this sectoral conception of commitment and alignment in African literature, we can equally trace the evolving patterns along a diachronic axis especially in the context of the written tradition. The early writings of freed African slaves in the New World were united by their commitment to the eradication of slave trading; in the colonial days, race retrieval and political independence constituted the objects of significant literary commitment – hence the considerable relevance of Negritude and other cultural nationalist movements in those days. In the immediate post-colonial era, the object of literary commitment has also changed from the initial critical stance of the writers to a situation where, at present, writers are being challenged by the class and ideological options in our societies to be committed to and aligned with the forces of neo-colonialism and imperialism on the one hand or those of the African revolution on the other. Each stage in this evolutionary paradigm must be seen as dictated by and relevant to the imperatives of its time and place.

In literature, as in real social and political life, non-alignment is an impossible position. To write or sing is to express a commitment. To be committed is to take sides in the conflictual essence of social reality. One's positions are either relevant or irrelevant in a given socio-historical setting, for each epoch presents its challenges to literature in the form of a two-part option: for or against progressive forces. Thus, a refusal to declare one's alignment in art is in itself a conscious position which almost always corresponds with acquiescence to the values and institutions that equilibrate existing social structures.

Here, one must enter a note of caution against that kind of liberal intellectual opportunism in African literary discourse which admits of the necessity for commitment and at once dissipates that admission in liberal equivocation about the subjectivity of commitment and the myth of the writer's freedom. Hear Chinweizu et al.

Treating the burning issues of the day is what is usually referred to as political *engagement* in literature. Though non-mandatory, the times may well demand that writers, like other citizens, be politically *engaged*, but to what side of a partisan affray? None can decide for the writer, as none can decide for the cook, the teacher, the soldier, doctor, merchant, lawyer, farmer, musician, athlete, or politician.[21]

It will be interesting to know whether a solidier in the battle-front can effectively disagree with his commander as to what side he should use his "art" to support! Or as to what side of the great divide the black South African writer should commit his art. Such liberal doublespeak as the above in the name of bourgeois "radicalism" is, to say the least, a dangerous development in the intellectual life of contemporary Africa.

A dialectical conception of commitment and alignment must insist on their socio-historical predication. Mao conceded the freedom of the artist but added a proviso: "as far as unmistakable counter-revolutionaries and wreckers of the socialist cause are concerned, the matter is easy: we simply deprived them of their freedom of speech".[22] Even Trotsky in his liberal admissions on the freedom of artists related artistic freedom to the needs of the Russian revolution. For Lenin, the freedom of literature and art was subordinated to the needs of the struggle to consolidate the Soviet state: for Sartre, commitment and alignment were conditioned by the peculiar needs of post-war Europe. In all these situations, what changes is the object of commitment and the relevant, historically compelled alignments, not the fundamental fact of commitment and alignment as irreducible constituents of literary practice.

In the context of the imperative of the anti-imperialist struggle in Africa, commitment and alignment must transcend a mere preoccupation with issues of *topical* nature and address questions such as *commitment to what?* and *on whose side?* These questions cannot, in our circumstances, be dismissed by any pretension to Pan-Africanist pluralism or some esoteric devotion to "freedom of the artist" couched in metaphors such as "self-apprehension" and "decolonization" and so on. The sides which artists assume in their works, by virtue of the pedagogical implications of those works in the educational system, are not less important than those which politicians take. Politics and literature have to do with power and hegemony in society.

Continuities from the Past

> The tradition of all the dead generations weighs like a nightmare on the brain of the living. And just when they seem engaged in revolutionising themselves and things, in creating something that has never yet existed, precisely in such periods of revolutionary crisis they anxiously conjure up the spirits of the past to their service. **Karl Marx**[23]

Either as an inexhaustible quarry of ancient myths or as a zone of decisive historical encounters, the African past has continued to exercise an irresistible fascination for the set of related practices that we have come to know as African literature. Singers and performers, writers and film-makers alike in modern-day Africa have been united in their endless recourse to artistic conventions, symbols and motifs from the past. Similarly, literary content has consistently explored themes, beliefs, practices and values from the period before and up to the coming of the West. The history of world culture illuminates now and again a certain tendency by the creative imagination to reach back to past ages in quest of values and motifs for the apprehension and ratification of contemporary experiences. Renaissance Western man reached back for the classics of ancient Greece and Rome just as the 18th Century was to be seized in a renewed feat of neo-classicism. In all instances of this retrospective fixation, there seems to persist an underlying belief (illusion?) that past ages were happier, more harmonious and progressive. Marx himself almost succumbed to this retrospective illusion when he tried to rationalize Western man's tendency to derive his aesthetic standards from the world of the ancient Greeks and concluded that it must have to do with our endless nostalgia for the infancy of our species.

In African literature (oral, written etc.) bourgeois discourse has come to consecrate the past as the repository of tradition. Here, tradition becomes the "stubborn past", an immutable complex of conventions and practices existing in the form of pearls and timeless crystals in the museum of ancestral memory to be resurrected at will for the purpose of validating contemporary experiences. We have already cautioned against the static "museum" view of tradition and advocated a more dialectical view in which tradition is seen as an active process of selection and exclusion, a selective continuity in which "convenient" aspects of past practices and conventions, in art and social habits, are invoked to give a sacrosanct colouring to the power structure of the present.

In all cultures, the precise forms which the retrospective glance takes have always been determined by factors of a historical nature, factors which actively condition the choices and exclusions which artists make from the past. In the African context, the constant recourse to ancestry is the expression of racial injury, an attempt by the creative imagination to transcend the distorting mists of present contradictions in quest of stabilizing images. It is the product of our unfortunate handshake with Western Europe and a tacit, if idealistic, rejection of the broken images of ourselves presented by imperialist historiography and supremacist myth-making in all their concrete forms. Even if we encounter the African past as a mythic reality in our literature, it must be understood in terms of this historical *first cause*. The sheer range of attitudes and approaches to the past which we encounter in our literature is an indicator of the extent of the historical disorientation in question. There are writers whose attitude is based on romantic idealism, the tendency to absolve the past of its imperfections. This tendency is most pronounced in early anti-colonial literature of the sort that has come to be associated with the Negritude writers. Camara Laye's *The African Child* and Senghor's early verse are replete with these "sweet" memories. This attitude, it needs to be pointed out, is historically justifiable in the light of the assimilationist strategy of French colonialist ideology.

A second attitude/approach to the past is that characterized by a mood of critical apprehension, a questioning of the past in a bid to clarify the experiences of the present. This attitude at times assumes an almost nihilistic, self-negating dimension as in Yambo Ouloguem's *Bound to Violence*. In other instances, as in Achebe's novels set in pre-colonial and colonial Igboland – *Things Fall Apart* and *Arrow of God* – or in Soyinka's *A Dance of the Forests* and *Death and the King's Horseman*, the writer relives the past in a fictive universe that strikes a realistic balance between glory and savagery without obliterating the dividing line between native frailties and alien barbarism. Says Ngugi: "The African past is not only one of egalitarian peasant communities . . . but also one of continued exploitation at the hand of the West".

A third and emergent approach to the literary appropriation of the past assumes the form of a certain historical re-evaluation of the past in the light of the ideological imperatives of the present. Ngugi and Mugo's historical play, *The Trial of Dedan Kimathi* and Armah's historical novels: *Two Thousand Seasons* and *The Healers* can roughly be said to belong in this category. In these works, there is a head-on collision between the ideological motivation of colonialism and that of champions of genuine African history. Thus, the imperialist version of African history is reconstructed with the genuine defenders of African values cast in a more positive light.

Against the foregoing background, it needs to be interjected that the conception of the past, our attitudes to it and the uses to which we wish to put it cannot be divorced from our ideological positions. The more romantic and fixated the African writer is to the past, the greater the tendency for him to become a slave to it and hence find friendship among those Europeans who would rather that Africa remains the way they found it in the 18th Century. It might be fascinating for a researcher to investigate the veracity of this proposition in terms of the award of excellence conferred on Leopold Senghor by the French National Academy!

On the other hand, those writers who proffer a "balanced" view of the African past or even insult our ancestors will equally be greeted as moderates and liberals, great artists whose works derive profundity from a certain aspiration to a universal spirit. Soyinka and Achebe, and not Ngugi, Osofisan or Armah, are more likely to get the Nobel Peace Prize for literature in their lifetime!

The upshot of the foregoing is that there is a strong ideological contest implicit in the various "uses" to which the African past is being put in our literature. If the historic opposition in the contemporary world – especially in Africa – is between capitalism and socialism, African literature cannot, in its attitudes to the past, be absolved from the responsibilities which these socio-economic systems define even in terms of viewing the past. Observed Marx and Engels: "In bourgeois society, . . . the past dominates the present; in communist society, the present dominates the past."[24] Ngugi illuminates this crucial distinction with greater clarity:

> In capitalist society, the past has a romantic glamour: gazing at it is *thus* a means of escaping the present. It is only in a socialist context that a look at yesterday can be meaningful in illuminating today and tomorrow. [25]

The challenge which this clarification poses for literary practice in the context of the anti-imperialist struggle in Africa goes beyond craft. It is essentially a matter of craft corrected by a progressive consciousness. Practices and motifs from the past cannot be excluded from even revolutionary literature, for in a period of social transition practices from an antecedent tradition will continue in present practices. Thus, aspects of the oral tradition will persist in African written literature until the historical conditions which account for their coexistence become irrelevant. The crucial point is the precise manner in which these past continuities – at the levels of myth, craft and values – should be appropriated by our literature in this neo-colonial age. Perhaps Mao's counsel on the matter should provide a guidepost:

> We must take over all the fine things in our literary and artistic heritage, critically assimilate whatever is beneficial, and use them as examples when we create works out of the literary and artistic raw materials in the life of the people of our own time and place.[26]

Aesthetics and Critical Values

A conspicuous manifestation of the wrong questions which bourgeois criticism of African literature has been asking these many years is its one-time preoccupation with the question as to whose *values* should inform the evaluation of African literature. Characteristically, the answer to this question has been formulated in terms of a simplistic polarization between African and Western values with the obvious conclusion that African values should inform the evaluation of African literature. This reductionism is of course contingent on the adoption of the bourgeois Western notion of aesthetics as a self-accounting profession whose responsibility it is to legislate the enjoyment and appreciation of art into a rigid discipline.

Ironically, however, much as racial and civilizational values have a bearing on the relative values ascribed to a body of literary works, it is also true that civilizational values manifest themselves in clear structural terms. The material conditions in the context of which aesthetic judgements are made, the process of educating taste as well as the overall conception of beauty and ugliness among members of a given society are all functions of those variables which distinguish one social class from another. In most African societies, we can distinguish at least three levels of aesthetic perception and valuation. These are the aesthetics of the rural peasantry, of the urban poor and of the bourgeoisie (both urban and rural).

In this formation, which roughly corresponds also to the broad configuration of social classes in Africa, the aesthetics of the bourgeois elite, who also furnish the ruling class, has acquired a hegemonistic status. The artistic appetite and standards of this class are conditioned and dictated from the familiar New York–Paris–London axis. The literary intelligentsia belongs to this class also, and accordingly derives its standards of aesthetic valuation from Western "high" literary culture which it proceeds to use its *power* to enthrone into an African aesthetic. In effect, when African bourgeois scholars organize a conference in quest of an African aesthetic, it is precisely the outlines of these elitist aesthetics that they are out to demarcate and crystallize.

Thus, to insist on a monolithic and undifferentiated African aesthetic in literature is the height of bourgeois arrogance, for it neglects and negates the heterogeneity and complexity of the African cultural universe.

The fundamental oppositions in African literature are between bourgeois African/European values and the values of the masses of African peasants and working classes. If the African bourgeois cultural intelligentsia have an in-house quarrel with their Western cousins, they ought to settle these amicably at their numerous conferences or on the pages of journals such as *Research in African Literatures* and *African Literature Today*.

The Limits of Literature

A final note of caution must be entered for the benefit of the student and aspiring scholar of African literature. A predominant feature of discourse on African literature is a disturbing note on messianism which almost elevates African writers to the status of a salvation army. Both the writers and their critics as members of the neo-colonial bourgeois class have been instrumental in creating this impression.

It must be conceded that literature, because of its peculiar raw material – human language – possesses an ideological force to the extent that it has to do with the fashioning of consciousness. Also to be conceded is the psychosocial necessity for fictional elevation and sublimation which the human psyche craves in response to the drudgery of everyday life.

But literature ought to be seen as an aspect – just one aspect – of the cultural expressions of society. The performer or writer in modern society is just another producer working in the cultural domain. His work can be pursued either to the detriment of society or to its glory. If society is to change for the better, it must depend on the collaborative efforts of all social forces, compelled to resolve their antagonistic relationship in a purposive unity forged by historical forces that place every occupation in a purposive context geared towards a definite progressive goal.

Thus, if kings rule badly and the police batter youth with the truncheons of oppression, let not the poet be called in to quell the riots in the streets with sweet or angry verse. But if the forces of the oppressed are galvanized in revolutionary struggle, there will be poets chanting the glory of the old order and others who will fight alongside the oppressed, sublimating their art to the dictates of revolutionary ferment. In such a situation, only the latter would be relevant. Mao Tse-Tung was sensitive to this intricate relationship between literature and politics when he said: "Literature and art are subordinate to politics, but in their turn exert a great influence on politics".[27] In effect, literature is instrumental to the political process only *by* and *according to* the laws of art.

Implications for Practical Criticism

The next three chapters are devoted to an exploratory application of the framework and categories enunciated in Chapter Four to the practical analysis and interpretation of African literary texts freely selected from the three conventional genres of literature. The intention here is to illustrate, even if schematically, the path trodden by dialectical hermeneutics of bourgeois scholars and critics who insist that a dialectical–materialist sociological approach to literature is antithetical to a rigorous consideration of matters of form.

In selecting texts for analysis in these chapters, I have tried to include works which cannot be said to articulate a revolutionary (in the sense of class struggle) view of society if only to debunk the bourgeois simplification that only certain works, namely, those of socialist revolutionary inspiration and vision, are amenable to radical sociological exegesis. It is specifically in this spirit that I have opted to explore the possibilities of a materialist reading of Achebe's novels set in what is erroneously called "traditional" Igbo society. These works have been the favourite victims of literary metaphysicians obsessed with a static notion of tradition and an exotic impression of the African world.

The preponderance of texts with an anti-imperialist ideological slant is a deliberate attempt to give substance to the overriding pedagogical and political mission of this book. No apologies need to be tendered for this position. Nor can a text like this one, whose primary thrust is mainly theoretical, aim at an exhaustive practical–critical treatment of texts and events in a literary universe whose creative energies are still very prolific. I have also avoided a discussion of oral literary pieces in line with my conviction that a textual rendition of such pieces amounts to a profane violation of their ontological status as organic events that are best discussed and evaluated in the active context of performance and the spontaneous celebration of the communality of experience in those societies where the oral mode of producing the literary is still predominant.

The emphasis in the ensuing exegeses is on the dialectical relationship among our cardinal categories – *context*, *content* and *form* – in their mutual and plural determinations and counter-determinations as conditioned by the specific ambience of the contemporary African world in its distinctive structural manifestations.

What is stressed throughout is that the literary text is a *prismatic dialectical image* of the African social totality in its specifying and universalizing essence.

Notes

1. Mao Tse-Tung, "Talks at the Yenan Forum on Literature and Art" in *Selected Works*, vol. 3 (Peking: Foreign Language Press, 1967) p. 90.

2. Early criticism and conference discussions of African literature were preoccupied with endless attempts at defining African literature.

3. Chinweizu et al., *Toward the Decolonization of African Literature* (Enugu, Fourth Dimension, 1980) pp. 10–16.

4. Chinua Achebe, *Morning Yet on Creation Day* (London: Heinemann, 1975) p. 56.

5. Ibid.

6. Mao Tse-Tung, "Talks at the Yenan Forum" p. 82.

7. Terry Eagleton, *Literary Theory: An Introduction* (Oxford: Basil Blackwell, 1983) p. 16.

8. Raymond Williams, *Marxism and Literature* (Oxford: O.U.P., 1977) p. 54. See also Tony Bennet, *Formalism and Marxism* (London: Eyre Methuen, 1979) ch. 1.

9. Adolfo Vazquez, *Art and Society: Essays in Marxist Aesthetics* (London: Aerlis Press, 1973) pp. 168–9.

10. Chinweizu et al., *Toward the Decolonization of African Literature*, p. 242.

11. Emmanuel Ngara, *Art and Ideology in the African Novel* (London: Heinemann, 1985) p. 46.

12. Raymond Williams, *Marxism and Literature*, pp. 145–150.

13. This is the central charge that launched Chinweizu's bourgeois manifesto poetics.

14. Mao Tse-Tung, "Talks at the Yenan Forum" p. 84.

15. Ngugi Wa Thiong'o, *Writers in Politics* (London: Heinemann, 1981) pp. 53–65.

16. Harry Slochower, excerpt from *The New Masses*, quoted in Maynard Solomon (ed.) *Marxism & Art* (New York: Vintage Books, 1973) p. 480.

17. Kyalo Mativo, "Ideology in African Philosophy and Literature", *Ufahamu*, vol. 8, no. 1, 1978, p. 133.

18. Chinweizu et al, *Toward the Decolonization of African Literature*, p. 252.

19. Raymond Williams, *Marxism and Literature*, p. 200.

20. Ibid., p. 204.

21. Chinweizu et al., *Toward the Decolonization of African Literature*, p. 254.

22. Quoted in Raymond Williams, *Marxism and Literature*, p. 203.

23. Karl Marx, *The Eighteenth Brumaire of Louis Bonaparte*, quoted in Maynard

Solomon (ed.) *Marxism and Art*, p. 54.

24. Karl Marx and Frederick Engels, *The Communist Manifesto* (Moscow: Progress Publishers, 1977) pp. 51-2.

25. Ngugi Wa Thiong'o, *Homecoming: Essays* (London: Heinemann, 1972) p. 45.

26. Mao Tse-Tung, "Talks at the Yenan Forum", p. 81.

27. Ibid., p. 86.

6 History and the Dialectics of Narrative in the African Novel

In the face of overwhelming empirical evidence to the contrary, it would be stupid to argue or pretend that the novel is an indigenous African form. Nor can scholarship predicated on the racial identity of a literary form, no matter how energetically polemicized, provide any meaningful insight into the manifestations of that form as an art form either within or outside its immediate genetic home.[1] The issue in correctly characterizing and understanding the African novel, therefore, transcends the narrow and wrong-headed controversy as to whether the novel is alien or indigenous to Africa. On the contrary, the general framework within which explorations into the identity of the African novel should be pursued is the whole matter of literary development, its modes and patterns as these are inexorably conditioned by socio-historical developments. In effect, the theoretical premise that informs the pronouncements on and analyses of the African novel in this chapter is essentially captured in David Craig's attempt to formulate a set of laws of literary development when he states that "the course of literary development – its lulls, peaks, dying branches and new shoots – is determined by the main course of history".[2] In broader terms, the theoretical inspiration of this chapter can be reformulated thus: *once born and nurtured in a given socio-historical environment, a literary form is propelled outside its native soil onto new ground by determinate historical factors which in turn will give it a local identity which, though reminiscent of its original "genetic" properties, will obey the laws of its new environment and baptize it into a new definition.*

This hypothetical generalization raises certain fundamental questions about the specific sociology of the African novel.

Problems in the Sociology of the African Novel

The instrumentality of the rise of capitalism and of the bourgeoisie as its pilot class in the rise of the Western novel can now be taken for granted. So also can its individualized modes of generation and consumption be assumed. And given the tacit adoption of liberalism as the dominant ideology of the bourgeoisie as a class, the novel could well be said to have furnished an important outlet for liberal ideology in the West especially up to the 19th Century. Similarly, in terms of form, the centrality of the schizoid hero as an archetypal figure in the cosmos of the Western novel led a writer like Lukacs in *The Theory of the Novel* to accept that feature as an immutable *condition* of the novel. And because the novel in its rising became a tradition unto itself, Western bourgeois literary theory and practice intervened to legitimize it in terms of certain basically formalistic categories. Thus in a tradition whose strongest voice to date is E. M. Forster in *Aspect of the Novel*, specific lexical categories were evolved as conceptual pillars for discussing the novel. Key among these are narrative technique, point of view, plot, structure, proportion, character, time, place, and style. It is crucial to interject here and point out that all these features and categories are axiomatic to the extent that we are discussing the novel in the "great" Western European tradition that we have come to associate with George Eliot, Charles Dickens, Jane Austen, Franz Kafka and James Joyce. They are also axiomatic to the extent that we are discussing the external formal manifestation of that novel.

In its rootedness in realist epistemology as a philosophical foundation, the novel form as part of the cultural arsenal of an emergent capitalism put itself freely at the service of all the vices to which its informing political economy was subject. Thus, the novel formed part of the literature syllabus of colonialist education in different parts of Africa. And to that extent, a certain familiarity with the Western novel was catalytic to the rise of the African novel. But it was by no means the only factor nor was it a factor *by* and *in* itself. Colonialist education was a factor in Africa's literary development, especially in the case of the novel, to the extent that it was instrumental in the creation of a colonized bourgeoisie. It was also the historic responsibility of this bourgeoisie either to face or betray the challenges of the colonial assault. At the level of cultural action, the intellectual arm of the bourgeoisie could either be assimilated into the dominant (Victorian) aesthetic tradition of the colonizers or use knowledge gained therefrom to combat colonialist culture. The latter option was naturally the more attractive and the novel form in particular found a prominent role in the resultant tradition of cultural nationalist literature. "Just as the emerging bourgeoisie was leading the political struggle, the emerging intelligentsia was expressing the new-found aspiration of the African people in the form of art".[3]

To centralize the rise of an African bourgeoisie and the imperative of nationalist politics in the rise of the African novel is not to exclude other factors. Some critics have argued for the existence of a tradition of narrative art in different pre-colonial African societies as providing a kind of contextual manure for the external impetus provided by formal familiarity with the Western novel. This is to be expected: literary forms as cultural seeds do not germinate and flourish in hostile terrains. Yet we cannot pursue the argument about the contribution of indigenous narrative traditions to its logical conclusion without running the fatal risk of wishing away the objective fact that Africa was colonized and therefore came under specific cultural influences as a result.

If liberalism provided the ideological substratum of the Western novel, nationalist politics and its attendant racial affirmative consciousness formed the main ideological thrust of the African novel in its earliest manifestations. In effect, the novelistic mode in the hands of pioneer African writers formed part of larger nationalist political discourse. Observes Emmanuel Ngara:

> The writings of committed, political ideologists and talented academics were an expression, in ideological terms, of a new social psychology, a new level of political and ideological awareness after an era of acceptance of and submission to colonial domination, cultural imperialism and capitalist exploitation.[4]

If we accept the adoption of a realistic referent as being at the core of the philosophy of the novel, its inherent specificity in terms of socio-historical conditioning becomes even more compelling. In this respect, we can argue that to the extent that they explore disparate *realities*, no unity is to be found among the English novel, the German novel, the French and the American novel respectively, even though they are all united by the hazy geo-political categorization as aspects of the "Western" novel. Given this fact of specificity, it would be the height of academic oversight to deny the African novel its distinctive historical specificity.

Against the background of its informing nationalist ideology, then, the sense of the *real* in the African novel is bound to assume a distinctively historical texture. In this respect, it may be instructive to recall that what a society considers real consists of a series of relationships: between people and between people and nature, the supernatural, and the objects with which they conduct the business of daily life at a specific time. Therefore, nothing precludes realism in the literature of a given society from incorporating elements of the supernatural for as long as those elements, as active constituents of the psycho-social world, affect people's actions at the level of material life experience. Thus, Tutuola's novels are no less realistic than those of Dickens. What distinguishes the two writers is the level of development of material forces of production and therefore consciousness in the respective social worlds that inform their works. Rightly regarded, therefore, realism should be seen in very historical terms.

However, definite ideological positions do have a conditioning effect on the slant and mode of literary depiction of the real. Therefore in categorizing the African novel to date, there seem to be two broad options: a stagist paradigm and an ideological paradigm. The first would group novels in terms of their diachronic insertion in the growing current of the African novelistic tradition. The main watersheds in this paradigm would be: the anti-colonial novel (for example *Arrow of God*, *The River Between*, *Chaka*); the novel of post-colonial disenchantment (for example *The Interpreters*, *A Man of the People*, *The Beautyful Ones Are Not Yet Born*,

Return to the Shadows); the novel of radical ideological commitment (e.g. *Petals of Blood* and *Violence, Time of the Butcherbird*). Implicit in this typology is a certain keen attention to the sensitivity of succeeding generations of African novels to the changing socio-political challenges in the African world. And to the extent that each of these phases (stages) is characterized by a certain reactive spirit, it could be suggested that a common ideational characteristic of the African novel to date is that it is an artistic negation of a series of political negations, not necessarily a complacent affirmation of the "moving spirit" of a dominant class. But to adopt this typology as definitive as I did in my book, *Towards a Sociology of African Literature*[5], is to succumb to a certain historicist fatalism which assumes that literary and socio-political developments progress along a line of direct correlation.

In any given historical development, the response of an art form cannot be measured with a scientific instrument such as a barometer or a thermometer. Thus, writers of the same generation, confronted by identical historical experiences and challenges, may respond in disparate ways thus suggesting the intervention of factors that are not immediately obvious in the conditioning of literary currents and fashions. If we take the anti-colonial phase of the African novel for instance, we discover that while Achebe's response in *Arrow of God* tends to focus on institutional (superstructural) aspects of the encounter between colonialism and the African society, Ousmane in *God's Bits of Wood* gives prominence to the economic fact of the production relations that underlay colonialism as an aspect of capitalism. Similarly, in the post-colonial disenchantment genre, we discover that while a writer like Achebe in *A Man of the People* heaps the blame for political misrule on individual actors, Armah in *The Beautyful Ones* discredits the neo-colonial state apparatus. The examples could be multiplied indefinitely for each of the stages outlined above.

In effect, there are serious ideological interferences in the manner in which a writer depicts what he considers the realities of his time and place. Some writers may pungently perceive the political issues at stake but depict them in a manner that is merely critical of them; others may depict the same realities in a manner that imbues social experience with a dynamics that suggests the possibility of change in a progressive direction. Yet others may depict reality metaphysically and show that human actions are unconscious enactments of supernatural machinations. In effect, we can designate these three dominant modes of realistic depiction in the African novel as follows: animistic realism, (for example Tutuola's *The Palmwine Drinkard*, Fagunwa's *The Forest of a Thousand Damons*, Amadi's *The Concubine*); critical realism (for example Armah's *The Beautyful Ones*, Achebe's *A Man of the People*), socialist realism (for example Ousmane's *God's Bits of Wood*, La Guma's *Time of the Butcherbird*, Ngugi's *Petals of Blood*).

It is necessary to add that each of these types of realism is necessitated by a specific stage (or form) of social consciousness and may be contextually appropriate for exploring the challenges necessitated by that level of consciousness.

At the level of formal realization, the attempts that have so far been made to distinguish the African novel in terms of certain stereotypical features are unscientific. The African novel, it needs to be pointed out, is not a monolithic and undifferentiated category. It is a complex of several ideologically related works of assorted aesthetic realizations. This is not to say that certain common features cannot be identified among closely related works. Attention has been drawn to such features as the use of oral continuities or the adoption of an African setting as distinctive formal attributes of the African novel. But on closer examination, it will be discovered that not all these features are manifest in all African novels and even when some of them are employed, their manifestation varies from author to author and from novel to novel. In order, therefore, to establish the formal identity of the set of related fictional products that we have come to know as the African novel, we need to return to the dialectical relationship among our categories: context, content and form. To the extent that a certain historical context defines the African novel, the narrative mediations of that context into definite works (i.e. *content* plus *form*) are bound to bear the stamp of their specific determination. For instance, because the African novel is the product of an ideological position that stands in opposition to capitalist imperialism and its attendant alienation, the schizoid hero, who is so relentlessly at the centre of the classical Western novel, hardly finds a place in the African novel. Nor do we have the rugged individualism and angst-ridden existentialist inwardness on which the schizoid hero thrives. On the contrary, most African novels feature heroes or heroic collectivities who are created to interrogate the values of capitalist society.[6] Besides this general feature, form in the African novel is as divergent as the African world itself and does not permit of such banal generalizations as find expression in clichés such as "the African personality" or "African culture". The decisive point which emerges from this observation is that *novels informed by a particular socio-historical context may share identical broad elements of content but will display divergent formal realizations, for it is mainly in terms of mediating context and content into form that the individuality of authors as artists is most manifest.*

In the rest of this chapter an attempt is made to proffer dialectical materialist explanations of African novels, most of which bourgeois criticism has mystified through its metaphysical hermeneutics. No apologies need to be offered here for the choice of the same overflogged novels, for the object of radical criticism is a transvaluation of received assumptions and not just to ignore those assumptions or accept them as given. Nor is anything to be gained from such ultra-leftism that consigns proven classics in a literary culture to the trash-can simply because those same works have constituted the favourite punching bags of bourgeois criticism.[7] Our specific challenge is to offer alternative explanations and interpretations of literary works as concrete aspects of the reality which we badly need to change.

The Materialism of Cultural Nationalism: Achebe's *Things Fall Apart* and *Arrow of God*

The impulse for a materialist reconsideration of Achebe's novels set in pre-colonial Igbo society is an act of rebellion against their systematic appropriation into the metaphysical aesthetics of traditionalist scholarship.[8] *Things Fall Apart* and *Arrow of God* have since become axiomatic reference points for diverse interests and opinions intent on rediscovering and commenting on "traditional African society" and "the culture conflict" inaugurated by the advent of colonialism, stock concepts which have since been adumbrated into a mini-catechism. Gradually also, these works have become part of the cultural raw material for the definition of an immutable African world. Little or no effort, however, has so far been made to situate analyses of the novels in the context of the specific socio-economic formation that characterized pre-colonial Igbo (African) societies and to understand the series of conflicts explored in the novels in terms of the collusion between that socio-economic formation and another one ushered in by the colonial encounter.

The contention being entered here is that both works constitute realistic depictions of social experience in the context of a pre-literate communal socio-economic formation at its point of impact with a nascent Western imperialist capitalist formation. It is precisely this unequal collision that provides the basis for conflict in the novels and also furnishes the ground rules for the resolution of the experiential conflicts through form.

In this respect, *Things Fall Apart* serves to furnish, albeit fictionally, the essential aspects of pre-literate communalism. Its fictional world is one in which the basic unit of social organization is the village which also serves as the locus for communal life and values. The village economy is essentially agrarian, depending for its subsistence on land as the principal means of production. Manual labour applied through basic iron tools – such as hoes or machetes – defines the dominant mode of production while production relations are essentially communalistic, characterized by co-operation and mutual assistance. Accordingly, because of the low level of mastery of nature and its laws, man is very much subject to the whims and caprices of elemental forces. If the rains do not come early or come in torrents, man's very survival is threatened as the possibility of a rich harvest is inextricably tied to the continued existence of the community.

It is this general background that animates and informs the realism in *Things Fall Apart*. Consequently, the Umuofia society is one in which a very high premium is placed on work – manual work. A man's social estimation is very much determined by the strength of his arm as manifested in his ability to cultivate the land and defeat his opponents in fights and wrestling matches. This accounts for society's adverse estimation of Unoka, Okonkwo's father. In a society where there is no conscious separation between artistic and manual labour, the individual who insists on being identified purely as an artist is doomed to public scorn, open condemnation and alienation. This, precisely, is the tragedy of Unoka's plight, for in the context of 20th Century Western society, Unoka would be a superstar! In Umuofia society, however, the indicators of social success are a full barn and a brimming household and the ability to prove one's mettle through physical prowess. These are qualities which Unoka lacks and which consign his efforts to the domain of "unproductive" labour.

On the contrary, Okonkwo's meteoric rise to fame and prosperity is almost exclusively predicated on his strength and will. And society measures his reputation in purely material productive terms: "He was a wealthy farmer and had two barns full of yams". Because there is as yet no conscious division of labour, Okonkwo is simultaneously a farmer, wrestler, warrior and leading political figure.

> Okonkwo was clearly cut out for great things. He was still young but he had won fame as the greatest wrestler in the nine villages . . . To crown it all he had taken two titles and had shown incredible prowess in two inter-tribal wars.[9]

Achebe's depiction of pre-colonial Igbo society as an essentially patriarchal one is largely realistic to the extent that it is based on a recognition of physical strength as a decisive factor in social life. Men and women are engaged in productive labour but the more exerting functions are reserved for the menfolk. Achebe is nevertheless critical of the excesses of this male-dominated society.

From this economic base arise certain beliefs, customs and practices which accord legitimacy and coherence to social experience. The *ozo* title, for instance, into which men of outstanding achievement are admitted, becomes a political-cum-juridical instrument not only for rewarding achievement but also for preserving social morality among its most privileged members. In addition, the religious beliefs and practices of the people arise from a purely instrumental conception of deity rather than from a blind self-surrender to the whims of immutable and inscrutable supernatural agencies. In the world of Umuofia, belief in the supernatural is a product of man's incomplete control over nature and his limited understanding of its mechanisms. This terrain is the breeding ground of fear and superstition and therefore of animistic worship.

> Darkness held a vague terror for these people, even the bravest among them. Children were warned not to whistle at night for fear of evil spirits. Dangerous animals became even more sinister and uncanny in the dark. A snake was never called by its name at night, because it would hear. It was called string.[10]

Nevertheless, man's conception of deity is essentially humanistic. Gods have a human face and their actions are predicated on human needs and necessities. For instance, when Okonkwo's lazy father, Unoka, resorts to augury to find an explanation for his poor harvests, the retort of the oracle is a direct reflection of society's work ethic with its premium on hard work: "when a man is at peace with his gods and his ancestors, his harvest will be good or bad according to the strength of his arm. Go home and work like a man." In this instrumental and symbiotic relationship between man and the gods, the gods that are accorded primacy are those that have a direct relevance to the land which is the principal means of production, hence the importance of the earth goddess:

> Ani played a greater part in the life of the people than any other deity. She was the ultimate judge of morality and conduct . . . The feast of the New Yam was held every year before the harvest began, to honour the earth goddess and the ancestral spirits of the clan.

It is perhaps in *Arrow of God* that Achebe gives the greatest stridency to the cultural dimension of pre-literate communal Igbo (African) society. This is not, however, to undermine Achebe's intense gaze on the material basis of cultural and spiritual life in his referent society. On the contrary, the various ideological and institutional mechanisms of that society are placed in sharp focus in order to place the colonial haemorrhage in bolder relief. Thus, the humanistic bias of this society is the first condition for its proper understanding. While in the Judaeo–Christian world view, deity precedes human existence: in the world of Umuaro, man creates god to serve his social and economic needs. Here, it needs to be pointed out that the supreme deity, Ulu, is a "synthetic" deity, fashioned by the peoples of the six villages that make up Umuaro to meet their need for collective security against the ravages of slave raiders.

> In the very distant past, . . . the hired soldiers of Abam used to strike in the dead of night, set fire to the houses and carry men, women and children into slavery. Things were so bad for the six villages that their leaders came together to save themselves. They hired a strong team of medicine-men to install a common deity for them. This deity which the fathers of the six villages made was called Ulu . . . from that day they were never again beaten by an enemy.[11]

In effect, the gods did not *exist* as objective entities but were essentially mental projections of human possibilities. In the world of these novels also, the physical approximations and mental pictures of the various gods are humanistic. For instance, when Ezeulu's son, Obika, returns home late at night to report that he had seen an apparition, Ezeulu quickly interprets the apparition as the god of wealth. It is instructive that the mental picture of Eru, the god of wealth, held by the community is an approximation of the physical attributes and material paraphernalia of wealth in the society. The god is said to be "dressed like a wealthy man", with "an eagle's feather in his red cap" and "carried a big [elephant] tusk across his shoulder". The point remains that Obika had merely been frightened by a flash of lightning in the dark at a particular place which the collective unconscious has grown to associate with the presence of Eru. It is the consciousness of Ezeulu as an older member of the society and, therefore, a custodian of the mythic and spiritual heritage of the society that fleshes out the young man's fear of darkness into a mental picture. The important point here, however, is that this mental picture of the god of wealth is rendered in human terms. In this socio-economic setting therefore, man creates god in his own image ("one day the men of Okperi made a powerful deity and placed their market in its care" p. 19).

Accordingly, the communal mode of production necessitates a broad republican political arrangement. In both Umuofia and Umuaro, political authority is vested in the council of elders and indeed the collectivity of the community. This point is much more pungently registered in the social setting of *Things Fall Apart* in which political and judicial decisions ranging from the declaration of war to inter-family adjudication are taken collectively. In *Arrow of God*, on the other hand, the historical necessity created by the slave raids necessitates a certain separation of secular authority from the purely religious functions. Ezeulu's significance is intricately tied to the psycho-social necessity that created his patron deity, Ulu. When he tries to mistake his otherwise purely religious functions for political ones, he runs into trouble with his community which quickly reasserts the supremacy of its communal will over Ezeulu's nascent individualism.

If, therefore, cultural nationalism defines the sensibility within which these novels are created, the culture which is being reaffirmed must be seen as the totality of the foregoing economic base and its legitimizing beliefs, practices and structures. Against this background, the historic clashes between both Umuofia and Umuaro on one hand and the forces of colonialism on the other must be seen as confrontations between two antithetical production formations. The Europeans were forcing capitalist structures down the throats of members of a pre-literate communal society. Both the production relations and the superstructural set-up necessitated by the two formations are grossly antithetical.

Consequently, a primary source of conflict between the respective indigenous societies and their British invaders is the question of land. This comes out in the land dispute between Okperi and Umuaro. When the white man intervenes on the side of Okperi against Umuaro, the latter society witnesses a major crisis, for land as the only means of production is organically entwined with the very life of the people. Similarly, when the Christian missionaries approached the elders of Umuofia for land to erect their church on, they are offered the evil forest which is not normally cultivated by the community. To meddle with the land and its people is to assault their very social and cultural institutions. It is in these terms that the colonialists' introduction of Christianity, courts etc. can be understood.

Against this background, it is an underestimation to insist that Achebe is mainly concerned with culture clash in these novels. He is in fact very keenly aware of and consistently exposes the economic exploitation which the colonialist assault entailed. In *Things Fall Apart*, the narrative voice insists:

> The white man had indeed brought a lunatic religion, but he had also built a trading store and for the first time palm-oil and kernel became things of great price, and much money flowed into Umuofia.[12]

The point, however, is that Achebe's depiction of the economic aspect of the colonial experience is embedded in critical suggestions while the experiences of his characters constantly reaffirm the centrality of economic factors in the life of his referent society.

To grasp the essence of the internal materialism of these works is to evoke questions about the literary/artistic strategies by means of which they are realized.

In this respect, the centralization of Aristotelian-type monumentalized heroes in these novels is an attempt to employ the strategy of typification to concretize the historical issues at stake. At first sight, both Okonkwo and Ezeulu would appear de-contextualized as individuals in a society where the community wields the decisive will. On the contrary, if we view them as instances of typification as an artistic strategy, they are essentially specific characters through whose experiences the crucial issues of the epoch are fictionally distilled and examined. The theoretical anchor for this contention is brilliantly articulated by the Soviet aesthetic theoretician, A. Bazhenova in the following terms:

> The typical character is a concentration of the unique thoughts, feelings and actions of an individual who becomes, due to the artist's creative power and his penetration of that character, one of the equivalents of a society, an age, a people, a nation, a class, a profession.[13]

Okonkwo, therefore, must be understood as an embodiment of the spirit of his age and the dramatization of the response of that *spirit* to forces hostile to the stability of his society and its culture. His decisive and heroic response to the colonialists must also be seen as a revolutionary anti-colonialist stance. When he stands up in open arrogant defiance of the colonialists, he is not defending culture as a superstructural proposition but the totality of the socio-economic formation and therefore cultural identity of his people. In this respect, his revolutionary stature must be seen in terms of Cabral's contention that in the colonial situation, the cultural values that would energize the national liberation struggle are lodged in the countryside and among the peasantry.[14] Okonkwo embodies the *spirit* of those values. Jean-Paul Sartre, in his preface to Fanon's *The Wretched of the Earth*, captures the legitimacy of the Okonkwo reflex when he writes:

> When the peasant takes a gun in his hands, the old myths grow dim and the prohibitions are one by one forgotten. The rebel's weapon is the proof of his humanity. For in the first days of the revolt you must kill: to shoot down a European is to kill two birds with one stone, to destroy an oppressor and the man he oppresses at the same time: there remain a dead man, and a free man.[15]

Ezeulu presents a somewhat more complex subtilization of the tragic implications of the colonialist assault. To the extent that his social significance (as a priest) is rooted in the superstructural realm of the social totality, he is more of an embodiment of the cultural values of his society than Okonkwo. As the personification of the spiritual values of Umuaro, Ezeulu is eminently placed to reflect the crisis of consciousness inaugurated in the society by the colonial intervention. Consequently, his psyche becomes the battleground for the reconciliation of the two conflicting value systems and their supporting institutions. He saves himself Okonkwo's kind of terminal tragedy by adopting a somewhat more "liberal" and dynamic attitude to the prevailing historical exigency without, however, severing his links with his patron deity and its sustaining society. Although he sends his son, Oduche, to the white man's school, he will not accept to be the white man's warrant chief. Even in adopting what could be regarded as a moderate position, Ezeulu prepares himself for a tragic role. Thus, while his society sees him as an ambitious, even treacherous man, the white man, Winterbottom, sees him as a stubborn tribal chieftain. It is the indignation attendant on being caught in between these antithetical expectations that defines the tragic essence of *Arrow of God* in general.

A proper appreciation of the tragic affiliations of this novel (and even *Things Fall Apart*) must be predicated on a clear epistemological distinction. Unlike the traditional Aristotelian concept, tragedy in *Arrow of God* is a function of human action (or inaction) at the material level which is complicated or made problematic by a given historical situation. In effect, Achebe's sense of the tragic in these novels compels a materialist epistemology which underlines the very instrumentality of the relationship between man and his gods in pre-colonial Africa.

In a society where the decisive political will is communal, it can be argued that Ezeulu's principal flaw consists in a certain egocentricity which places individual self-assertion above the will of the collectivity and even the imperatives of public office. But in the context of the historical conjunctures of the moment, what constitutes his undoing is that he responds to the pressures of colonialism (which are collective in nature) in a rather individualistic manner. His tragedy, then, is essentially one of a basic dislocation between individual action and the demands of a historical imperative requiring collective assertion.

At the level of structure, Achebe's mastery of novelistic art finds expression in a certain sense of balance which presents the experiences in their dialectical essence. Just as the structure and institutional practices of pre-colonial society are presented in their contradictory essence so also are the motivations and values of colonialism exposed. This feature is perhaps more pronounced in *Arrow of God*, a novel in which the colonial presence has become entrenched. Captain Winterbottom furnishes a typification of the stock prejudices at the core of colonialist ideology. His personal responses to his African (Nigerian) environment are permeated by prejudices which are reminiscent of Joseph Conrad's *Heart of Darkness*. He is perennially haunted by his obsession with the primitivity of the native and his customs: "He would wonder what unspeakable rites went on in the forest at night, or was it the heart-beat of the African darkness?" (p. 29). In his racist psyche, the Nigerian land is one vast expanse of unrelieved primitivity perennially haunted by uncanny and malevolent presences: "This dear old land of waking nightmares!" Accordingly, he frowns at European officials interacting with "natives" and sees his African workers and subjects as lower animals. Of his servant, Boniface, he says: "He's a fine specimen, isn't he? He's been with me four years. He was a little boy of about thirteen – by my own calculation, they've no idea of years – when I took him on. He was absolutely raw." (p. 35).

Without, however, diminishing the place of racial bigotry in colonialist ideology, Achebe relieves Winterbottom's excesses through another white character, Tony Clark, who adopts a more liberal attitude to the natives. Mr Clark interacts freely with Africans and accords some measure of respect to their institutions. But his individual "progressive" stance does not diminish the assumptions and prejudices that underlie the British policy of Indirect Rule.

One aspect of these novels that has attracted excited comments is the use of language. Achebe's creative use of the grammatical features and rhythm of Igbo speech and elements of Igbo oral lore has been variously interpreted and richly described. What remains unfinished, however, is to proffer a sociological explanation of the place of language in Achebe's referent society. Like in all pre-literate communal societies, language in the societies of *Things Fall Apart* and *Arrow of God* is not just a means of communication. It is, on the contrary, the expression of what Lukacs calls the immanence of meaning in being. These are societies in which language serves as a veritable accompaniment to the process of production of material life. Art (poetry, folktales etc.), philosophy, science and politics are all embedded in the matrix of social language because there is as yet no overt fragmentation of experience into different specializations each requiring its own mode of discourse. This, according to Lukacs, "is a homogeneous world, and even the separation between man and world, between 'I' and 'you', cannot disturb its homogeneity".[16] Language in this social totality becomes a purveyor of the "metaphysical" nature of experience. Thus between the world of the folk-tale and that of real life, there is a certain contiguity. Thus when in *Things Fall Apart*, Achebe weaves folktales into the plot structure, he is merely reiterating this basic contiguity.

From the foregoing then, the importance of Achebe's portrayal of pre-colonial society in these novels lies in his ability to deploy the realistic essence of novelistic fiction to recover and expose the dynamism of preliterate African communalism at an important historical moment.

Proletarian Consciousness and the Anti-Colonial Struggle: Ousmane's *God's Bits of Wood*

At a theoretical level, Ousmane's acclaimed masterpiece derives its undisputed candidature for classical status from the fact that it represents a fictional elaboration of the materialist thesis that existence precedes essence. This proposition is here domesticated in the context of French colonialism in Africa with a view to placing the accent correctly on the production relations in the colonial venture. In effect, although *God's Bits of Wood* shares a common generic affinity with works like Achebe's *Arrow of God* as an anti-colonial novel, its distinction lies in its adoption of a radical, ultra-realistic and even socialistic view of the colonial question. For Ousmane, colonialism was first and foremost an economic undertaking in an exploitative capitalist sense and its cultural and ideological impacts must be assessed against this principle.

This radical ideological stance, it can be argued, derives from certain facts in Ousmane's biography. Of all the significant African writers, he has the distinction of not having had the benefit of Western higher education. More importantly, he has the singular advantage of having experienced life variously as a fisherman, plumber, bricklayer, apprentice mechanic, dockworker and trade unionist. As he rightly maintains, he received his education in "the University of Life".[17] These exposures compel the kind of proletarian consciousness and sense of solidarity with the masses which permeates and pervades the experimental fabric of *God's Bits of Wood* and the rest of Ousmane's work. It is also this ideological stance that has made it inevitable that he should be aligned with writers like Ngugi and La Guma for instance.

Specifically, *God's Bits of Wood* is a fictionalization of a historical experience, namely, the railway workers' strike of 1947–8 along the Dakar–Niger line which is here reconstructed and imbued with greater ideological clarity.

At the crux of the thematic contention of the novel is the recognition that colonialism as an aspect of imperialism (the highest stage of capitalism) was primarily a system of economic exploitation of African workers by their European masters. In order to concretize this concern, the railway line is depicted as a symbol of industrial capital and the antagonistic relationship between it and labour. The railway workers and their families have become almost totally dependent on the railway line for their livelihood. "Every inhabitant of Thies, no matter who he was, depended on the railroad, and on the traffic between Konlikoro and Dakar."[18] Yet in spite of lifetimes spent working in the railway establishment, the workers are alienated from the fruits of their labour and live a thoroughly marginalized life. Thus, in the strike action which dominates the novel, the question of wages and working conditions becomes the central issue among the workers as an organized and conscious group. We learn this much from the sagacious Mamadou Keita at the beginning of the strike.

> It is true that we have our trade, but it does not bring us what it should. We are being robbed. Our wages are so low that there is no longer any difference between ourselves and animals. (p. 8)

This basic theme constitutes the launching pad for the exploration of other related issues and a subtle way of reiterating the dialectical relationship between economic realities and other realms of experience. Typically, colonialist exploitation relies on violence to maintain its stranglehold on the exploited workers. Consequently, when the striking workers and their dependants and supporters gather in the various locations, they are routed and beaten down with characteristic colonial ferocity by the police. Ousmane is careful to render these scenes of brutality with humanistic pathos without, however, presenting the struggling workers in a helpless light. While the menfolk put up a heroic fight against the guns and truncheons of the militiamen and the police, the heavy boots of the oppressors crash down on the skulls of helpless infants and disabled women. We learn with obvious sympathy of the death of Maimouna's helpless baby, the breaking of Houdia M'baye's neck and the massacre of defenceless women – Penda, Samba N'Doulogou and Old Niakoro – in Dakar.

Despite the heavy accent on economic exploitation and physical violence in the novel, Ousmane shows a rather keen perception of the effects of the colonial experience on the cultural values and institutional structures of his referent society. But he predicates this perception on an ideological perspective that firmly recognizes cultural and institutional practices as contingent on economic realities. Therefore, the real experiences of the striking workers and their families become points of departure for highlighting the haemorrhage of colonialism on indigenous Senegalese culture. At the onset of the strike, little Ad'jibidji displays an increasing alienation from her cultural roots attendant on colonial education – to the utter discomfiture of her grandmother, Old Niakoro. The old woman laments the progressive corrosion of indigenous culture in very apt terms:

> What use is the white man's language to a woman? To be a good mother you have no need of that. Among my people, who are your father's people, too, no one speaks the white man's language, and no one has died of it! Ever since I was born . . . I have never heard of a white man who had learned to speak Bambara, or any other language of this country. But you rootless people think only of learning his, while our language dies. (p. 4)

Beyond this overt affirmation of cultural identity, however, the specific experiences of the strike compel certain changes and re-evaluations of accepted practices and beliefs. The railway as an economic institution implies a change in mode of production from peasant agriculture to dependence on a machine, a shift whose realities are driven home by the strike.

> When the smoke from the trains no longer drifted above the savannah, they realised that an age had ended – an age their elders had told them about, when all of Africa was just a garden for food. Now the machine ruled over their lands, and when they forced every machine within a thousand miles to halt they became conscious of their strength, but conscious also of their dependence. (p. 32)

This realization graduates into a certain consciousness which is quickened by the hardship and deprivations attendant on the strike. As the salaries and wages of the menfolk are stopped, the very livelihood of their dependants is threatened while the very institutions on which their society depends are threatened either to extinction or are forced to make fundamental adjustments. The women who hitherto had remained dependent on the men are forced by hunger and hardship to go out in quest of material sustenance for their children, thus changing themselves from a passive dependent group to an active one. "And the men began to understand that if the times were bringing forth a new breed of men, they were also bringing forth a new breed of women". (p. 34) More importantly, the men who had previously been content with acquiring many wives and bringing forth innumerable children are also compelled by economic adversity to reconsider polygamy. Nor are the whites spared the changes which the strike brings about. The uneasy cordiality between them and their African workers disappears and is replaced by fear, insecurity and suspicion. "The white women went to the market only if there was a policeman at their side; and there had even been cases when the black women refused to sell to them". (p. 33)

Ousmane strives to steer the narrative away from any suggestion that the crucial point in colonialism was racism. There are among the whites people who see their mission in racial terms just as there are others who see the negroes just as another set of humans who are sufficiently dignified to demand decent working conditions and adequate wages. Dejean is the French equivalent of Achebe's Winterbottom, an unrepentant racist to whom the African is a congenital infant ("I know them . . . they are children"). On the other hand, there are colonial officers like Isnard whose humane attitude to Africans stands in direct opposition to the racism of Dejean.

> One night someone had knocked at his door, and when he opened it he found a Negro woman on the point of giving birth on his threshold. There was no doctor available at that time for such a case . . . and the woman had not enough time left even to return to her own home. Isnard had taken her in and helped her: he had cut the umbilical cord with his teeth and then had bathed the baby and cared for the woman. (p. 31)

This show of bourgeois humanism does not, however, affect the solidarity among the whites as representatives of colonialism nor does it begin to question the characteristic production relations of capitalism.

Similarly, among the African characters, there are heroes and backsliders, patriots and opportunistic traitors in line with Ousmane's essentially dialectical design. Just as people like Bakayoko and Ramatoulaye epitomize unflinching commitment to the cause of the strike so also do people like El Hadji Mabigue and Beaugosse represent a betrayal of the consciousness which underlies the strike action. Yet it is this contradictory nature of relationships and motives which propels the action of the novel forward towards a resolution in favour of the galvanized will of the workers.

Yet the fact of contradiction, the presence of conflicting interests, divergent motives and material limitations among the African strikers and their sympathizers is not allowed to nullify the central ideological anchor of the text. The mobilized consciousness and energy of the workers is posited as a revolutionary force in an antagonistic and oppositional tussle with the forces of imperialist capitalism. In the context of this struggle, the presence of saboteurs, backsliders and traitors as well as the reality of hardship and suffering fall into place as necessary aspects of a revolutionary situation. It is in steering the logic of the plot towards eventual victory for the workers that Ousmane reaffirms his confidence in the efficacy of struggle and mobilization in re-establishing the value of labour in the production process.

In terms of aesthetic realization, the formal profundity of *God's Bits of Wood* can be explored, and perhaps better understood, in the context of the possibilities made available by socialist realism. Outside its orthodox definition in the statutes of the Soviet Union of Writers of 1934, socialist realism can now be understood in broader terms to mean a mode of depicting reality informed by an ideological position that not only desires socialism but also perceives the experiences depicted according to a logic that has socialism as its goal. Consequently, the term has since escaped from its original Soviet home to acquire relevance in discussing works of writers and artists as diverse as Pablo Neruda, Ngugi Wa Thiong'o, Bertold Brecht and Louis Aragon. Perhaps one crucial distinction that needs to be made is that between socialist realism inspired by experiences in "actually existing" socialist societies on the one hand and situations, as in Africa, where socialist realist artistic expressions constitute part and parcel of the struggle for the institution of socialist relations of production and political structures on the other.

Broadly speaking, the essential attributes of socialist realist expression include (a) the use of simple accessible language, (b) a sympathetic portrayal of characters from among the oppressed, and (c) a sense of patriotism defined in terms of concern with the struggle for socialism. To a great extent, these attributes are richly represented in the formal configuration of *God's Bits of Wood*. It needs reiterating here however that it is not only the formal outlook of the book that compels this interpretive model but also the expressed ideological alignment of Ousmane himself.

The ultra-realistic landscape of *God's Bits of Wood* can now be taken for granted. But Ousmane's depiction of character deserves greater elaboration. The fictional world of the novel swarms with people – "God's bits of wood" – who in their sheer diversity of material conditions, physiological states, views and alignments represent a *total* picture of the antagonistic and contradictory forces at play not only in the novel but in the larger colonial confrontation. What needs to be pointed out however is that

Ousmane explores his essential preoccupation largely through an *inside* presentation of characters from among the oppressed and dispossessed. There is a certain self-immersion into the inner worlds of the characters, especially the womenfolk, which suggests a depth of psychological insight far superior to what casual observation can yield. A classic instance is Maimouna, the blind woman. She is heroic, dignified, creative and resourceful. She has an ability to transcend the limits of her physiological disability to provide useful inspiration and counsel to the strikers. Nor is her heroic spirit daunted by the white man's dastardly murder of her baby. It is a credit to Ousmane's socialist humanism that a character like Maimouna is not depicted as an object of pity.

> Maimouna was blind, but this is not to say that she was pitiable . . . She held her splendid, smooth-skinned body like some goddess of the night, her head high, her vacant glance seeming to contemplate an area above people, beyond the world. (p. 16)

Similarly, Houdia M'Baye, the mother of a child aptly named "strike" is portrayed to evoke the horror and extreme marginalization in which the dependants of the railwaymen have to exist. A mother of nine, whose husband, Badiane, had fallen in the strike, Houdia M'Baye evokes pity to the extent that her wretchedness and that of her scrawny offspring constitute an indictment of colonial vandalism.

Not all the women evoke such pity. There are others like Penda and Ramatoulaye whose tenacious commitment to the cause of the strike transcends fraternal bonds and calls to question society's erstwhile relegation of the womenfolk. If viewed against the background of the traditional attitude to women in most African societies, Ousmane's female characters in this novel are deliberately placed in the forefront of heroic action as an ideological statement.

The all-inclusive collectivistic nature of characterization in *God's Bits of Wood* raises the question of the relationship between the individual and the collective wills in the historical process. As much as possible, Ousmane avoids the lure of individuation of the heroic function but instead democratizes the heroic responsibility among his numerous characters. Informed of course by the materialist contention that history is an index of the existential struggles of active people in active relationships, Ousmane's strategy of characterization removes heroism from the realm of the fictional to the social. Here, Bakayoko's candidature for heroic status becomes pertinent. As the leader of the strike, he provides that informed leadership without which class struggles degenerate into anarchy. In every sense, Bakayoko is a negation of the Aristotelian model of the hero – tragic or otherwise. He is neither rich nor notable. But he possesses such qualities as the intelligence, tact and drive which revolutionary leadership demands. Yet he also embodies certain contradictory and even repulsive qualities which discourage direct empathy with him. He is almost callous, indifferent to emotional blackmail from both family and friends. Yet as an approximation of revolutionary leadership, the contradictory character of Bakayoko as an individual is submerged by the redeeming value of his leadership for the rest of his society. But it needs to be underlined that Bakayoko is by no means the hero of *God's Bits of Wood* nor does individualized heroism constitute a significant part of the artistic and ideological agenda of the novel. If anything, it is the galvanized will of the collective that wields the decisive heroic function.

But by far the more striking aspect of Ousmane's craftsmanship in this novel is his ability to capture, through apt description, the faint details of environment and human circumstances. In scene after scene, event after event, Ousmane closes up on those details which most powerfully reinforce his thematic concern. Here, for instance, is a description of Thies, one of the settlements inhabited by the railway workers and their dependants:

> Hovels. A few rickety shacks, some upturned tombs, walls of bamboo or millet stalks, iron barbs, and rotting fences. Thies: a vast, uncertain plain where all the rot of the city has gathered – stakes and crossties, locomotive wheels, rusty shafts, knocked-in jerricans, old mattress springs, bruised and lacerated sheets of steel. And then, a little farther on, on the goat path that leads to the Bambara quarter, piles of old tin cans, heaps of excrement, little mountains of broken pottery and cooking tools, dismantled railway cars, skeletons of motors buried in the dust, and the tiny remains of cats, of rats, of chickens, disputed by the birds . . . Constantly hungry, naked children, with sunken chests, swollen bellies, argued with the vultures. Thies: a place where everyone – man, woman and child – had a face the colour of the earth.

The evocative power and point-blank proximity of such descriptions falls into place when one realizes that Ousmane has equally distinguished himself as a film-maker of international repute. His technique of presentation in *God's Bits of Wood* can therefore be described as cinematic not only in terms of its overall montage effect but mostly in terms of its particularistic incisiveness. This technique acquires even greater stridency when Ousmane is probing the deep recesses of human psychology or just describing the physical appearance of significant characters.

> Houdia M'Baye remained where she was, rocking the baby in her arms, thinking. This ceaseless hunger, which swelled the bellies of the children while it defleshed their limbs and bent their shoulders, called up pictures in her mind, pictures of an earlier, happier time. (p. 51)

Structurally, dialectics governs the design of *God's Bits of Wood*. Actions elicit reactions, people contradict one another and either succumb to or transcend their own internal contradictions in a dialectical movement whose inner logic is however guided by an authorial ideology which has the struggle for and optimism about socialism as its underlying ethic. Although the novel consists of different episodes located in different locations, the railway line connects these places and the actions which take place in them and relocate them within a fictional logic in which the struggle between African labour and colonial capitalist exploitation becomes the overriding problematic. Individual and group actions and idiosyncracies in their contradictory essence become meaningful only in the context of this overriding conflict. Men and women redefine themselves and their values accordingly. While the strikers press for family allowances, equal pay for equal work, and old age pensions, there are still some among their rank and file who secretly wish to return to work. There are also others in the society like Mabigue and Beaugosse who sabotage the will of the people; there are yet others like N'Deye Toiti whose obsession with the cultural values of the colonizers constitutes a compromising obstacle. Just as there are people like Bakayoko whose commitment to the struggle is impeccable, there are also religious leaders for whom tutelage is divine. Hear Mabigue, for instance:

> I know that life is often hard, but that should not cause us to turn our backs on God. He had assigned a rank, a place, and a certain role to every man, and it is blasphemous to think of changing His design. The *toubabs* are here because that is the will of God. Strength is a gift of God, and Allah has given it to them. We cannot fight against it. (p. 44)

Yet in spite of setbacks and contradictions, Ousmane artfully propels the logic of the plot in the direction of victory for the workers. And when victory comes in the end, it is subtly reaffirmed that the workers had waged their struggle in pursuit of their rights, not as an act of anarchist indulgence or racial hatred: "happy is the man who does battle without hatred".

Class Struggle and the Socialist Vision: Ngugi's *Petals of Blood*

Up to date, *Petals of Blood* constitutes simultaneously Ngugi's most ambitious novel as well as a classic of epic proportions in the emergent tradition of anti-imperialist literature in Africa. In terms of Ngugi's specific career, this novel embraces the major themes and artistic strands of his earlier work. Thus, the confrontation between indigenous Kikuyu society and colonial culture in *The River Between*, the economic, physical and psychological violence of the Mau Mau emergency period in *Weep Not, Child*, the pervasive betrayal of the hopes and aspirations that fuelled the independence struggle in *A Grain of Wheat* as well as the limited variations on these themes that recur in his volume of short stories, *Secret Lives*, are all synthesized and placed in the context of the gigantic theme of imperialism and the struggle to negate and transcend it in pursuit of the socialist alternative in contemporary Kenya and Africa. It is precisely in the ability to unify these diverse themes into a coherent artistic statement that the decisive significance of *Petals of Blood* resides.

Beyond this power of synthesis, however, the novel derives additional force in terms of Ngugi's ability to articulate his themes within a consciousness informed by a greater ideological clarity than he had displayed in his previous work. In *Petals of Blood*, Ngugi's consciousness is decidedly anti-imperialist while his ideological alignment is unambiguously socialist in a Marxian sense.

> In so many ways the Kenya peasantry is the real actor in the novel. The turning of peasants into proletarians by alienating them from the land, is one of the most crucial social upheavals of the twentieth century.[19]

It is principally against this political and ideological background that the experiences, themes and novelistic techniques explored and adopted in the novel can most meaningfully be understood.

In general, *Petals of Blood* is a complex exploration of human experiences, motivations and dilemmas in a historical context. While the concrete socio-historical canvas is furnished by Kenyan history and society from pre-colonial through the colonial and contemporary neo-colonial periods, it is the interconnections among the lives of the four major protagonists – Munira, Wanja, Abdulla and Karega – that humanizes this canvas. These characters are, as it were, centres of consciousness for relating the experiences of individual Kenyans (and Africans) to the reality of life in the colonial and neo-colonial situations. The experiences of these characters, as we shall see subsequently, are classic illustrations of the dialectical relationship between men, as members of specific social classes, and their environment. This proposition finds greater illumination if we examine the broad range of themes through which Ngugi explores it.

The transformation of Ilmorog from a peaceful pastoral settlement into a major seat of capitalist investment provides a dynamic locus for the action of the novel. Old Ilmorog had been a pastoral haven, replete with myths and legends of ancient heroism. Because of its essentially peasant agrarian economy, production relationships had been mainly communal and, as with all such societies, the relationship between humankind and nature had been governed by animism. Just as drought brings misery and uncertainty, the arrival of rain brings exhilaration and joy.

> At the beginning of April it started raining. The eyes of the elders beamed with expectation of new life over Ilmorog: their wrinkled faces seemed to stretch and tighten with sinews of energy.[20]

In this environment, the only signs of modernity are the village school presided over by Munira, and Abdulla's drinking house. It is precisely these two institutions that bring the protagonists together; Karega as Munira's co-teacher and Wanja as Abdulla's barmaid. It is therefore in this environment that their past lives, present experiences and future expectations meet and mix. To a large extent, their lives become also matrixed with the plight of Ilmorog but not in a deterministic manner.

Consequently, when a devastating drought afflicts Ilmorog, they are at the forefront of a campaign to draw the attention of the political leadership to their plight. Their epic march to the capital attracts national and international attention to Ilmorog thus bringing about a radical physical transformation of Ilmorog into a centre of capitalist investment. It is part of Ngugi's overall dialectical design however that the Ilmorogians' campaign for a better life brings hunger, pauperization and violence disguised as capitalist development. Thus, in the New Ilmorog, Abdullah is extremely marginalized, inhabiting the slum area symbolically called New Jerusalem; Karega takes to trade unionism to galvanize the consciousness of the working class to the ills of the system represented by the directors of the Ilmorog Theng'eta Brewery; Wanja takes to big time prostitution while Munira's psychological balance is so shattered that he takes to esoteric religious fanaticism. Thus, in its "accidental" transformation, Ilmorog brings with it new production relations, new tensions in private lives and reveals the essential contradictions in the very political economy, namely capitalism, that brought about the transformation in the first place.

This outline, though broad, nevertheless encapsulates a number of themes through which Ngugi explores the nature and extent of imperialist control and exploitation of the neo-colonial state in Kenya in particular and Africa in general. As he indicated at the launching of the novel, the nature and limitations of imperialism constitute the core of the novel's preoccupation:

> Imperialism . . . can never develop a country or a people.
> This was what I was trying to show in *Petals of Blood*: that imperialism can never develop us, Kenyans. In doing so, I was only trying to be faithful to what Kenyan workers and peasants have always realised as shown by their historical struggles since 1895.[21]

Hence the broad range of themes explored in the novel amount to an x-ray of different realms of contemporary African experience as they are governed by the forces of imperialism.

The capitalist invasion carries with it all the familiar contradictions: there is the dispossession of the peasantry of their land as epitomized in the expropriation of the old woman Nyakinyua's land: "We shall sell by public auction . . . all that piece of land situated in New Ilmorog . . . property of Mrs. Nyakinyua" (p. 275); there is the emergence of a class of parasitic bourgeoisie represented here by Chui, Kimeria and Mzigo – the Directors of the Ilmorog brewery; there is also the pauperization of the erstwhile peasantry and their replacement with a new urban elite of property owners. Thus, as Abdulla is condemned to a peripheral existence of trading in merchandise of inconsequential value in the slums of the New Ilmorog, people like Mzigo rise to positions of unearned pre-eminence and wealth.

A conspicuous aspect of Ngugi's preoccupation with contemporary African socio-political reality is the searchlight which he throws on the close relationship between political functionaries in neo-colonial Africa and imperialist economic interest. Nderi Wa Riera, the MP for Ilmorog, is a personification of this phenomenon. For him, the people's mandate is a licence to amass wealth and barter his nation's interests for profit in joint business ventures with imperialists. For him, even the hunger and misery unleashed on his people by a devastating drought is converted into a commodity; an opportunity to attract capitalist investment. Characteristically, his brand of politics thrives on empty rhetoric, vacuous promises and deceit coated in the idiocy of liberal equivocation. He resurrects primordial ethnic sentiments through rituals (tea parties, oath-taking ceremonies etc.) only to keep the people perpetually divided. But Ngugi is quick to reveal that the people see through his antics. Thus, in a memorable and very dramatic scene, the peasants of Ilmorog stone Nderi wa Riera: "suddenly, a stone flew and hit Nderi on the nose. This was followed by a hailstorm of orange-peels, stones, sticks . . . He suddenly took to his heels, wondering what had gone wrong." (p. 183)

In this setting also, the law, the church, the educational system are exposed as conduits and mechanisms for the propagation and protection of the interests of the ruling class. Inspector Godfrey who is charged with investigating the murder of the directors of the Ilmorog brewery realizes that he is paid to protect capitalist investment: "His duty as a policeman was to help maintain stability, law and order, upon which depended the successful growth of all the industries and foreign investments." (p. 335). Similarly, an institution like Siriana High School is established as a breeding-ground for the production and reproduction of the likes of Chui, Kimeria and Mzigo and the ideas that prop them up in positions of economic and political power. Priests like Reverend Jerrod provide a spiritual justification for the crimes of capitalism.

Perhaps the most crucial aspect of the thematic insistence of *Petals of Blood* is its solid predication on a certain anti-imperialist historical consciousness. A fervent, even passionately nostalgic, concern with the history of Kenyan nationalism, whose highest point was the Mau Mau war, has become an axiomatic component of Ngugi's artistic and ideological sensibilities. In *Petals of Blood*, this obsession is so intricately matrixed in the content and form that to understand the book is to become sympathetically engrossed in the vicissitudes of Kenya's national history. In the lives of the principal characters, especially Abdulla, there are indelible imprints of that history and their fates and fortunes, hopes and aspirations are conditioned by its imperatives. Abdulla's amputated limb is a physical testimony to the sacrifices which the peasants had to make in the struggle for independence. It is precisely this experience that equips him to play the role of ideological guardian to the rest of the Ilmorogians, especially during their epic march to the capital. Through Abdulla's copious reminiscences, the legacy of national heroes like Dedan Kimathi, Ole Masai and MeKitelili are resurrected as part of a whole process of historical reconstruction whose object is to challenge the more scandalous dislocations of Kenyan history by colonialist historiography:

> There are many questions about our history which remain unanswered. Our present day historians, following on similar theories yarned out by defenders of imperialism, insist we only arrived here yesterday. (p. 198)

It is Abdulla's reminiscences that fill this vacuum by not only furnishing the travellers with stories of his exploits in the Mau Mau war but also inspiring them with tales of the exemplary heroism of men like Ole Masai and Dedan Kimathi. "Actually, some of us had not seen Dedan although we acted in his name." (p. 140) The central point that emerges from the various historical reflections in the novel is to draw a distinction between patriots and traitors. While the true heroes and patriots like Abdulla are cast aside in the neo-colonial period, those who had collaborated with the imperialists emerge as government officials and big time business barons in active collaboration with imperialist interests. This tradition of authorized treachery and betrayal is one into which the neo-colonial KANU government from Kenyatta to Moi fits perfectly. This much has been orchestrated in the political and artistic writings of Ngugi and other Kenyan patriots. There is a consensus among this group that Kenyan independence, like that of most African countries, is a sham.

> Independence means self-determination and self-government. An independent nation is one with the autonomy to make decisions which will advance the welfare of its people. It is a nation that controls its own resources and has the political and economic scope to utilize these resources, human and natural, free of foreign interference.
>
> Independence in this sense has little relevance to our current situation. We find ourselves enclosed in a dependent country, wholly subservient to foreign interests. Our economy is geared to the needs of foreigners – both of our ex-colonial masters and other western capitalist nations.[22]

The process of historical reconstruction is, however, cast in clearer ideological perspective by Karega. Karega rejects the subservient ideology of colonialist education in quest of libertarian education. Accordingly, he rejects the view of African history proffered by "eminent" black scholars in the universities. "He just wanted to know the truth. But what truth? Weren't they all, shouldn't they all be on the side of blackness against whiteness?" (p. 200) Yet his conception of history is not that of ancestor worship but a dynamic and dialectical one which would seem to summarize the accent in Ngugi's own historical consciousness.

> I mean we must not preserve our past as a museum: rather, we must study it critically, without illusions, and see what lessons we can draw from it in today's battlefield of the future and the present. But to worship it – no . . . I don't want to continue worshipping in the temples of a past without tarmac roads, without electric cookers, a world dominated by slavery to nature. (p. 323)

While evoking the complex faces of imperialism and capitalism, Ngugi's consciousness does not stop at problematizing the contemporary Kenyan (African) situation. Through highlighting the contradictory and conflictual essence of capitalism, Ngugi's ultimate thematic insistence is to underline the inevitability of a revolution of the workers and peasants and the overthrow of the dispensation of the comprador bourgeoisie.

Imperialism: capitalism: landlords: earthworms. A system that bred hordes of round-bellied jiggers and bedbugs with parasitism and cannibalism as the highest goal in society. This system and its profiteering gods and its ministering angels . . . These parasites would always demand the sacrifice of blood from the working masses. These few who had prostituted the whole land, turning it over to foreigners for thorough exploitation, would drink people's blood and say hypocritical prayers of devotion to skin oneness and to nationalism even as skeletons of bones walk to lonely graves. The system and its gods and its angels had to be fought consciously, consistently and resolutely by all the working people! . . . Tomorrow it would be the workers and the peasants leading the struggle and seizing power to overturn the system of all its preying bloodthirsty gods and gnomic angels, bringing to an end the reign of the few over the many and the era of drinking blood and feasting on human flesh. (p. 344)

Against the timid imputations of bourgeois critics, the decisive ideological thrust of *Petals of Blood* does not weaken its artistic identity. On the contrary, the strength of the novel derives precisely from the sheer aesthetic force of its informing and objectified ideology. Here the dialectic of content and form is so intimate that there is no valid statement that can be made about any aspect of the formal realization of *Petals of Blood* that is not anchored to its express ideological mooring.

Symbolization is a primary artistic vehicle by means of which meaning is presented in its ideological essence. It begins right from the very structuration of the broad experiential span that constitutes the material of the text. Drawing from his familiar biblical quarry of symbols, Ngugi gives the novel a four-part epic structure that runs as follows: Walking . . . Toward Bethlehem . . . To be Born . . . Again – La Luta Continua. In plain terms, the plot of the novel conforms to a logical pattern which reinforces its revolutionary vision. *The peasants and workers of Ilmorog walk towards the capital city and in the process are reborn in a new consciousness about the real mechanism of neo-colonialism and capitalist exploitation. And thus equipped, they are ready for the struggle to overthrow their exploiters, a struggle which is continuous and self-renewing.* Thus, the biblical story of the journey of the Magi to herald the birth of Christ is here appropriated artistically to portray a revolutionary message. Myth, symbolism, structure and ideology meet and mix in one dialectical image that gives coherence to experiences and situations of dizzying diversity.

Similarly, events, objects and phenomena acquire a symbolic value circumscribed by the overriding ideology and vision of the novel. But these symbols exist and acquire meaning only in a dialectical context. The drought that afflicts Ilmorog is a natural disaster but it serves also to attract attention to the miserable plight of the rural peasantry in neo-colonial Africa. Yet, although Ilmorog gets the attention it deserves, this in itself becomes a curse, for the massive capitalist invasion brings about class antagonism, poverty and unprecedented misery for the masses. Abdulla's donkey is an archetypal symbol of suffering and perseverance whose services lighten the yoke of the great trek of the Ilmorogians: "They kept on making comparisons between the donkey-pulled carriage and the bull-pulled wagons that the colonial settlers used to own: They too were on a mission of conquest – of the city." (p. 134) Similarly, the Trans-Africa highway which runs through Ilmorog to connect other major cities of Africa is both a major artery of capitalist cargo as well as a link among African peoples suffering identical plights in the hands of capitalism. Children "sing, in shrill voices of the road which will surely carry them to all the cities of Africa, their Africa, to link hands with children of other lands". (p. 263)

By far the most central of the system of symbols in *Petals of Blood* is that which anchors the title to the very experience of the novel. Aptly captured in the opening epigraph from Derek Walcott, the symbol of the petals of blood is grotesque and frightening in its very negation of the regenerative associations of petals and flowers. This symbol is a recurrent motif in the novel. Our attention is first drawn to it in the Ilmorog village school when Munira takes the children out into the fields for a nature study lesson. One of the boys makes a startling discovery: "I have found another. Petals of blood . . . it has no stigma or pistils . . . nothing inside." Subsequently, we learn that the plant whose flowers bear the "petals of blood" is indeed the Theng'eta plant. In old Ilmorog, the plant which had been both a stimulant, an intoxicant and a medicinal herb had been used for ritual occasions requiring great inspiration and purity of vision.

> Theng'eta is the plant that only the old will talk about . . . It is only they who will have heard of it or know about it. It grows wild, in the plains, the herdsmen know it and where it grows, but they will not tell you. Nyakinyua says that they used to brew it before Europeans came. And they would drink it only when work is finished, and especially after the ceremony of circumcision or marriage or itwika, and after a harvest. It was when they were drinking Theng'eta that poets and singers composed their words for a season of Gidiandi, and the seer voiced his prophecy. (p. 204)

After the capitalist invasion of Ilmorog, it is this otherwise mystical plant that is appropriated as the raw material for the Ilmorog Theng'eta Brewery. In other words, a plant that had served to unite and purify men and women in pre-capitalist society becomes an object of exploitation in a capitalist setting. Consequently, the red petals of the Theng'eta plant become symptomatic of the harvest of blood which capitalist exploitation will necessarily yield. Accordingly, the contemporary Kenyan society with its class conflicts and antagonisms is depicted as inevitably bound to violence. The prophetic implication of this symbol will appear to have been vindicated when Munira, intent on destroying an evil world, sets fire to Wanja's brothel, killing the directors of the Ilmorog brewery. It is, however, in the violent overthrow of the capitalist system which is sustained on the people's blood by the working classes that the symbolic value of the title of the novel ultimately resides.

Ngugi's characterization in *Petals of Blood* displays three dominant features which have become constant features of his novelistic technique: the actions and responses of the characters are socio-historically conditioned; the lives of the major characters are intricately linked and their "secret lives" as individuals within a social totality are probed through very incisive psychological portraiture. Munira is reminiscent of Mugo in *A Grain of Wheat*, an intensely insecure and cowardly man who habitually withdraws from situations involving competition and violent expression. Given his weak spirit, reality of neo-colonial exploitation and bourgeois decadence in the New Ilmorog drive him into religious fanaticism and false consciousness. On his part, Abdulla is a living vestige of the independence struggle. He is infinitely resourceful, resilient and wise. His effort to reconstruct his life in Ilmorog after the trauma of amputation during the war is shattered by the capitalist invasion of Ilmorog which marginalizes him and makes nonsense of his sacrifices during the Mau Mau emergency. On her part, Wanja is a typical Ngugi woman, an *élan vital* combining great adaptive skills with dynamism, enterprise and forbearance: "I am a hard woman and/know I can carry things inside my heart for a long time." Although a drop-out from school, Wanja displays an incredible ability to survive in a hostile world. She resists exploitation by the menfolk but instead uses her relationships with the men as a stabilizing influence for her own self-realization. Her fiery rebellious spirit, which is aptly captured in her frequent association with fire, helps her to rise above the status of a common prostitute.

In his portrayal of these characters, however, Ngugi shows the dialectical relationship between the individual and the collective/societal realms of experience. All the characters are subjected to the same socio-historical forces – rural poverty, subjection to the vagaries of nature, betrayal by the bourgeoisie, exploitation by local and foreign capitalists. But they respond to these situations in ways that individualize them without however obliterating the reality that their different experiences are conditioned by the class character of their society. It is when they are confronted by the frustrations of life in New Ilmorog that their diverse experiences begin to galvanize into a kind of class consciousness. Again, they attain this consciousness to varying degrees. Munira sees the exploitation and decadence of the society as manifestations of an evil world requiring divine purgation: "Munira had been so convinced that this world was wrong, was a mistake, that he wanted all his friends to see this and escape in time." When, therefore, he sets Wanja's brothel on fire, he sees himself as doing the will of God: "Christ, after all, had beaten the traders who had been spoiling God's temple." (p. 332) On his part, Karega grasps these features as manifestations of capitalist exploitation of labour which requires active resistance by the working class. "We want a world . . . in which the wealth of our land shall belong to us all, in which there will not be parasites dictating our lives, in which we shall all be workers for one another's happiness and well-being." (p. 327)

Ngugi is also conscious of the class alignments of his characters. He creates Chui, Mzigo and Kimeria for the specific purpose of inveighing against capitalism.

The characters do not exist as isolated "witnesses" to these experiences. Ngugi weaves an intricate web of relationships and interrelationships among them which unites their "secret lives" into a gigantic metaphor of human struggle with historical forces threatening annihilation. Karega's mother had worked in Munira's father's farm; Munira and Karega had lived in perennial mutual suspicion over Wanja's love; Wanja had been Abdulla's barmaid and also Munira's and Karega's mistress, and so on. This intricate web is animated by an almost clinical depth of psychological realization of the characters which enables us to encounter them in their private worlds.

Psychoanalytic characterization lends to Ngugi's narrative method a certain fluidity which enables him to forge a dialectical linkage among events, objects and persons with the result that there is hardly any dividing line between the prosaic realities of mundane experience and the subliminal terrain at which these realities also acquire mythic and symbolic resonance. Munira as a school teacher encounters the plant with "petals of blood" in the company of his pupils in old Ilmorog; he, along with the other characters, partakes of the Theng'eta ritual administered by old Nyakinyua. Later, when he sees Wanja's brothel as the symbol of worldly sin and evil, he sets it ablaze and retires to Ilmorog hills to watch the flames: "He stood on the hill and watched the whorehouse burn, the tongues of flame from the four corners forming petals of blood." (p. 333) Similarly, spatial and temporal demarcations dissolve as experience is explored from within the consciousness of individual characters with their powers of reflection, introspection, and projection. Munira's reminiscences provide the bulk of the narrative. Through him, Ngugi is able to reconstruct the phases in the development of Ilmorog from its small pastoral beginnings. Through Nyakinyua, glimpses from legend, myth and ancestry flow in to fill out the grey regions of the narrative. Abdulla furnishes the historical aspect while Karega's infinitely analytical mind provides ideological clarity to the warring concourse of events and experiences. The result is a narrative structure in which the past, the present and the future are constantly evident in the actions and utterances of characters.

In the final analysis, what emerges in *Petals of Blood* is a gigantic dialectical image which is, however, devoid of mystery but one which is nevertheless sufficiently intricate to discourage mechanical one-dimensional interpretations. As Gregory Shaw observes in a somewhat related context,

The dialectical image is subversive of the external order; establishing its own order and its own hierarchy of values, it creates its own world. This inner dialectic seeks, in fact, to re-create or revise the world and translate it into the categories of mind. It seeks, in a sense, to supplant the "original" act of creation, to submerge creation in an apocalyptic flood of images.[23]

But the flood of images which constitutes the "inner world" of *Petals of Blood* is relentlessly animated by the history and experience of contemporary Kenya and neo-colonial Africa. It is only in that context that the novel as an artistic statement begins to be meaningful.

The foregoing observations are reaffirmations not only of the historical predication of the African novel but, more crucially, of the derivativeness of its formal expressions from history, the history of Africa's resistance to colonialism and neo-colonialism.

Notes

1. A great deal of the attempt to define and defend the integrity of the African novel has been predicated on racial and emotional grounds rather than the objective laws of literary development. See, for instance, Chinweizu et al., *Toward the Decolonization of African Literature*; Chinua Achebe, *Morning Yet on Creation Day*, pp. 491–53. I have countered some of these views in my book, *Towards a Sociology of African Literature* (Oguta: Zim Pan African Publishers, 1986), ch. 2.

2. David Craig (ed.) *Marxists on Literature* (Harmondsworth: Penguin, 1975) p. 137.

3. Emmanuel Ngara, *Art and Ideology in the African Novel* (London: Heinemann, 1985), p. 15, See also, Emmanuel Obiechina *Culture, Tradition and Society in the West African Novel* (Cambridge: Cambridge University Press, 1975) pp. 14–17.

4. Ngara, p. 22.

5. Chidi Amuta, *Towards a Sociology of African Literature*.

6. Chidi Amuta, "History, Society and Heroism in the Nigerian War Novel", *Kunapipi*, vol. 6, no. 3, 1984, pp. 57–85.

7. See Terry Eagleton, *Criticism and Ideology* (London: Verso, 1976).

8. For typical positions in this critical fashion, see Bernth Lindfors (ed.) *Critical Perspectives on Chinua Achebe* (London: Heinemann, 1979).

9. Chinua Achebe, *Things Fall Apart* (London: Heinemann, 1985) p. 13.

10. Ibid., p. 31.

11. Achebe, *Arrow of God* (London: Heinemann, 1974) pp. 14–15. All further page references are to this edition.

12. Achebe *Things Fall Apart*, p. 126.

13. A. Bazhenova, "The Creative Process and Typification" in *Marxist–Leninist Aesthetics and the Arts* (Moscow: Progress, 1980) p. 243.

14. See Amilcar Cabral, *Return to the Source* (New York: Monthly Review Press, 1973), pp. 39–56; pp. 57–74.

15. Jean-Paul Sartre, Introduction to Frantz Fanon *The Wretched of the Earth* (Harmondsworth: Penguin, 1967) p. 19.

16. Georg Lukacs, *The Theory of the Novel* (Cambridge, Mass: M.I.T. Press, 1978) p. 32.

17. Interview in *Positive Review*, no. 3, 1981.

18. Sembene Ousmane, *God's Bits of Wood* (London: Heinemann, 1976) p. 13. All further page references are to this edition.

19. Ngugi Wa Thiong'o, *Writers in Politics* (London: Heinemann, 1981) p. 94.

20. Ngugi Wa Thiong'o, *Petals of Blood* (London: Heinemann, 1977) p. 20. All further page references are to this edition.

21. Ngugi, *Writers in Politics*, p. 97.

22. *Independent Kenya* (Anonymous) (London: Zed Press, 1982) p. 13.

23. Gregory Shaw, "Art and Dialectics in the Work of Wilson Harris", *New Left Review*, no. 153, 1985, p. 128.

7 Drama and Revolution in Africa

"Commitment" in contemporary African drama has taken a decisive turn. The main subject is revolution: its necessity or impossibility, its heterogeneous socio-historical context, its prospects and possible directions.   **Biodun Jeyifo**[1]

Politics and Ideology in Contemporary African Drama: Theoretical Observations

From its communal ritualistic "roots" through the colonial equivalents of the Christian morality play to the early stirrings of a literary tradition, African drama has in the recent past acquired an increasingly sharper "engaged" (in a political sense) focus. This is not to say that the primordial relationship between drama and politics has ever been in abeyance in the African world but rather to restate the theoretical truism that this relationship in its essential historical determination has become more manifest in contemporary Africa in response to familiar but specific historical developments. In the more elitist literary tradition of African drama which forms our immediate subject here, the political challenges which have confronted practitioners of other literary forms have not eluded the dramatist. Drama either as literature or as theatre has been compelled to display a sense of commitment. In West Africa, for instance, where earlier works of drama were dominated by a certain preoccupation with the metaphysical and the supernatural, we can perceive a shift to more secular political concerns especially since the late 1960s. This development is evident in both the careers of individual playwrights as well as in the trends within individual national literatures. From plays like *A Dance of the Forests* and *The Strong Breed*, which have a pronounced supernatural presence, Soyinka has scripted and produced works such as *Kongi's Harvest*, *Madmen and Specialists*, *The Road*, and *Opera Wonyosi* which explore aspects of the political and social problems of contemporary Nigeria. The same pattern appears also in the career of Ola Rotimi who has moved from his adaptation of *King Oedipus* (*The Gods Are Not To Blame*) through historical drama (*Kurunmi*, *Ovonrawen Nogbaisi*) to political satire (*Our Husband Has Gone Mad Again*) and, of late, reformist and revolutionary drama (*If . . .* and *Hopes of the Living Dead*, respectively).

If *commitment* as a blanket term defines the dominant political temper in much of recent African drama, it is not a phenomenon without internal differentiation in terms of regional, national attitudinal and, most crucially, ideological variations. While broad distinctions of theme and consciousness can be made, say, among and within East African, West African, and South African drama respectively, we get closer to a scientific analysis if we base our distinctions on features informed by ideological considerations because, ultimately, we have to answer the question: commitment to what and to whom? Biodun Jeyifo has, for instance, identified two broad patterns of alignment and social preoccupation in committed African drama.[2] The first pattern tries to answer the question: commitment to whom? In this respect, he distinguishes between those plays like Ama Ata Aidoo's *The Dilemma of a Ghost*, Soyinka's *Kongi's Harvest* etc. which deal with the political, social and cultural problems of the elite on the one hand and others like Hussein's *Kinjeketile* and Ngugi's *The Trial of Dedan Kimathi* which shun the elite and deal with the experiences of peasants, workers, the urban and rural masses and their leaders. Furthermore, in this regard, it is also possible to distinguish between plays in which the emphasis is on individual will on the one hand and others which underline the class or group determinism of individual action on the other. These distinctions are ultimately ideological rather than artistic in essence.

To the extent that all significant African playwrights to date belong to the petty-bourgeois class of teachers, civil servants etc., the recent emergence of radical leftist playwrights like Ngugi, Hussein, Osofisan, Sowande and others is partly evidence of greater ideological clarity within the ranks of committed African playwrights, thus necessitating a deeper theoretical insight into the relationship between drama and revolution in the contemporary African setting. This need is made more urgent by the unanimity and optimism with which revolution as a theme has been orchestrated by these playwrights.

> Very consciously, very deliberately, active historical contents are played off against the old myths, the supernatural and magical explanations of man's existence within society and nature. And no wonder, for quite often these plays deal with the more basic, more concrete problems that confront Africa and Africans: foreign domination, hunger, poverty, the degradation and oppression of the "little people", that is of Africa's vast urban and rural masses. The sights are focused more sharply on all the means of liberation, as much from foreign and domestic oppression, as from the systems of thought and the mystifications of reality inherited from previous ages unencumbered by the problems of the present epoch.[3]

The above formulation contains the *raison d'être* for the rise of revolutionary drama in Africa. In other words, *the rise of revolutionary drama in a given society requires the existence of social, economic and political situations requiring revolutionary intervention.* But more than the other forms and perhaps only next to poetry, drama is very amenable to revolutionary expression and can become very instrumental to revolutionary situations for reasons that are intrinsic to the nature of both drama and revolution. Drama is addressed to a group mind, is a collaborative art, relies on action for its actualization and appeals to a combination of senses, thus exploding the barrier of literacy which shackles the other forms in their written expression. By its nature also, a revolution is a collective activist phenomenon with far-reaching implications for the social, political and cultural lives of society.

Drama in the service of a revolution is like all other cultural effects – painting, music, dance etc. – which may be called into the service of a particular revolution. But drama as an art form can be revolutionary in two ways: either by articulating and exploring revolutionary themes or by utilizing novel and hitherto unused techniques to realize its themes and effects. While the subject of Euripides' *The Bacchae* may have been "revolutionary" in the context of Athenian slavocracy, its dramatic method remains within the confines of Aristotelian (idealist) tragic prescriptions. On the contrary, there may not be anything so revolutionary in an immediate sense about the content of Brecht's *Mother Courage*, yet its revolutionary affiliation is subsumed within the aesthetic revolution implied by Brecht's concept of the epic theatre. It would appear that drama is at its most revolutionary when a talented playwright expresses a revolutionary theme through equally revolutionary dramatic techniques.

The immediate sociology of revolutionary drama in Africa is furnished by the realities of imperialist domination, rural and urban poverty co-existing with oases of affluence and opulence. Mass participation in literary culture reflects these realities and is in turn complicated by the deliberate "hoarding" of literacy by the African ruling classes thus limiting the access of the masses to cultural expressions requiring literate competence and participation. Given this situation, revolutionary drama in Africa is faced with the challenge of addressing the present polarization between the *literary* and *popular* traditions as two parallel and diametrically opposed formations in African drama.[4] The imperative is towards greater popularization and the evolution of an alternative theory and practice of performance. Given its socio-historical ambience, a truly revolutionary African theatre must, at the level of technique, marry elements of traditional festival drama with folk opera under the intellectual and ideological guidance of the best achievements in the radical literary tradition with a popular audience in mind. In terms of content, such drama must be articulated from the position of a clear class analysis of society.[5]

In order to illuminate the progress already made in this direction, we shall examine four plays which variously illustrate aspects of the foregoing submissions. Two plays (*The Trial of Dedan Kimathi* and *I Will Marry When I Want*), in which Ngugi has collaborated with others, are informed by an actual struggle for a revolutionary alternative while Femi Osofisan's *Once Upon Four Robbers* and *Morountodun* represent attempts to proffer radical, revolutionary "explanations" for contradictions in contemporary Nigerian society with a view to quickening revolutionary consciousness in the immediate target audience.

Historical Reconstruction and Class Struggle in Anti-Imperialist Drama: *The Trial of Dedan Kimathi* and *I Will Marry When I Want*

To be familiar with contemporary Kenyan politics is to come face to face with the uses and abuses to which the African ruling classes have subjected history, for at the heart of the conflictual essence of Kenyan politics is the question as to which is the "correct" version of Kenyan history in the pre-colonial and colonial periods. While imperialist interests through their domination of vital media outlets in Kenyan culture have insisted on a colonialist supremacist view of Kenyan history, the ruling KANU government has mediated this extreme position by deliberately playing down those aspects of the nationalist history that involved the masses, especially the Mau Mau guerrilla heroes. In a bid to confront, nullify and transcend these misrepresentations, patriotic Kenyan intellectuals have insisted on seeing the essence of modern Kenyan nationalism in the Mau Mau and other related anti-colonial struggles waged by the masses of Kenyan peasants and workers. The latter position has necessitated a programme of historical reconstruction which has been pursued by both progressive historians and literary artists alike.[6] A significant aspect of this project is the rehabilitation of heroic figures who have suffered denigration and vilification in the hands of colonialist and imperialist historians and writers. Ngugi and Micere Mugo's *The Trial of Dedan Kimathi* must be understood as a dramatization of this process of historical reconstruction and rehabilitation.

The specific point of focus in this play is the heroic stature of Dedan Kimathi, leader of the Mau Mau struggle. But in the course of the play, this specific project is enlarged and ideologically corrected to symbolize the present struggle of Kenyan workers and peasants against imperialism and its many local agencies. This point emerges as a conspicuous part of the playwrights' motivation, as they state in their introduction to the play:

> We agreed that the most important thing was for us to reconstruct imaginatively our history, envisioning the world of the Mau Mau and Kimathi in terms of the peasants' and workers' struggle before and after constitutional independence. The play . . . [is] an imaginative recreation and interpretation of the collective will of the Kenyan peasants and workers in their refusal to break under sixty years of colonial torture and ruthless oppression by the British ruling classes and their continued determination to resist exploitation, oppression and new forms of enslavement.[7]

Based on the actual trial of Kimathi in 1956 by the British colonialist authorities, *The Trial of Dedan Kimathi* explodes its specific historical predication to become a gigantic metaphor of the history of struggle among African peoples in the past and present, as well as a way of envisioning a future of triumph for patriotic and progressive forces. It is in this ideological context that the quest for the meaning of the play must be rooted. Its lean plot line is provided by the preparations to try Kimathi, the actual trial, the attempt to rescue him and a loud suggestion of his dastardly and cowardly execution. Around this outline are woven strands of experience, themes and motifs which reaffirm the general value of struggle in the evolution of culture and consciousness.

The atmosphere of the play is characterized by unrelieved tension between the galvanized revolutionary will of the peasants and the ferocity of the omnipresent colonial army and police. The underground solidarity of the people baffles the colonialists and creates a permanent sense of insecurity and panic among them. To the colonialists' imagination, every women, every child is a "Mau Mau terrorist", a fact which only testifies to the mass character of the nationalist struggle. It is so intense that the Woman in the play can hide a pistol in a loaf of bread and still "dramatize" helplessness before an inquisitive colonial soldier! Similarly, the Boy accepts the need to dedicate his life to the cause for which Kimathi is being held.

Given this background, values, institutions and meanings become part of the binary opposition between the two sets of *wills* that are in conflict in the play: progressive nationalist will against the combined repressive and exploitative will of colonialism and contemporary capitalist imperialism. In the play, colonialist violence is counterposed against the libertarian violence of the freedom fighters; the law of the oppressor against the people's injured sense of justice. And in each case, Kimathi is consistently portrayed as the champion of positive and progressive values.

In the process of depicting these polarizations, the playwrights avoid a simplistic binary opposition. Contradictions among the people are revealed as in the fight between the Boy and the Girl. But such contradictions are exposed in order that the necessary clarification of consciousness can be effected. The Woman comes in handy to explain the petty conflicts between the Boy and the Girl as typical of the phenomenon of interiorized violence whereby the oppressed masses destroy one another as an unconscious response to their pauperized and marginalized conditions:

WOMAN: It is the same old story. Everywhere. Mombasa. Nakuru. Kisumu. Eldoret. The same old story. Our people . . . tearing one another . . . and all because of the crumbs thrown at them by the exploiting foreigners. Our own food eaten and leftovers thrown to us – in our land, where we should have the whole share. We buy wood from our own forests; sweat on our own soil for the profit of our oppressors. Kimathi's teaching is: unite, drive out the enemy and control your own riches, enjoy the fruit of your sweat. (p. 18)

There is here an attempt to raise the consciousness of the oppressed with a view to saving them from self-destruction and thereby directing their attention to the proper sources of their condition. The Boy whose father had died a victim of capitalist exploitation and neglect is better suited to imbibe the Woman's lesson, having *lived* the reality of poverty and exploitation: "I have fought with dogs and cats in the rubbish bins, for food." For him, the challenge is to rise above the limitations imposed by his deprivation and champion the cause for which Kimathi is being tried:

> WOMAN: The day you understand why your father died: the day you ask yourself whether it was right for him to die so; the day you ask yourself: "What can I do so that another shall not be made to die under such grisly circumstances?" that day, my son, you'll become a man. (p. 19)

In order to further ground the experience of the play in the contemporary opposition between imperialist exploitation and progressive forces, Kimathi's "trial" is enlarged into an x-ray of the major agencies of capitalism. Thus, each of the Priest, the Indian, Business Executive, Banker and Politician as a symbolic character acts out a role in accordance with the interest he represents in the imperialist and neo-colonial schemes of things. Each of these characters represents an interest group in the capitalist domination of contemporary Kenya. In their various encounters with Kimathi, each of them exposes, through self-revealing dialogue, its complicity in the under-development of Kenya. In obvious self-mockery, the Banker tells Kimathi:

> Confess. Repent. Plead guilty. Co-operate – like the surrendered generals. Tell your people to come out of the forest. We need stability. There never can be progress without stability. Then we can finance big Hotels . . . International Hotels . . . Seaside resorts . . . Night Clubs . . . Casinos . . . Tarmac roads . . . oil refineries and pipelines . . . Then tourists from USA, Germany, France, Switzerland, Japan, will flock in. Investment, my friend, development, prosperity, happiness. (p. 40)

This bourgeois theory of development is quickly countered by Kimathi: "It is not true that it was your money that built this country. It was our sweat. It was our hands." It is the dialectics of these exchanges between Kimathi and the agencies of imperialism that constitute the essence of the "trial". While the colonialists' judiciary tries Kimathi for his patriotic and progressive stance, the whole of imperialism puts itself on trial by virtue of its relentless association with and espousal of negative and oppressive values. Henderson is the embodiment of the negative values of imperialism and is made to play the symbolic role of trial judge in the play in an obvious ironic bid to expose the fraud in the imperialists' sense of justice.

As a necessary complement to its revolutionary topicality and anti-imperialist fervour, *The Trial of Dedan Kimathi* relies on a variety of innovative dramatic strategies for its realization. There is a rich use of mime to fill out specific temporal gaps and to provide vital historical anchorage for much of the action. For instance, the play begins with a mimetic flashback scene, "Black People's History", in which the main phases of the history of the exploitation of African peoples are re-enacted. These correspond to the slave trade, the exploitation of black labour in the New World and the contemporary anti-imperialist struggle. Similarly, when the Banker claims that he is "the maker of modern Kenya", there is a mime scene to counter this claim in which we find "Coolies and Swahilis building the Railway".

As a vital complement to the use of mime, Ngugi and Mugo employ an extensive flashback in order to recapture the essence of Kimathi's heroism and revolutionary vision. The scene in question takes place in a guerrilla camp in the Nyandura forest, ostensibly a recall of a most significant episode in Kimathi's career as a nationalist guerrilla commander. Here, not only Kimathi's humanism but also his disdain for traitors is revealed. More importantly, a rare insight is provided into the hero's revolutionary vision:

> We must learn from our past strength
> Past weaknesses
> From past defeats
> And past victories . . .
> Here in the forest
> . . . We must plant seeds for a
> future society
> Here in the forest armed in body
> mind and soul
> We must kill the lie
> That black people never invented anything
> Lay for ever to rest that inferiority
> complex
> Implanted in our minds by centuries
> of oppression
> Rise, Rise workers and peasants of Kenya
> (p. 68)

The strength of such flashback scenes derive from their close articulation into the contemporary anti-imperialism of the experience as a whole. Consequently, throughout the play, there is a certain fluidity in the handling of both time and space. As an aspect of an anti-illusionary device, the past, the present and the future dovetail in a continuum that is forged by mime, flashback and narrative. Similarly, the courtroom in which Kimathi is being tried is one and the same place with his prison cell where he encounters the main agencies of imperialism. The characters complement this fluidity through role-playing – Henderson is both judge, prosecutor, police investigator and imperialist soldier. Even the three formal movements into which the play is divided do not strike us as separate sequences of events but as a continuum. The overall effect is to reaffirm the dialectical complexity of historical experience. The playwrights indicate this much in the prelude to the play:

> The play is in three movements which should be viewed as a single movement. The action should on the whole be seen as breaking the barrier between formal time and infinite time, so that past and future and present flow into one another. The scenes (street, cell, courtroom) should also flow into one another.
>
> There is impersonation, merging of characters and reflection of history emphasizing the complexity, duality and interrelationships of people and events. (p. 2)

The popular appeal of the play and the mass character of its historical preoccupation are further enhanced through a rich use of song and dance. The songs are rendered mainly by peasants as a means of reinforcing their solidarity both with Kimathi and with one another in the struggle against imperialism. Most significantly, in the flashback scene on Kimathi's life as a combatant, the place of culture (especially popular song and poetry) in the liberation struggle is nostalgically re-created. Out of fresh historical experiences emerge new cultural forms through which the people remake themselves in struggle.

> When our Kimathi ascended
> Into the mountain alone
> He asked for strength and courage
> To defeat the whiteman
>
> He said that we should tread
> The paths that he had trodden
> That we should follow his steps
> And drink from his cup of courage
> (p. 62)

If history provides the tissue of this play, Ngugi and Mugo mediate that history by reaffirming the truism that it is people through conscious will and action who are the subject of history. Kimathi's heroic stature is an objectification of this thesis and its transformation into a metaphor for revolutionary action.

If the revolutionary message of *The Trial of Dedan Kimathi* is likely to be somewhat muted by its essentially "literary" and, therefore, elitist medium, Ngugi and his fellow patriotic artists in Kenya have since realized the need for the cultural aspect of the struggle for social justice to be waged *with* the people. If the freedom of the people is the object of revolutionary art, such art must of necessity not only objectify the material conditions and experiences of the people but must also communicate directly to them through language and techniques that belong in their aesthetic and cognitive worlds. If such art, especially drama, manages to enlist the participation of the people as actors in the drama of their own life struggles, true revolutionary drama is born. Such drama will need to make two sacrifices: firstly, it will need to explore a new language. Here *language* is understood not only in terms of verbal signals but also in terms of the totality of communicative devices deployed in literary communication; secondly it will need to extend the methods and standards of artistic performance to accommodate the participation of ordinary people and their level of artistic perception and socialization. If drama makes these two accommodations, its revolutionary potentials are greatly enhanced, for it appeals directly to and involves the active consciousness of the people to whom the responsibility of revolutionary action ultimately belongs.

To a great extent, the circumstances in which *I Will Marry When I Want*[8] was produced testify to the foregoing logic. The play was conceived of and staged in the company of peasants and workers at the Kamiriithu Cultural Centre at Limuru. It was also the workers and peasants who physically constructed the theatre with the two Ngugis merely providing intellectual and ideological direction and guidance. The result is a "theatre of the oppressed" in which the peasants and workers acted out their predicament in the context of a neo-colonial society riven by class contradictions. The performances, which ran for weeks, were widely attended by a cross-section of Kenyan society drawn especially from the urban centres – the home of the ruling class. It is no wonder then that on account of both the popularity and revolutionary appeal of the play, its further performance was banned by the Kenyatta government whose agents also burnt down the theatre and clamped Ngugi wa Thiong'o into detention without trial. Ngugi copiously recalls these circumstances in his prison diary *Detained*, and in his volume of essays *Barrel of a Pen*.

Against this background, then, *I Will Marry When I Want* is best understood as an attempt to dramatize, in plain terms, the reality of exploitation of the workers and peasants by an evil alliance of foreign capital and indigenous middlemen under the guise of economic development. The manipulation of the people's consciousness is disguised by Christian religious propaganda. This general perception and its underlying questioning of the legitimacy of capitalist production relations in contemporary Kenyan society provides the thematic basis of the play.

The plot is straightforward but carefully crafted around the centrality of the class question in capitalist society. Kiguunda, a farm labourer possesses a piece of land which his employer, Ahab Kioi, covets. Both Kioi and his business partner, Ikuua Nditika, will not stop at anything in their bid to secure the farmer's land for a factory project which they propose to undertake in conjunction with their Western partners. Simultaneously, Kioi's son is engaged in a dubious love affair with Kiguunda's daughter. These two unequal relationships provide the basis for conflict in the play and also furnish material for the exploration of the realities of social experience in a class society. Not only are we exposed to the hypocrisy and cowardice of the propertied bourgeoisie but also their constant recourse to a repressive use of the law to cow their victims. But the awakened consciousness of the workers and peasants is able to penetrate this cocoon of deceit and rise in open defiance of the oppressors. When Kiguunda discovers the ploy of Kioi, he challenges and subdues him physically only to discover that the "law" cannot but be on the side of the rich.

The overriding preoccupation of the play, then, is the nature of capitalist exploitation and its implications for every facet of life among members of different classes in society. Thus, the "love" affair between Kiguunda's daughter and Kioi's son is depicted as one based on inequality. Hence the young man summons his "loved" one by merely hooting at his car horn and will not suffer the inconvenience and condescension of being seen in the house of his father's slave. "He . . . never enters the house/He just hoots and whistles from the road." (p. 32) Njooki reminds Kiguunda of the class character of love: "Rich families marry from rich families,/The poor from the poor!" (p. 32)

Similarly, religion is emptied of its metaphysical appearance and given a concrete class meaning. For the oppressed, the concept of divinity is important to the extent that it can liberate from poverty and want. On their part, the rich see salvation in terms of wealth and material contentment irrespective of the source of such wealth. It also means the absence of libertarian violence and protest. Ndugire, a traitor in the Mau Mau days turned business tycoon, amplifies this facet in his testimony:

> My name is Samuel Ndugire
> I am a man who has received the tender mercy of the Lord,
> It was the midnight of December twelve,
> And he told me:
> Ndugire . . . the only good freedom is that of the soul
> Leave your fishing net behind
> Follow me now,
> And I shall make you a fisher of men . . .
> Since then my affairs started improving.
> I and my sister-in-Christ
> Were given a few shops by God
> (p. 46)

In other words, the end of capitalism justifies its meanness! What emerges, however, is the truth that in class society, there are two Gods: the God of the poor and that of the rich and that they are worshipped for different purposes.

It is part of the strength of the play that the facts of exploitation and alienation are objectified through the life experiences of ordinary people on a day-to-day basis. Kiguunda has to toil endlessly in Kioi's farm in return for a pittance and a life of squalor and chronic want. Supporting evidence emerges from the experiences of Gicaamba, himself a factory worker. His entire life is also an endless ritual of work in return for a subsistence wage. His own alienation is placed in the context of international capitalism and becomes a vital complement to Kiguunda's exploitation in the hands of a local landlord.

> GICAAMBA: The power of our hands goes to feed three people:
>   Imperialists from Europe
>   Imperialists from America
>   Imperialists from Japan
>   And of course their local watchmen.
>   But son of Gathoni think hard
>   So that you may see the truth of the saying
>   That a fool's walking stick supports the clever
>   Without workers,
>   There is no property, there is no wealth.
>   The labour of our hands is the real wealth of the country.
>   (p. 37)

This is not however a play that only laments the tragedy of the oppressed but above all one which also inspires them to rise above their limitations by challenging the conditions of their oppression. Gradually, through occasional flashbacks and reminiscences of the heroic heritage of the Mau Mau and the heroic struggles of their ancestors, both Gicaamba and Kiguunda are strengthened in their growing consciousness of the evil nature of the present society. Consequently, at the climactic moment of the play, Kiguunda is able to confront and subdue Kioi, even if for a brief moment while the awakened consciousness of the people identifies, in stark clarity, the class nature of their social predicament.

> GICAAMBA: The question is this:
>   Who are our friends? And where are they?
>   Who are our enemies? And where are they?
>   Let us unite against our enemies
>   (p. 114)

Throughout the play, there is an underlying ethical predilection governed by an overriding ideological viewpoint. Right and wrong in society are defined by the objective conditions of life and are, therefore, circumscribed by class position. For Kioi and Ndugire, *good* and *justice* flow from private property and those who oppose it will perish in hell fire: "But how can a country progress/Unless led by the rich?" (p. 87) On the contrary, the mobilized and sensitized consciousness of the poor conceives of the good society in terms of equality: "A day will surely come when/If a bean falls to the ground/It'll be split equally among us" (p. 115) Alongside this ethical polarization is an equally far-reaching schism at the level of other values (cultural, institutional, aesthetic etc.). Conditioned into the decadent values of the bourgeoisie wearing the façade of Western civilization, the Kiois and Ndugires have come to perceive reality through

"Western eyes". In their obsession with private property and accumulation, they believe in the myth of workers' and peasants' stupidity:

> KIOI: These workers cannot let you accumulate!
>   Every day: I want an increment.
>   Workers are like the ogres said to have two insatiable mouths.
>   When they are not demanding a rise in wages
>   They are asking you for an advance.
>   My mother is in hospital!
>   My child has been expelled from school,
>   Because I have not paid his school fees!
>   My wife has just delivered!
>   (p. 78)

Explanations for the pitiable conditions of the poor workers are sought either in Christian morality ("This business of not being satisfied . . . with one's station in life . . . comes from not being a good Christian") or in some other "cultural" domain ("I don't blame them. Many of them cannot read or write."). In order to stupefy the poor into a state where they can be better exploited, the rich have to recruit them into their (the rich's) value system. Thus, the Kiois will only interact effectively with the Kiguunda family if the latter can have a Christian white wedding. This of course is a ruse designed to drive Kiguunda into such financial desperation that he can readily sell his land to Kioi and his foreign partners!

In terms of artistic and dramaturgic significance, *I Will Marry When I Want* derives its popular appeal from its rich operatic structure. There is a heavy accent on music which is furnished by an assortment of religious and folk songs performed by the major characters. The strength of this form is enhanced by a certain fluidity in the structure of the play; there is an easy oscillation from song and dance to action. The songs are not, however, merely ornamental. They are constantly amplifying and reinforcing the central ideological contention of the play and its thematic elaborations. Here, the religious songs stand out prominently. In their various renditions of these songs, both the rich and the poor expose their antithetical conceptions of sin, heaven, salvation and damnation and thus underline the class determination of social consciousness.

As the instrument for thematic elaboration and intensification, music and dance in this operatic form become means of cultural reaffirmation. This is especially urgent in view of the acquiescence of the upper classes to Christian and bourgeois Western values. In this respect, the flashback into traditional Gikuyu nuptial rites and its musical accompaniment is introduced as a counterpoint designed to ridicule the artificiality and contemporary dysfunctionality of the church wedding into which the Kiguunda are about to be lured. Njooki reaffirms this:

> There's no marriage which is not blessed
> Except the one founded on measured love

Or on bank savings!
My wedding for instance was very blessed
Though I didn't take it to their churches
(p. 64)

She adds quite instructively:

Marriage is between a man and a woman.
Marriage is a covenant between two people,
Their flesh and soul becoming one
Without money coming into it . . .
Today it's not one human that marries another
But property marrying property,
Money marrying money,
This House marrying that House,
Hearts being taken to the market
(pp. 62–3)

The dialectics of social experience in a class society find further objectification through a blatantly polarized characterization. The characters are created to embody class values within the conflictual essence of the play and its informing society. Kiguunda, a peasant, is aware of his condition but does not, initially, possess the necessary consciousness to give this awareness a political significance. Because he *lives* the reality of exploitation, he realizes the futility of his existence, the unequal relationship between him and his employer and the uses to which religion (Christianity) is being put in his progressive dehumanization and alienation. He is a potential rebel. Wangeci, his wife, acts as a dampening influence on this potentiality. She is content with exploiting openings within the existing system for the material benefit of her immediate family. In her acquiescence, she is impatient with her husband's attempt to acquire a clearer class perspective. Her cynicism, it is later revealed, is a product of the experience of betrayal in the Mau Mau struggle.

As part of the dialectical design of the play, the Ngugis create Gicaamba apparently to prop up Kiguunda and help sharpen his consciousness. Gicaamba is eminently equipped for this role by his background as a factory worker. He helps to place in perspective Kiguunda's experiences as a peasant. Together, they constitute the vital alliance between the peasantry and the working class in the African revolution.

On the negative pole of the dialectical balance of the play are the characters created to typify the greed and hypocrisy of the propertied class. Ahab Kioi, his wife Jezebel, Samuel Ndugire and Nditika are posited as personifications of capital in its antagonistic relationship with labour. Accumulation and appropriating greed define their responses to the lower classes. They are all united by their subscription to common values, interests and beliefs. These include belief in the stupidity of the masses, in inequality as an act of God, in illiteracy as synonymous with lack of wisdom, and in love for foreign business partners over and above the interests of their nation. In their artistic realization, they are somewhat excessively parodied with the result that they emerge as caricatures more than realistic depictions. When, for instance, Kiguunda asks for water to drink, Jezebel tells the waiter: "Go and fetch water from the drum outside,/You know the one near the pig-sty." (p. 81) This apparent weakness in characterization can be rationalized as an inevitable consequence of the ideological insistence of the play. It would appear that these characters are deliberately overblown in order to expose the hollowness and puncture the bloated hypocrisy of the African comprador bourgeoisie. Their names, such as Ahab or Jezebel, are symbolic points to this process of demystification.

Beside its very realistic experiential referent, the play operates equally successfully at a symbolic level. As typifications of the reality of class conflict and antagonism, the characters are symbolic projections on the inevitable logic of the class struggle. Thus, when Kiguunda physically subdues Kioi, what we witness is a dramatization of a larger possibility. But Ngugi and Ngugi do not deceive their audience into thinking that the subjugation of the parasitic bourgeoisie will be an easy victory hence Jezebel shoots and injures Kiguunda and the law (which is always on the side of the ruling class) is called in to "discipline" Kiguunda. This concession does not, however, deprive the play of its optimistic accent. The victory of the oppressed which is foreshadowed in the ending is conditional on their coming into an awareness of the fact that "There are two sides in the struggle,/The side of the exploiters and that of the exploited".

It is this vital consciousness that the play is designed to foster and galvanize among the victims of oppression in today's Africa.

Contemporary Contradictions and the Revolutionary Alternative: *Once Upon Four Robbers* and *Morountodun*

If Nigerian literature offers, in the African instance, a vibrant example of a national literature that has come into its own, it also bears testimony to the effects of socio-political change on the evolutionary pattern of a national literature. If the "great tradition" of Nigerian literature has come to be associated with such names as Chinua Achebe, Wole Soyinka, J. P. Clark, Christopher Okigbo etc., the post-war period of the 1970s and 1980s with its sudden rush of artificial wealth and attendant inequalities has produced an alternative tradition which one may conveniently refer to as the left hand of the great Nigerian tradition. In drama, the new writings of Femi Osofisan, Kole Omotoso, Bode Sowande and Tunde Fatunde are characterized not just by their accent on political commitment but on a certain ideological predilection that is class-partisan and sees socio-political salvation mainly in terms of the revolutionary transformation of society. Within this emergent tradition, Femi Osofisan is prominent not only in terms of output but also in terms of stylistic and technical accomplishment. To date, Osofisan's plays can be seen as attempts to use the medium of drama to proffer materialist explanations of the major contradictions in Nigeria's neo-colonial society. In this regard, such contemporary issues as bureaucratic ineptitude, indiscipline, armed robbery, and peasant revolts have formed the major preoccupations of his plays with each contradiction being adduced as evidence of the unworkability of the present pseudo-capitalist system in the country. It is against this background that two of his more significant plays to date – *Once Upon Four Robbers* and *Morountodun* – are examined here.

Once Upon Four Robbers[9] is an attempt to provide a fictional re-interpretation of the social scourge of violent robbery which has engulfed Nigeria since the end of the Civil War in 1970. Successive Nigerian governments have insisted on dealing with the problem at a symptomatic rather than at a causative level. The state has resorted to public execution of robbers backed by draconian decrees. Such executions have been carried out in full view of the public either as a live audience or as a television audience.

Osofisan's play can, therefore, be seen as an attempt to counteract and challenge the government's position which is informed by the perspective of the ruling class. Specifically, the artistic theses that form the basis of *Once Upon Four Robbers* are that: (a) armed robbery is the product of a system rooted in inequality, (b) the cure to armed robbery and associated societal problems lies in a revolution that redefines production relations thus removing the sources of inequality and aggressive competition, and (c) that the violence with which the state confronts violent robbers cannot but beget greater violence on the part of robbers and others whom objective conditions compel to defy the terrorism of the state.

Osofisan explores these propositions through an artistic strategy that places the armed robbers at the centre of action thereby revealing their motivations and thought processes. Contrary to the propaganda of the state, it is revealed that the robbers, like other members of the society, act out of love of life; they are merely in pursuit of life through death. More importantly, they show a very keen awareness of the mechanism of the system and seek survival and identification through robbery and violence. In a social world characterized by aggressive competition, private property, crass materialism, unemployment and poverty for the weak majority, the underprivileged who crave a good life must resort to violent defiance. Besides, the violence which attends the operations of the robbers is a form of political protest against the inequality in the society. Says Angola, one of the robbers: "There are many citizens who must be made to account for their wealth, and the poverty of their workers. Such accounts can be settled only one way." (p. 17) Through violence, of course!

Osofisan strives to emphasize a strong class consciousness among the robbers thereby exonerating them from that kind of sponsored official prejudice which dismisses them as bloodthirsty vagabonds and anarchists. Throughout the play, all the robbers see their actions in terms of the need to settle a score with a society whose ruling and propertied classes (often one and the same) deprive the majority of a fair chance. Says Angola: "Too many people ride their cars along the sore-ridden backs of the poor". In spite of the certainty of death in their kind of occupation, the robbers see their actions as the early signs of the possibility of a revolutionary overthrow of the parasitic class. On the execution block, Major tells the Sergeant:

> Man is so fragile, so easy to kill.
> Especially if he robs and lies, if he wantonly breaks the law. Serg, today that law is on the side of those who have, and in abundance, who are fed and bulging, who can afford several concubines. But tomorrow, that law will change. The poor will seize it and twist its neck. The starving will smash the gates of the supermarkets, the homeless will no longer yield in fear to your bulldozers. And your children, yes, your dainty, little children will be here where I stand now, on the firing block.
> (p. 53)

Even the rank and file of the military, those charged with the task of executing and terrorizing robbers on behalf of the state are posited within the class contradictions in the society. They are mere tools in the hands of the ruling class; although pauperized by the property and power relations, they are literally "programmed" into defending a system which they scarcely understand. In this arrangement, even relationships between members of the same family are governed by the logic in the larger society. Between Hassan (one of the robbers) and the army sergeant who is his brother, there is a schism. Says the Sergeant: "I joined the victors" while Hassan insists on his right to a decent life in a country that he calls his: "I have sworn never to be a slave in my own father's land. All I wanted was the right to work, but everywhere they only wanted slaves." (p. 56) Hassan's criminal activities become part of a deep-seated psychological response to an upbringing characterized by strictness, a preparation for a meaningless future: "I want to pay back all those lashes, and the lies, of teacher, priest and parent." (p. 56)

Not even the market women are spared in the logic of the jungle – "eat or be eaten" – which governs relations in a market economy. Faced with the challenge of surviving in a society where the basic necessities of daily existence are commoditized, the women cannot but prey on one another and on the society. This much is revealed in the "Song of the Market" which forms the anthem of the market women:

> The lure of profit
> has conquered our souls
> and changed us into cannibals:
> oh praise the selfless British

who with the joyous sound
of minted coins and gold
brought us civilization!

We make inflation
and hoard away
as much as we may relish
essential commodities
like sugar and salt
like milk and oil . . .

The lust of profit
keeps us in this world
this life that is a market:
refuse to join and perish,
rebel and quench!
(pp. 28–29)

Although divergent in their various endeavours, motivations and levels of consciousness, the robbers, soldiers and market women are presented as members of "a class in itself", victims of private property and its hold on the state.

The freshness of *Once Upon Four Robbers* does not, however, derive solely from its central ideological caveat. In this, as in his other plays, Osofisan articulates a revolutionary vision of society through a creative fusion of elements of Yoruba oral art and Brechtian theatre. In this particular instance, the formal inspiration derives from the oral art of story-telling, hence the title is a play on the stock beginning of most stories. The story-telling function is performed by Aafa, a man equipped for this function by both his age and calling as a sorcerer in the pre-colonial Yoruba tradition. Thus, there is a sense in which the experiences in *Once Upon Four Robbers* are rendered as a story, albeit one with a specific and recognizable socio-historical referent.

Thus, a central formal attribute of the play is the constant oscillation between the world of illusion (of the story) and of reality. The constant creation and breaking of the illusion of reality which is here achieved through the mystical spell of Aafa is a conspicuous aspect of Brechtian dramaturgy. Further aesthetic distantiation is achieved through a combination of role-playing (the soldiers feign the foibles of their superiors at the execution ground), an informal beginning in which the actors select and wear their costumes in full view of the audience, and an equally informal and inconclusive ending in which the Aafa problematizes the experience of the play by challenging the audience to choose between the soldiers and the robbers in terms of ideological significance.

The use of trance heightens the alienation effect. Alhaja, possessed by her role, is transported from the world of reality and sheds her earthly identity, encountering a transcendental "reality" in the process. Thus transfigured, Alhaja sheds the stigma of being just an armed robber in the present and becomes a universal symbol of motherhood in a decadent and anarchic society that destroys her offspring. The mythic milieu of her transfiguration is provided by Yoruba mythology and the object is a lament of the agonies of motherhood in a turbulent and anarchic society. "And all alone I will swell with the terrible burden of unwanted seed, unwanted because condemned to die. I will swell, I will explode, bearing the laughter of new corpses." (p. 51)

There is in this play, as in most of Osofisan, a strong poetic tinge which some critics have attributed to the strong influence of Soyinka on the language of this playwright.[10] Unlike Ngugi's plays, for instance, where no conscious effort is made to heighten speech through deliberate stylization, the texture of Osofisan's language is lyrical and metaphoric. In a passage reminiscent of the Old Man in Soyinka's *Madmen and Specialists*, Hassan reminds Sergeant of his mortality

> HASSAN: You're an animal, you're flesh, you're blood and urine, not a bloody uniform! Take it off! Take the damned thing off and reveal yourself, you smelling primate. Let's see if you're not skin like me. If we didn't come from the same womb. You eat and belch and you sleep with women, you're a bloody human being. So don't answer me like a uniform. I said, you have eyes, you can see, you know what is going on everywhere, what is happening to people like us, so how can you remain unmoved?
> (p. 55)

The sense of poetry in *Once Upon Four Robbers* is accentuated by a lavish use of songs mainly derived from Yoruba oral culture which in their thematic pungency reinforce the central ideological contention of the play. In a manner reminiscent of the chorus in classical Greek drama, the songs here provide oblique comments on the experiences in the play. They also give the various characters an opportunity to criticize even their very roles and perceptions. In the latter respect, Osofisan's songs partake of a certain Brechtian essence.

It is perhaps at the level of characterization that Osofisan displays his familiarity with the contradictory essence of social experience. Although joined in the popular mind as an undifferentiated gang of terrorists, the robbers in this play show a certain individuality of perception which reveals them as intensely human. The four robbers represent variations on a common theme; crime as socially generated. Alhaja is intensely maternal and in her humanistic views embodies the moral dimension of Osofisan's revolutionary consciousness. In a symbolic gesture, Alhaja gives food and life to the soldiers preparing the stakes for the execution of Major. Similarly, the Aafa complements Alhaja's role by trying to divest the robbers' acts of terror. Even between Angola and Major, there is a divergence of views on method. Major is a survivalist, intent on quitting the hazardous trade after a major haul. Angola accuses him of cowardice and bad faith. On his part, Hassan is part of the gang as an act of defiance and rejection of the status of a slave in his fatherland. In spite of these divergencies, however, Osofisan does not allow them to dissipate their consciousness of their class predicament in interpersonal quarrels. Nor is any attempt made to convert them into a revolutionary vanguard.

The revolutionary appeal of *Once Upon Four Robbers* lies ultimately in the alternative and obviously radical "explanation" which it offers for one of the most conspicuous symptoms of the dysfunctionality of capitalist social relations in contemporary Nigeria (and Africa). Thus conceived, the crucial significance of the play is mainly pedagogical; an attempt to compel the African mind to abandon idealist explanations of and solutions to social problems. The function of such drama in Africa today is to nurture popular consciousness in a revolutionary direction.

In *Morountodun*, Osofisan borrows from myth and history certain experiential metaphors for the exploration of revolutionary change in the contemporary Nigerian society. The mythic inspiration comes from the legendary heroism of Moremi of Ile-Ife, a woman who singlehandedly mobilized to save her society from the menace of Igbo invaders. The historical substratum of the play derives from the Agbekoya peasant revolt which took place in parts of Oyo State in 1969 while the Nigerian Civil War was still raging. But the immediate socio-political context which these two realms of experience are invoked to confront is the class antagonism and various deformations and abuses of the state apparatus which had become rife in Nigeria by 1979. *Morountodun* is, therefore, better understood as simultaneously a reconstruction of both myth and history in the service of contemporary reality with specific reference to the issue of social and political change.

While myth functions to ratify the experiences within a national setting, the history of the Agbekoya revolt provides an ideological framework for the realization of the plot. Class conflict, therefore, is at the centre of the play. But this conflict is not presented in the form of a simple polarization between the rich and the poor but in more complex and contradictory terms. Thus, Titubi the heroine, although nurtured in the comfort and material opulence of the *nouveau riche*, represented by her mother (Alhaja), is seasoned by experience into a rejection of the values of her social class by her exposure to the experiences of the peasants in the countryside. In committing class suicide, she also comes to a re-evaluation of the myths that sustain the values of the ruling class. The version of the Moremi myth on which her heroic stature is predicated is a fundamental reformulation of the ancient myth which is here shorn of its feudalistic orientation and given a more progressive and anti-establishment outlook. Declares Titubi at her moment of recognition:

> I had to kill the ghost of Moremi in my belly. I am not Moremi. Moremi served the state, was the state, was the spirit of the ruling class. But it is not true that the state is always right.[11]

Nor can it be said that the rest of the characters are arranged along a line of simple binary oppositions dictated by class alignment. What obtains rather is a deliberate resistance to the lure of typification and rigid symbolization. The various characters embody and manifest the contradictory essence of social experience without, however, losing track of the basic class alignments in society. In the hands of a more vulgar socialist dramatist, one would expect the police superintendent, for instance, to unrepentantly champion and defend the state. On the contrary, he is made to display a startling awareness of the contradictions and antagonisms in the society of which he forms part. Defying his official role as defender of the ruling class, he tells Alhaja:

> One of these fine days you'll wake to the noise of shooting in your kitchen. Your markets will be on fire, your pretty houses, your banks and insurance houses, the entire street will be burning. And there'll be nowhere for you to hide.
> (p. 70)

In spite of Osofisan's insistence on portraying characters in their dynamic and dialectical essence, we do not lose sight of the pattern of alignments in the confrontation between the oppressed peasantry on the one hand and the state and the ruling class on the other. This much at least is revealed in the impeccable solidarity among the revolting Agbekoya peasants. Marshal as the symbol of the aspirations of the peasant movement is the purveyor of the revolutionary ideology of the play. He is dogged ("We'll fight with our bare hands. Till Death."), ideologically convinced and committed ("The well-fed dog has no thought for those who are hungry.") and believes in the efficacy of libertarian violence in a situation where mindless authoritarianism thwarts the will of the people ("Let all prisons fall.").

The obviously revolutionary ideology of the play finds dramaturgic reinforcement in the essentially Brechtian approximations of the technique. As is typical of the epic theatre, much of the theme is realized through *narration* while the experiences are explored through an essentially dialectical route; conflict, contradiction and opposition are the essence of this drama. There are no stereotypes; everything and everybody changes into their opposites and back again in a purposive direction dictated by a compulsion to a revolutionary redefinition of social reality. Accordingly, the dialogue is equally dialectical in essence, constantly exploding accepted axioms and beliefs through a combination of folk witticism and proverbs in order to challenge the audience into a reflective rationalistic participation.

More crucially, Osofisan makes no attempt to confound his audience in a belief that the experiences dramatized constitute reality. The illusion of reality is constantly exploded by the Director who intervenes at the beginning and in the end to problematize the experiences depicted by situating them in the context of contemporary social experience. Even at the end of the play, the adoption of a problematic open ending is designed to sensitize the audience into resolving the contradiction inherent in

Marshal's decision to return to the battle front even after consummating his marriage to Titubi. Furthermore, the essentially narrative realization of temporal and spatial dimensions in the play renders them fluid. Actions dovetail and coalesce while characters, through role-playing, *are not* what they are.

The upshot of the excellent fusion of revolutionary content and technique in *Morountodun*, then, is the emergence of a certain textual ideology which also reinforces Osofisan's avowed commitment to the revolutionary option in Nigeria's quest for a viable society. Perhaps Marshal speaks for his creator and for the oppressed people of Nigeria when at the end of the play he asserts, almost in a trance:

And who knows, maybe it will be time
then to rest our weapons and let them grow
to rust . . . until the next cry of desperation.
And maybe afterwards our own children
will have a decent chance to grow up like
human beings, not like animals having to
scrounge for left-overs in the sewer of
history.
(p. 78)

Notes

1. Biodun Jeyifo, *The Truthful Lie: Essays in a Sociology of African Drama* (London/Port of Spain: New Beacon Books, 1985) p. 54.

2. Ibid., p. 47.

3. Ibid., p. 62.

4. I have dealt, at a very theoretical level, with the problems of popularization in Nigerian literary culture in my essay, "Toward a Popular Literary Culture in Nigeria", *Critical Arts*, vol. 3, no. 1, 1983, pp. 56–64.

5. See Biodun Jeyifo, "Literary Drama and the Search for a Popular Theatre in Nigeria" in Y. Ofunbiyi (ed.) *Drama and Theatre in Nigeria: A Critical Source Book* (Lagos: Nigeria Magazine, 1981) pp. 411–421.

6. This process of historical reconstruction is a conspicuous part of the writings of Kenyan radical intellectuals. See, for instance, *Independent Kenya* (London: Zed Press, 1982).

7. Ngugi wa Thiong'o and Micere Githae Mugo, *The Trial of Dedan Kimathi* (London: Heinemann, 1976) p. iv. All further page references are to this edition.

8. Ngugi Wa Thiong'o and Ngugi Wa Mirii, *I Will Marry When I Want* (London: Heinemann, 1982). Subsequent references to the text are to this edition. The play was first composed, performed and published in Kikuyu under the title *Ngaahika Ndeenda*.

9. Femi Osofisan, *Once Upon Four Robbers* (Ibadan: Bio Educational Service, 1980). All further page references are to this edition.

10. See, for instance, Eliane Saint-Andre, "Political Commitment in Nigerian Drama (1970–1983)", *Commonwealth*, vol. 7, 1984, pp. 36–50.

11. Femi Osofisan, *Morountodun* (Lagos: Longman, 1982) p. 70. All further page references are to this edition.

8 Poetry and Liberation Politics in Africa

The poet speaks not for himself only but for his fellowmen. His cry is their cry, which only he can utter. That is what gives it its depth. But if he is to speak for them, he must suffer with them, rejoice with them, work with them, fight with them. **George Thomson**[1]

Poetry and Politics: The Dialectic of Commitment

All arguments as to whether modern African poetry in its written (and therefore elitist) form can cultivate a popular audience are beside the point. Written poetry in Africa, and indeed everywhere, is part of a general fragmentation process in which poetry is reified away from its original integration with the very rhythm of collective speech, and therefore with socially redeeming action and converted into an object of individual contemplation. Furthermore, the phenomenon of written poetry testifies to the reality of class differentiation of society, in which literacy as a critical factor in the composition and consumption of written poetry is differentially available to members of different classes and groups. In capitalist and pseudo-capitalist societies, written poetry is therefore the exclusive preserve of the intellectual arm of the bourgeois and petty-bourgeois classes. To that extent, such poetry is primarily addressed to members of the same class and their approximations. Even if the bourgeois poet strives, through technical innovations such as the adoption of simple ideas and the rhythm of popular speech, to reach a popular audience, his efforts will not nullify his essential alienation, for the original creative force of poetry belongs to that spontaneity of relationship between the poet and his live audience which was the norm in the oral tradition of all societies. Writes George Thomson:

> (Bourgeois) poetry has lost touch with the underlying forces of social change. Its range has contracted – the range of its content and the range of its appeal. It is no longer the work of a people, or even of a class, but of a coterie. Unless the bourgeois poet can learn to reorientate his art, he will soon have nobody to sing to but himself.[2]

The essential alienation of the bourgeois poet and the privatist exclusivity attendant on the written form do not, however, nullify the possibility of using poetry as one means of social change.[3] This possibility in itself inheres in the generic peculiarities of the poetic mode. As a means of communion between poet and people, poetry has the specific advantages of both breaking down the barrier between reason and emotion and obliterating the distinction – a concomitant of prose narrative – between time and space. As a result, poetry can become readily instrumental in historical situations requiring the galvanization of feelings and emotions in pursuit of a collective cause. But the language of such historically functional poetry cannot be legislated by professional criticism and literary theory. *Every historical epoch writes its own poetry or rather expresses itself in appropriate idiom in the poetry of its most committed and sensitive minds.*

In this respect, the bourgeois poet in Africa hovers between two compelling possibilities. As a member of the bourgeois class, his high-class literacy and relatively privileged social status compel the popular mind to ally him with the ruling and propertied classes. On the other hand, the ruling class views the poet as potentially subversive and therefore holds him in perennial suspicion and would readily cast him into preventive detention if the need arose.

Because the art (all art) which he practises stands in eternal opposition to the dehumanization which tyranny and private property constitute, the poet tends to turn his back on his ruling and propertied colleagues and instead pitches his tent with the people in their struggle for justice and humane existence. Thus, in situations requiring direct involved heroic intervention in defence or pursuit of progressive values, poets have often found themselves fighting on the side of the people. This is why poets as diverse in nationality and outlook as Christopher Caudwell, John Cornford, Louis Aragon, Christopher Okigbo, Maxim Gorky and Dennis Brutus have dedicated their art and sometimes their lives to the pursuit of freedom.

In the African world, this historical necessity, in which the poet as a man of culture devotes his art and life to the pursuit of justice and freedom, has become part of the very legitimacy of the poetic undertaking. To be a significant poet in Africa at a time like this is to stand up and be counted in the struggle against foreign domination and class and racial injustice. This historical imperative constitutes also the sore point of much of critical and polemical conflicts in discourse on African poetry at the present time. That the issue of the poet's political commitment should be controversial is in itself evidence of the critical place of ideology even in matters of poetry. Over the ages, two "tribes" of poets have emerged: those who use their art to legitimize, uphold and advance the cause of the status quo and those who use their talents to challenge the ruling class and thus champion the cause of those who bear the burden of oppression. All attempts to strike a balance are opportunistic and hypocritical.[4]

In the African world, this polarization constitutes the core of the legacy of commitment in poetry, for African poetry, either in the oral or written tradition has a legacy of commitment. But the question has to do with the object of such commitment. There have always been poets who either praised or denounced tyrannical kings either in the oral or written tradition. Changing historical challenges have only altered the precise beneficiaries and targets in this equation. This historical and ideological imperative should constitute the starting point for the understanding and evaluation of African poets, not their fidelity to some Euro-modernist or "traditional" models.

This is not however to suggest that there is a necessary correlation between ideologically progressive poetry and artistic profundity on the one hand and reactionary verse and aesthetic mediocrity on the other. What is being underlined is the political and ideological choices which specific historical situations define for poets and their art. The aesthetic mediation of any one choice is a different matter but one which in any event is pivotal to a distinction between the poet and the non-poet.

Consequently, there is a need to historicize and contextualize evaluations of individual African poets and their works. We can, for instance, distinguish between the responses of Senghor and that of David Diop or Aimé Césaire to French colonialism and its ideological and cultural policies; the former idealistic and romantic and the latter combative and materialist. Yet the necessity of a Senghor *as* and *when* he sang his "sweet songs", cannot be discountenanced considering the extent of the psychological damage done to the negro by colonialist mythology. Nor does this recognition redeem Senghor from the fold of idealist artists.

In situations requiring direct action in the pursuit of freedom, the poet who lends his art to the service of freedom restates the truism that socially redeeming political action is the highest form of artistic expression. Such action rearranges people, structures and institutions, thereby re-humanizing them, which is the ultimate object of all art. In present day Africa, armed struggle against colonialism, the struggle to end the unjust system of apartheid and the various struggles by progressive intellectuals, workers, students and peasants to end class inequality and oppression present decisive challenges that need to be addressed as vigorously on the cultural front as on other fronts. The poetry of Agostinho Neto, Dennis Brutus and Odia Ofeimun typify the use of a cultural form to intervene in these historical situations. It is to these specific poets of the African people that I now turn.

Private Experience as Public Protest: Dennis Brutus's *Stubborn Hope*

To come to grips with the scourge of apartheid: its daily assault on all that is decent about humanity, is to know a *system* whose exploitative and repressive essence permeates all areas of human endeavour. Said Dennis

Brutus recently: "I see apartheid as having, not only economic, political and military dimensions, but also a *cultural* dimension."[5] Thus, in addition to the political and economic efforts being made to dismantle apartheid, there is now a whole heritage of cultural responses to that evil system. In literature, anti-apartheid writing manifests itself in two dominant forms: a moderate tradition that denounces apartheid by revealing its so-called "human face" and a combative, uncompromising tradition that not only exposes the underlying materialism of the system but invites responses that are totally geared towards its nullification annd transcendence. In the former tradition are to be located writers like Alan Paton and Athol Fugard while the late Alex La Guma, Pitika Mthuli and Dennis Brutus, among others, typify the latter.

In many ways, Dennis Brutus represents the deep involvement of men and women of culture in the struggle to end apartheid and inaugurate a new and free society in South Africa. His involvement is not, however, limited to the area of poetry alone. Brutus has been in the forefront of several international campaigns against the apartheid regime ranging from his role as president of the South African non-racial Olympic committee, which succeeded in excluding South Africa from the Olympic Games, to his current efforts to get American universities to disassociate from South Africa. This level of involvement has meant a life of persecution, imprisonment and exile.

Brutus' career as a poet, which is an accompaniment to his other involvements, is conditioned by the same socio-political pressures as his political action. In essence, the struggle for freedom constitutes the overriding concern in Brutus' poetry.

> It must be absolutely basic for a human being to be free, it is part of our psyche, our nature. It's as elemental as the need to breathe or to eat or to sleep, to excrete, or to make love.[6]

To the extent that written poetry in general is an essentially private and personal medium, Brutus' verse derives its strength from its ability to utilize personal, even subdued, experiences to express very public concerns, thus smashing the cultic esotericism of expression and individualistic thrust of much of contemporary African poetry (especially Anglophone West African poetry). Says Brutus in this respect:

> It seemed to me at some point that merely to indulge myself either in the kind of traditional balladry or, on the other hand, high-brow expression or whatever it was was boring and inauthentic and it wasn't worth doing at all. *I would either make this kind of expression which was both public and personal or not write at all.*[7]
> (my emphasis)

As we shall see subsequently, in trying to grapple with the personal and collective implications of apartheid, Brutus is merely exploring the general through the specific by stressing their dialectical relatedness.

Stubborn Hope represents an advancement, politically, on Brutus's earlier verse. In the poems collected in *A Simple Lust*, he had tried to express various aspects of his South African experience through occasionally dense metaphor and a predominantly subdued and meditative tone, paying particular attention to the formal norms of poetry. In *Stubborn Hope*, however, it would appear that the experience of exile and the compelling need for urgent militant action against apartheid forces him to abandon his earlier approach in favour of more direct, declamatory and structurally uncomplicated verse. Yet there is no significant loss in artistic effect while the political force is everywhere in evidence. We shall return to this aspect subsequently.

Most importantly, *Stubborn Hope*[8] presents a diversity of themes and concerns derived from the apartheid situation which lends a fairly total picture of the South African experience.

To the extent that Brutus's verse emanates from personal sources, the primary thematic tool by which he bridges the chasm between the personal and public realms is his centralization of love. Here, love is not conceived of as an abstract concept but as a metaphor of the poet's deep and abiding sense of patriotism. Thus, the land of South Africa is depicted in a multiplicity of images as a woman. Far from degenerating into an amorous and pornographic pastime, the relationship between poet and the land-woman is often characterized by violence, turbulence, uneasiness and even outright anguish. Yet these aberrations do not mar the original feeling of affection.

> I know my love can endure, resist all things – even as storm and footprints scar
> her ravaged face and leave her dearness still unmarred.
> (p. 6)

There is a persistent indication that a certain abnormality inhibits the poet from actualizing his affection for his land. The abnormality, the obvious aberrations of apartheid, is depicted as a disease condition.

> How are the shoots of affection withered at the root?
> What lops the tendrils that reach out
> and what blights the tender feeling buds?
>
> All that I dreamed – and doubtless you –
> and that we fondly hoped and planned
> how was it poisoned and with what?
> (p. 17)

Brutus' sense of patriotism which is here rendered in amorous terms does not compromise the activist and combatant dimension to his commitment. While adoring the land-woman, Brutus is intensely aware that given the distortions of apartheid, a certain therapeutic violence is required to cleanse it of the scourge of injustice and oppression. Thus, while still remaining within the limits of the love metaphor, he depicts such violence as an inevitable part of his affection and patriotism.

If in time I can endure no longer
the torturing of unrequitedness
and claw your contours with deliberate clumsiness
I beg you to remember
such violence may be
pervasion of frustrated tenderness
(p. 52)

Out of the feeling of torture, affection and consummate patriotism the excruciating pain of exile emerges as a prominent concern in *Stubborn Hope*. This feature, which arises naturally from the poet's physical separation from the land, is not a private concern. It is portrayed as the reward for all patriots opposed to apartheid. In the poem, "Our Allies Are Exiles", Brutus powerfully laments the plight of all his compatriots in exile, especially writers and artists.[9] For each of them, exile is a negation of his being, a necessary sacrifice for freedom at home. The pain of exile consists in a double futility: a wasted life and a wasted death.

Our allies are exiles
to their earth unreturnable
or corpses that rot in alien earth.
(p. 85)

Exile offers only a passing succour; it renews the longing for home and enkindles patriotism.

I have been bedded
in London and Paris
Amsterdam and Rotterdam,
in Munich and Frankfurt
Warsaw and Rome –
and still my heart cries out for home!
(p. 94)

There is in these poems an abiding sense of incarceration which is both physical and mental. Prison and imprisonment which are recurrent themes in Brutus' poetry and all of South African literature become obsessions, permanent scars which follow the poet wherever he goes. This point falls into place when one recalls the series of prison terms which Brutus had to serve before he finally left South Africa.

Sirens contrail the night air:
Images of prisons around the world,
reports of torture, cries of pain
all strike me on a single sore
all focus on a total wound
(p. 50)

Freedom as the corollary of imprisonment and not incarceration as a permanent condition is the ultimate object of Brutus' commitment. We are constantly reminded that the poet's alienation from his land-woman and his exile are the result of denials of freedom by the system at home. The subject of freedom in South Africa calls to mind such authoritarian obscenities as the obnoxious Pass Law, the colour bar, the Immorality Act, the Sharpeville and Soweto massacres as well as the now daily ritual of cold-blooded massacres of black youth to satiate the appetite of the gods of Western capitalist investment. The prime symbol of the denial of freedom remains, of course, Nelson Mandela. Brutus remembers Mandela quite nostalgically, as he revealed in a recent interview with Biodun Jeyifo:

> We broke stones together on the island (Robben Island), we spent some time together, but we were not able to talk to other prisoners. I had known Nelson outside prison at the time we were all working on the National Convention; and when he went underground he spent part of the time hiding at my home.[10]

Brutus' preoccupation with freedom goes beyond mere contemplation and wishful longing. In the poem, "I am a Rebel and Freedom is My Cause", the poet/patriot cuts the image of a crusading freedom fighter canvassing international support and sharing in the hopes of freed mankind everywhere.

> I am a rebel and freedom is my cause:
> Many of you have fought similar struggles
> therefore you must join my cause:
> My cause is a dream of freedom
> and you must help me make my dream reality:
> For why should I not dream and hope?
> Is not revolution making reality of hopes?
> (p. 95)

In *Stubborn Hope*, an occasional sense of utter desolation and despair mingles with angry resolve to emphasize hope. Endurance becomes a stoic acceptance of suffering as a concomitant of the struggle for freedom while hope itself is a reaffirmation of the will to succeed. The path of optimism is littered with potholes of self-doubt, self-reproach and even outright apprehension.

> There are times
> when our repudiation of ourselves
> is so complete
> the acceptance of our corruption
> so absolute
> the thrust of our concupiscent propensities
> so unarguable
> that capitulation,
> surrender
> – nay more!

the embrace of despair
is almost final
(p. 17)

It is to the credit of Brutus' revolutionary optimism that he is able to transcend the pangs of understandable despair and disillusionment to reaffirm his hope in freedom and the triumph of justice. This much is the emphasis in the title poem, "Stubborn Hope", in which the poet stresses the value of endurance in the struggle against apartheid:

Somewhere lingers the stubborn hope
thus to endure can be a kind of fight,
preserve some value, assert some faith
and even have a kind of worth.
(p. 22)

As we had hinted earlier, the essence of the formal freshness of *Stubborn Hope* derives from the technical (and, invariably, ideological) departure which Brutus makes here from his earlier verse especially as contained in *A Simple Lust*.

In contrast to the considerable length of a sequence like "Letters to Martha", for instance, the poems that constitute *Stubborn Hope* consist of short and direct statements on specific experiences and themes. At times the poems are just epigrammatic statements, as in "Perhaps":

Perhaps all
poems
are simply
drafts
(p. 55)

To complement this directness of expression, which is obviously aimed at democratizing or popularizing the consumption of the verse and thereby advancing its political message, Brutus shuns convoluted sentence structures and unnecessarily long lines. This twist is celebrated in apparent self-mockery in the poem, "When Will I Return":

When will I return
to the tightly organised
complexly structured
image and expression
rich in flying tangential associations
that buttress, ore-vein or embroider
and sing with a complexity of feeling
and richness of expression
(p. 13)

Consequently, the themes are not far-fetched. This does not, however, make the poems simplistic. On the contrary, these short poems derive their strength from a certain metaphoric intensity which enables them to appeal at more than one level of meaning simultaneously. This quality derives largely from a certain economy in the use of images which is exhibited in two patterns. One is in the form of an extended metaphor. A simple image is elaborated throughout an entire poem or a situation where a short poem consists of just a series of related images, thereby deriving its force from the combined associative potentials of these images. This pattern finds expression in "How are the Shoots of Affection Withered?" where the image of a diseased plant with withering tendrils, droopy branches, blighted buds etc. is used to capture the political climate in South Africa. The second pattern is displayed in the elegy "For Frank Teruggi":

> A single rose
> a single candle
> a black coffin
> a few mourners
> weeping
> (p. 89)

In aid of directness of expression, the poet displays a consistently keen sense of audience which manifests in a certain striving for audience participation. Such audience anticipation takes the form of short declamatory lines as in the poem, "Stop":

> Stop
> I ask you to think for a moment
> to think of pain
> of hunger,
> to think of people who are not free,
> to think of death . . .
>
> Stop.
> Now.
> Think.
> Now.
> Then stand
> And lift your fist
> and shout your anger
> and your resolution;
> Shout "Africa"
> Three times
> Now.
> Africa.
> Africa.
> Africa.
> (pp. 53–4)

By the time we come to the end of such poems, the poet is no longer a lone voice! We are compelled to join him.

By far the more involved dimension to Brutus' poetic method in this volume is a certain sense of dialectics which presents experiences and issues in their essential contradictoriness, thereby resolving certain key oppositions. In individual poems, no single emotion is allowed such dominance as to overwhelm the audience in an undirectional empathy. Hope is counterposed to despair, courage to cowardice, tenderness to violence, freedom to unfreedom, love to hatred, justice to injustice and beauty to ugliness. It is in the ability to project and resolve these binary oppositions that the real strength of Brutus' verse resides.

The ultimate revolutionary significance of *Stubborn Hope* is to be sought in the sheer proximity between the directness of its unarguably artistic essence and specific aspects of the actual struggle against apartheid. Here, more than previously in Brutus, the poetic word conjoins with political action and both are united by the poet's commitment to freedom and justice.

The Poetic Essence of National Liberation: Agostinho Neto's *Sacred Hope*

It is not possible to begin to understand the poetry of Agostinho Neto outside the context of his deep involvement in and championship of the struggle for independence in Angola. Although a medical doctor, Neto, like Che Guevara in Cuba, devoted himself to the larger task of healing his people of the exploitation and oppression of Portuguese colonialism and its fascist repression. For this commitment, however, Neto had to suffer endless persecution and numerous prison terms without trial. In 1951, Neto was arrested for collecting signatures for the Stockholm Peace Appeal; in 1955, he was arrested for leading a youth movement in Portugal; in 1960, Neto, now leader of the MPLA, was again arrested and at a rally organized by the people of his village in protest, thirty people were killed by Portuguese colonial police. He was subsequently "exported" from his country first to a prison in Lisbon and then to Cape Verde, Santo Antão and Santiago where he continued to be held under house arrest. On his release in 1962, Neto, who had escaped to the MPLA headquarters in Leopoldville, Congo Kinshasa, was elected president of the movement.[11] It was in this capacity that he continued leading the armed struggle until Angola became independent in 1975. It is against this background that the sense of persecution in Neto's verse is to be understood and appreciated.

> Neto's crime was an articulate projection to Salazar's cynical and brutal use of the Angolan people – a transgression which is scarcely surprising. The plight of the people of Angola is not a school for indifference, and one of the dominant themes of Neto's poetry is the relationship between his personal predicament and the experience of the people among whom he grew up.[12]

The significance of Neto's poetry in the struggle for Angolan independence is subsumed within the overall active involvement of literature and culture in the strategy of the MPLA. Right from the onset, Angolan youth recognized the necessity to wage the liberation struggle as much at the political and military levels as at the cultural level. In the latter sphere, poetry played a prominent role. By 1948, a group of Angolan students studying in Portugal had founded the magazine *Message*, in which they published patriotic verse, rejecting colonial values and reaffirming the dignity of the Angolan people.

> Under the rallying cry . . . "Let's Discover Angola", they rejected the colonial values. Poetry became the principal means by which they struck roots among the people, writing for the people, making of the despair and suffering of the people on the sterile lands and in the shanty towns the material of poetry, rediscovering a land and customs which had been deformed in the distorting mirror of the oppressor, and creating a modern national literature which gave voice to the people's aspirations.[13]

Beyond this affirmative role, it is on record that patriotic poetry transposed into war songs was widely invoked by young MPLA combatants in the battle field: Neto's poetry occupied a prominent position in this active deployment of art in the service of struggle.

The poems collected in *Sacred Hope* span several years in Neto's career as well as various stages in the struggle for national liberation. Consequently, the themes range from the need to use valuable elements from the past to shape the future to reflections on the deprivations and sufferings of the people under colonial rule.

As in the work of Brutus, however, it is hope in the future that forges the essential unity among these poems.

For Neto, the historical experience of the people is the first condition of art, hence he writes from a position of absolute immersion in their plight. His voice is their voice and it reveals the various dimensions of their plight under colonial tutelage. In this respect, there is a strong sense of realism in the poems which is able to capture the subtle nuances of life among the common folk while constantly relating this to the relations of dominance and subordination which define the colonial equation. In the poem, "Saturday in the Muceques", he writes:

> *Muceques* are poor neighbourhoods
> of poor people
> Comes Saturday
> and they become a part of life itself
> transformed into despair
> into hope and mystic anxiety . . .
>
> Anxiety
> in the skeleton of wooden poles
> threateningly inclined
> holding up a heavy zinc roof

and in backyards
sown with excrement and bad smells
in furniture dirty with grease
in tattered sheets
in mattressless beds
(pp. 7–9)

Yet in depicting the nasty and brutish conditions under which the colonized live, Neto does not succumb to despair but sees the people's suffering as a launching pad for liberation action.

In men
seethes the desire to make the supreme effort
so that Man
may be reborn in each man
and hope
no longer becomes
the lamentation of the crowd.
(p. 9)

Much as he is engaged with the realities of the colonial "present", Neto's verse is also a means of positing a cultural antithesis to the hegemony of colonial values. Thus, the landscape of his verse is furnished by prominent landmarks in Angola in particular and Africa in general. The River Congo, the Kalahari Desert and the Maiombe forest become means of authenticating experience and reinforcing the poet's rootedness in the identity of his people. In this respect, Neto's verse shares with Negritude poetry a certain nostalgic recreation of rural Africa and its vital rhythms. But for Neto, affirmation of racial cultural identity is a complement to liberation action, not a substitute for it.

His is not idle romantic affirmation but a resolve to retrieve continental identity and pride through struggle, addressed to compatriots in the entire black world.

Now is the hour to march together
bravely
to the world of
all men

Receive this message
as a fraternal greeting
oh any black of the streets and bush villages
blood of the same blood
(p. 30)

A keen awareness of the exploitative essence of colonialism pervades these poems. The stock instruments of this exploitation – forced labour, the train, police batons etc. – are invoked to animate the landscape. Images of men sweating under forced labour, of railway workers "under the weight of the engine and the din of the third class" build up into a gigantic metaphor of exploitation of Africans by the Portuguese.

> Long months separate them from theirs
> and they go filled with longing
> and dread
> but they sing
>
> Tired
> exhausted by work
> but they sing
>
> Filled with injustice
> silent in their innermost souls
> (p. 24)

The poet's identification with the exploited and downtrodden is complemented by his experience of the brutality of the colonialists. The most persistent indicator of this brutality is his numerous incarcerations and forced exiles. In this respect, Neto's prison poems lament a certain sense of alienation from his people, an alienation which finds concrete expression in the recurrent longing for the warmth and affection of loved ones. The attendant yearning for love is not just personal and amorous but collective and ultimately political.

> Against the dilemma of today
> of being submissive or persecuted
> are our days of sacrifice
> and audacity
> for the right
> to live thinking to live acting
> freely humanly
>
> Between dreams and desire
> when shall we see each other
> late or early
> tell me love
> More justly even grows
> the longing to be
> with our peoples
> today always and ever more
> free free free.
> (p. 62)

The poet cherishes freedom, not for its own sake and at all costs but in the context of his people's struggle to regain their dignity after the years of humiliation and denigration. Consequently, even in prison, the poet's attitude is one of stoic defiance and pride towards his persecutors.

even if they beat me
I will say nothing
even if they offer me riches
I will say nothing
even if the *palmatoria* crushes my fingers
I will say nothing
even if they offer me freedom
I will say nothing
(p. 63)

Yet in spite of the repression of armed tyranny, hope emerges as the dominant theme in most of Neto's poems. The constant reaffirmation of optimism and faith in the future is not just an anodyne to drown the pangs of present adversity but a way of imbuing the sacrifices implicit in the struggle for freedom with a sense of purpose. The struggle becomes a painful process of building for future success; looking forward to a time when the poet/combatant shall lose his anonymity and emerge distinguished in a new "catalogue of human glory".

Neto's poetry is characterized by a general contemplative tone which is unhurried, painstaking and shrewd in its attempt not to compromise the organic proximity between the poet and his people. Consequently, the emotions which permeate and exude from his verse are those of patriotic heroism and sympathetic identification with those who bear the burden of oppression.

My mother
   (all black mothers
   whose sons have gone)
You taught me to wait and hope
as you hoped in difficult hours . . .

It is I my mother
hope is us
your children
gone for a faith that sustains life
(p. 1)

Nevertheless, Neto is not sentimental. Nor does he wallow in self-pity or succumb to the humiliating weight of tyranny. It is this stoicism that is powerfully captured in the frequent occurrence of the phrase "with dry eyes" in many of the poems.

At times, however, the general contemplative tone yields to an exuberant lyricism that is almost celebrative and euphoric as we witness in the poem, "The Bush Path". Yet even in such moments of apparent emotional outburst, the poet never loses grip of his historic mission. Such sudden bursts of vigour become invitations to compatriots for intensification of the freedom struggle.

Let us start action vigorous male intelligent
which answers tooth for tooth eye for eye
man for man
come vigorous action
of the people's army of the liberation of men
come whirlwinds to shatter this passiveness . . .

Let us not wait for heroes
let us be heroes
uniting our voices and our arms
each at his duty
and defend inch by inch our land
(pp. 74–75)

Structurally, Neto's poetry thrives on a lyrical repetitiveness of images
and syntactic patterns in a manner reminiscent of motifs in jazz. In
"Aspiration", the constant repetition is an instrument for heaping up
evidence in support of a particular point.

John was lynched
his brother whipped on his bare back
his wife gagged
and his son continued in ignorance.
(p. 26)

The recurrent images are those associated with right (blackness, the colour
of poverty and also of dignity), violence and liberation. Throughout, the
evocative power of the images is enhanced by the scientist's keen eye for
precision and details.

One consequence of this keen attention to structure is a strong sense of
rhythm which comes across even in translation. But the pursuit of rhythmic
effect is never at the expense of the poet's political commitment and
ideological alignment. If anything, rhythm is a device for drawing and
focusing attention on specific aspects of his larger historical preoccupation.

Fires
    dance
        tom-tom

Rhythm in light
rhythm in colour
rhythm in sound
rhythm in movement
rhythm in the bleeding cracks of bare feet
rhythm in torn off nails
But rhythm
rhythm

Oh sorrowful voices of Africa!
(p. 25)

Perhaps the most trenchant summation of Neto's achievement is contained in Basil Davidson's prefatory remarks to *Sacred Hope*: "Chants of sorrow, these are also songs of joy. Poems of departure, they are also poems of arrival."

Poetry as Political Polemic: Odia Ofeimun's *The Poet Lied*.

Odia Ofeimun belongs in what I had earlier referred to as the "left hand" of the Nigerian literary tradition. Having come into adolescence with the dawn and early sunset of Nigeria's nationhood, Ofeimun (born in 1950) belongs to the generation of Nigerian writers for whom overt radical political commitment can be regarded as a given. For this generation which includes Niyi Osundare, Ossie Enekwe, Funso Aiyejina, Dubem Okafor and the much younger Harry Garuba, the civil war of 1967–70 symbolized the psychological, moral and physical devastation not only of the newly independent nation but also of their own hopes and expectations as adolescents in an emergent society. For Ofeimun, however, the compulsion towards a radical stance is increased by certain biographical facts. He has worked variously as a reporter, factory labourer, clerk, and party official at different times, coming to higher education largely as a struggling man.

The Poet Lied is therefore his attempt to come to terms, through an artistic medium, with the reality of the Nigerian civil war and its aftermath society with its succession of deceitful military regimes. More important from an artistic/literary point of view is the fact that *The Poet Lied* inaugurates a fresh departure in Nigerian (and African) poetry, namely, the use of poetry as criticism of poetry. The freshness and desirability of this departure derives from the fact that it holds out the vital promise of banishing the redundant and artificial dichotomy which bourgeois scholarship has maintained between literature and politics.

More directly, Ofeimun's title poem is at a general level an attack on that brand of bourgeois individualist poetry which, in dwelling on the collective tragedy of the Nigerian civil war, adopts an aloof, personalist and ambiguous stance. There is now abundant evidence to confirm the view that *The Poet Lied* is largely an artistic critique of J. P. Clark's *Casualties* which also deals with the civil war.[14] In his own collection, J. P. Clark displays characteristic bourgeois attachment to abstract moral ideals and pretension to objectivity. Consequently he sacrifices the collective essence of the national tragedy on the altar of personal lamentations and cynical moralizing.

Despite protestations to the contrary by Clark, Ofeimun's title poem can only be read as an attack on Clark's war poems to the extent that the high points of its thematic indictments correspond to the verifiable weaknesses in Clark's presentation of the war experience and the underlying ideological alignment of that presentation. The "poet" who forms the target of the artistic bludgeoning in the title poem can only remain a type.

He is variously accused of aloofness ("He meant to escape the acute fever/the immoderacy of the rabble") and inhuman indifference to a crushing national disaster.

> For him as for the many handy serfs
> to whose lot it fell
> to whitewash the public idols
> with termite-eaten insides,
> there was no place for raised fingers
> even when human adders
> gobbled the peace of the market place
> even when famine snaked through
> his neighbours' homesteads
> he saw no need for raised fingers . . .[15]

The poetic critique also extends to matters like the appropriateness of craft to the experiences and situations explored.

> When he wrote, he pasted weather reports,
> colourless snippety, thumps of items
> about friends who died, comrades slain
> in the frenzied billows of civil strife.
> (p. 27)

In his bid to posit, in dialectical terms, an alternative to the kind of artistic and ideological falsifications that he indicts in his title poem, Ofeimun includes in his volume specific poetic *statements* on the political crises and civil war that ravaged Nigeria between 1964 and 1970. Whether he is dwelling on the more public issues raised by these experiences or lamenting personal losses of friends and relations, there is in Ofeimun's verse a certain attention to lyricism, to structural coherence and an acuteness and urgency of tone which reinforces the collective nature of the tragic experiences and reaffirms the organic relationship between poetry and politics. In "Exodus '67", a poem on the onset of violence in the Nigerian polity, he writes:

> *the iroko is spitting fire*
> *if you have a child strap him to your bosom*
>
> Chapters that the writing down would demean
> Chapters that rend our talking drums
> Chapters that tongues will fail,
> ram down the crags of memory
> (p. 16)

Although he experienced the war from the Federal side of the battleline, Ofeimun writes from a patriotic nationalist stance. Thus, he is anguished by the contrast between the relative peace and normalcy in the Federal areas and the suffering, anguish and devastation on the Biafran side.

> Over there, tuppence pieces
> of shattered limbs write
> the vanity of outspoken shells . . .
>
> Here, maniacal orgies
> topple the nights
> to provide us with alibis? . . .
>
> We lynch the memory of our dead
> in unthinking cups of wine
> we chew the mistakes of our dead
> to make sure the stench of the past
> will never really die.
>
> A blade of disgust
> confounds my dangling hopes.
> (p. 19)

Far from degenerating into a utopian nationalist, however, Ofeimun is able to use his poetry to explore the question of guilt in the national tragedy within a framework informed by class consciousness and analysis. While J. P. Clark had conceived of all and sundry (irrespective of class position) as "casualties" of the war, Ofeimun makes a clear distinction and lays the blame for the holocaust squarely at the doorstep of the Nigerian ruling class:

> The guilty are too well-fed to pass
> through the needle's eye of our scorn
> the noose of public contempt
> hangs idle at the market place
>
> A halo, a brazen halo
> fashioned by praise-singers and clowns
> distinguishes the head-gear
> of patent nation-wreckers . . .
> (p. 30)

Beyond the civil war, we get in *The Poet Lied* what amounts to the most engagingly direct and accomplished patriotic verse in Nigeria to date, taking as its object the various aspects of the Nigerian experience in neo-colonialism. Just as the civil war provides its launching pad, the post-war society with all its aberrations – the squandered oil boom, the scandalous social inequalities, the ethical morass and tyranny form the crux of Ofeimun's agenda. For Ofeimun, these conjunctures dictate an uncompromising commitment.

> I cannot blind myself
> to putrefying carcass in the market place

pulling giant vultures
from the sky
(p. 1)

In this context, poetry becomes a medium of communion between the poet and his fellow travellers along the road to national regeneration. The poet's responsibility is to communicate to his fellows from the wellspring of those experiences which define the conflictual essence of their experience, challenging them to alter themselves and their circumstances.

Ofeimun writes from a position of impeccable patriotism akin to but contextually different from what we have identified in the instances of Dennis Brutus and Agostinho Neto. Unlike his older compatriots (J. P. Clark, Wole Soyinka, Christopher Okigbo), the reality of the Nigerian nation is not at issue in Ofeimun's poetry. His sense of patriotism finds expression through the familiar archetypal love metaphor in which land and woman become interchangeable. "A garland of subversive litanies/ should answer these morbid landscapes/my land, my woman."

The overriding consciousness that informs most of the poems in this volume is a critical one. The poet focuses his critical gaze on a variety of aberrations in Nigeria's neo-colonial society ranging from graft and corruption to the hypocrisy of the ruling class. These poems are a searing critique of an aberrant society.

We hurtle down
driven by storms they could not harness
our fathers who went before us
along the same potholed roads
we hurtle down
breaking and getting broken on our way
(p. 34)

As a logical consequence of this ardent critical temper, however, Ofeimun confidently affirms his confidence in the possibility of revolutionary change in the Nigerian society. In effect, there is a strong visionary quality to his art.

In the new day
when the whole land grunts swollen
with new births
and snails have changed house
and the rivers have changed valleys
and we who stood on our side of the lagoon
have no landmarks by which to know
the other side
in the rains high flood and thunder
we will not cry world's end
(p. 31)

The formal accomplishment of Ofeimun's poetry derives from a combination of two aesthetic strands: a vibrant echo of oral verse forms reminiscent of Okigbo and a strong sense of realism which harnesses the contradictions of daily experience to poetic effect. The former strand furnishes the distinctive collective voice of the poems, creating a cognitive context in which the entire Nigerian national society shrinks to the size of a large family. Consequently, even personal losses and disappointments acquire meaning only within the context of a deep sense of collective loss. Echoes of the late Okigbo recur in the frequent adoption of the town-crier's mien, the invocation of aspects of rural lore to complement and spotlight the decadent atmosphere of the urban area. On the other hand, there is an unmistakable sense of realism in the poems which relentlessly underlines the poet's proximity to and familiarity with the life experiences of his country's masses. This strategy is complemented by Ofeimun's manifest ideological alignment linking him with the people.

In the final analysis, then, Ofeimun emerges as a radical nationalist poet whose ideological alignment finds homologous expression in an equally involved tone and a disturbingly stark invocation of the realities of life among the oppressed masses of Nigeria.

Notes

1. George Thomson, *Marxism and Poetry* (New York: International Publishers, 1946) p. 65.
2. Ibid., p. 58.
3. Denys Thompson, *The Uses of Poetry* (Cambridge: Cambridge University Press, 1974) p. 171.
4. Ngugi Wa Thiong'o also distinguishes between these two types of writers in *Writers in Politics* (London: Heinemann, 1981) p. 75.
5. Interview with Biodun Jeyifo et al. in *The African Guardian*, 20 February 1986, p. 44.
6. Interview with William Thompson in *Ufahamu* vol. 12, no. 2, 1983, pp. 76–7.
7. Interview with Jeyifo.
8. Dennis Brutus, *Stubborn Hope* (London: Heinemann, 1978). Quotations refer to this edition.
9. In this particular poem, Brutus alludes to such writers as Alex La Guma, Lewis Nkosi, Cosmo Pieterse and Ezekiel Mphalele, sardonically and humorously savouring their tireless efforts in pursuit of freedom even in exile. Brutus himself lives in exile in the US.
10. Interview with Jeyifo.
11. These biographical details are contained in Marga Holness's Introduction to Agostinho Neto, *Sacred Hope* (Dar es Salaam: Tanzania Publishing House, 1974) trans. Marga Holness.
12. Arthur Merwin, "Agostinho Neto: To Name a Wrong", in Ulli Beier (ed.) *Introduction to African Literature* (Harlow, Essex: Longman, 1979), pp. 142–5.

13. Marga Holness, Introduction to Neto, *Sacred Hope* p. xx. All further page references are to this edition.

14. When *The Poet Lied* was published, J. P. Clark threatened Longman Ltd. with legal action, alleging that he is "the poet" of the title. Consequently, Longman discontinued the distribution of the book in Nigeria.

15. Odia Ofeimun, *The Poet Lied* (London: Longman, 1980). p. 26.

9   Beyond Decolonization

The main thrust of the discussion so far can now be garnered but only in the form of tentative projections on the challenges confronting literary theory, criticism and pedagogy in the African setting.

As the global social and economic picture increasingly reflects the class configuration in capitalist societies; as nations of the world resolve themselves more and more into clubs of haves and have-nots, roughly corresponding to a North–South equation, and as the more affluent and developed nations consciously and aggressively guard their gains and interests in the face of growing poverty in the less privileged societies, the challenge confronting members of the less privileged societies can only be that of a rigorous application of mind to matter. As workers whose stock-in-trade is ideas, the African intelligentsia must realize that the very ideas that are responsible for our underdevelopment cannot liberate us from that condition.

For the literary scholar, this unsettling realization must compel not only the adoption of an alternative anti-imperialist theoretical framework but also, more fundamentally, a relocation of the frame of discourse. Even if literary discourse elsewhere were to be consigned to the region of superstructural practice, the political and historical predication of African literature in general dictates that literary discourse must drink from the same pool as political and economic discourse. It is not possible, even it if appears convenient, to practise literary theory and criticism as an abstract, value-free and politically sanitized undertaking in a continent which is the concentration of most of the world's afflictions and disasters. These realities are those of squalor, desertification and drought, hunger, disease and monumental ignorance coupled with artificial macro-economic problems foisted on the masses of Africans by a greedy ruling class in collaboration with the merchants of debts and cannons in New York, Washington, Tokyo, Paris and London. It is not possible to talk of literature and beauty or even to remain intelligent and credible in any area of academic discourse without taking our bearings from these unsettling realities. The approach which these problems dictate for literary and cultural discourse in general is not simply that of scuttling into the warm embrace of ancestry for aestheic values and artistic models in the name of decolonization.

On the contrary, an anti-imperialist consciousness must permeate the series of related practices that we know as African literature: creative praxis, theoretical, critical and pedagogical practices respectively. African writers, some of them unconsciously, have continued to objectify the social, historical and psychological implications of imperialism and neo-colonialism in their various works. For these writers, creativity is praxis, a mode of intervention to change reality through inspiring a new consciousness of the African condition. This is why the essays, interviews and political actions of most of our writers have posited them variously as teachers, prophets, moral stabilizers, activists and so on. *This point of literary creativity as a form of praxis is the starting point for an anti-imperialist aesthetics of African literature.*

Theoretical practice, in order to complement the effort of the writers, must of necessity begin from a materialist epistemology, exploring the aesthetic implications of an ideological antithesis to imperialism. Such theorizing, as ideo-praxis, should draw inspiration from the thoughts of those like Fanon, Cabral, Ngugi, Mondlane – all of whom have underlined the place of culture in the struggle for an alternative African society. In addition, such theoretical practice must link up with the heritage of radical thought from Marx and Engels to the most contemporary postulations in radical aesthetics from all over the world. The African past with its rich heritage of artistic and philosophical models can only form part of the material for the reformulation of an anti-imperialist aesthetics, for a truly dialectical aesthetics must of necessity take into account the interaction between the past and the present which is the basis of the idea of tradition in the first place.

At the level of critical practice, the challenge is for a political criticism even though all criticism is somehow politically predicated. To the extent that the various works in African literature are fictional mediations of the contemporary African experience, critical explications of these texts must progress from the known to the relatively *unknown*. The need to historicize our explications and evaluations dictates that critical practice insists on the dialectical relationship between the *context* of the work and its specific *content* and *form*. This methodology ensures that there is a marriage between theory and practice, thus removing the halo of mystique that has continued to surround bourgeois criticism of African literature to date. In effect, we must insist that the experience and formal realization of literature is a knowable area, not one of metaphysical inscrutability that can only be commented on through timid statements. If, in referential terms, our literary and general social criticism derive from the same source (i.e. the material conditions of life of the African people), the way to ending the present alienation of our literary discourse from social discourse will have been opened.

These observations have far-reaching pedagogical implications. The teaching of African literature in African universities, colleges and schools constitutes one of the most effective ways of transmitting the values contained in that literature into the consciousness of the young and the uninformed. The world view of those who fashion the literature syllabi in most of Africa's educational systems is conditioned by a conception of literature that is colonial. Literature for them is a means of perpetuating the existing relations of domination and subordination that have kept Africa in perennial bondage. The dominant bourgeois pedagogy has merely consecrated this conception into a credo that informs the annual churning out of graduates for whom the study of literature constitutes part of a programme of admission into the culture and value system of the United States, Britain, France, or even Portugal. As unemployment queues lengthen and privileges accruing to fresh graduates contract, bourgeois pedagogy is becoming increasingly dysfunctional. An alternative pedagogy, a pedagogy of the oppressed, is urgently called for. Such a libertarian pedagogy would not only challenge the values that inform today's curricula of literary studies in Africa but will replace "neutral" texts with those that present the African experience in its starkness and from a class-partisan perspective. The understanding of reality with a view to changing it should be the object of the new pedagogy of African literature. In addition, literary study must take into cognizance the literary productions of the peasants in the rural areas and the workers and unemployed in the urban slums and ghettos.

Ultimately, the effort to create, theorize on, criticize, enjoy and participate in literature in Africa (as elsewhere) ought to be one and the same with the struggle to banish those conditions which dehumanize humankind and threaten the nobility of art itself. The business of literature ought to begin from the creation of the conditions necessary for economic and political freedom, for it is from these that cultural freedom flows. A literary culture that sets itself this vital task cannot but be defined in rigorous activist and radical political terms that go far beyond the bourgeois insistence on superstructural decolonization. To insist otherwise is to advance the cause of imperialism and deepen the exploitation and oppression of our peoples.

Select Bibliography

Primary Texts Studied

Achebe, Chinua, *Things Fall Apart* (London: Heinemann, 1959).
—— *Arrow of God* (London: Heinemann, 1974).
Brutus, Dennis, *Stubborn Hope* (London: Heinemann, 1978).
Neto, Agostinho, *Sacred Hope* (Dar es Salaam: Tanzania Publishing House, 1974).
Ngugi Wa Thiong'o, *Petals of Blood* (London: Heinemann, 1977).
—— and Micere, Mugo, *The Trial of Dedan Kimathi* (London: Heinemann, 1976).
Ngugi wa Thiong'o and Ngugi wa Mirii, *I Will Marry When I Want* (London: Heinemann, 1982).
Ofeimun, Odia, *The Poet Lied* (London: Longman, 1983).
Osofisan, Femi, *Once Upon Four Robbers* (Ibadan: Bio Educational Services, 1980).
—— *Morountodun* in *Morountodun & Other Plays* (Lagos: Longman, 1982).

Theoretical and Critical Sources

Achebe, Chinua, *Morning Yet on Creation Day* (London: Heinemann, 1975).
Ake, Claude, *Revolutionary Pressures in Africa* (London: Zed Press, 1978).
Amuta, Chidi, "Criticism, Ideology and Society: The Instance of Nigerian Literature", *Ufahamu*, vol. XII, no. 2, 1983.
—— "Towards a Popular Literary Culture in Nigeria" *Critical Arts*, vol. 3, no. 1, 1983.
—— "The African Writer and the Anti-Imperialist Struggle: Ngugi's Prison Memoirs", *Journal of African Marxists*, no. 6, 1984.
—— *Towards a Sociology of African Literature* (Oguta: Zim Pan African Publishers, 1986).
Armah, Ayi Kwei, "Larsony or Fiction as Criticism of Fiction", *Positive Review*, no. 1, 1978.
—— "Masks and Marx: The Marxist Ethos vis-à-vis African Revolutionary Theory and Praxis", *Présence Africaine*, no. 131, 1984.
Aronson, Ronald, "Historical Materialism, Answer to Marxism's Crisis", *New Left Review*, no. 152, 1985.
Awoonor, Kofi, *The Breast of the Earth* (New York/Enugu: NOK, 1975).
Barthes, Roland, *Critical Essays*, trans. Richard Howard (Evanston: Northwestern University Press, 1972).
Bennet, Tony, *Formalism and Marxism* (London: Eyre Methuen, 1980).

Cabral, Amilcar, *Return to the Source: Selected Speeches* (New York/London: Monthly Review Press, 1973).

—— *Unity and Struggle*, trans. Michael Wolfers (London: Heinemann, 1980).

Chinweizu, et al. *Toward the Decolonization of African Literature* (Enugu: Fourth Dimension, 1980).

—— *The West and the Rest of Us* (Lagos: NOK, 1978).

Craig, David (ed.) *Marxists on Literature* (Harmondsworth: Penguin, 1975).

Eagleton, Terry, *Criticism and Ideology* (London: Verso, 1978).

—— *Literary Theory: An Introduction* (Oxford: Blackwell, 1985).

—— "Capitalism, Modernism and Post-Modernism", *New Left Review*, no. 152, 1985.

Egudu, Romanus, *Four Modern West African Poets* (New York: NOK, 1977).

—— *Modern African Poetry and the African Predicament* (London: Macmillan, 1978).

Emenyonu, Ernest, *The Rise of the Igbo Novel* (Ibadan: O.U.P. 1978).

Fanon, Frantz, *Toward the African Revolution* (New York: Grove Press, 1967).

—— *Black Skin, White Masks* (New York: Grove Press, 1967).

—— *The Wretched of the Earth* (London: Lawrence & Wishart, 1979).

Fox, Ralph, *The Novel and the People* (London: Lawrence & Wishart, 1979).

Gerard, Albert, "Is Anything Wrong With African Literary Studies?" in Bernth Lindfors (ed.) *Research Priorities in African Literatures*, (Munich/New York: Hans Zell Publishers, 1984).

Gramsci, Antonio, *Selections from Prison Notes* (London: Lawrence & Wishart, 1982).

Hauser, Arnold, *The Social History of Art*, vol. 1, trans. Stanley Godman (London: Routledge & Kegan Paul, 1977).

Hegel, G. W. F. *On Art, Religion, Philosophy*, ed. J. Glenn Grey (New York/Evanston: Harper & Row, 1970).

Hsu, Kai-Yu, *The Chinese Literary Scene* (Harmondsworth: Penguin, 1976).

Irele, Abiola, "Literary Criticism in the Nigerian Context", *The Guardian*, 15 June 1985.

Iyasere, Solomon, "African Oral Tradition – Criticism as Performance: A Ritual", *African Literature Today*, no. 11, 1980.

Jameson, Fredric, *Marxism and Form* (Princeton: Princeton University Press, 1974).

—— *The Political Unconscious* (New York: Cornell University Press, 1981).

—— "Post Modernism, or the Cultural Logic of Late Capitalism", *New Left Review*, no. 146, 1985.

Jeyifo, Biodun, *The Truthful Lie: Essays* (London/Port of Spain: New Beacon, 1985).

Kharin, Yo, *Fundamentals of Dialectics*, trans. Karstantin Kostrov (Moscow: Progress Publishers, 1981).

La Guma, Alex, "Culture and Liberation", *World Literature Written in English*, vol. 18, no. 1, 1979.

Lenin, V. I. *Critical Remarks on the National Question* (Moscow: Progress Publishers, 1976).

—— *On Literature and Art* (Moscow: Progress Publishers, 1967).

Lindfors, Bernth. "The Blind Men and the Elephant", *African Literature Today*, no. 7, 1975.

—— "Armah's Histories", *African Literature Today*, no. 11, 1980.

—— "Are There Any National Literatures in Sub-Saharan Africa Yet?", *English in Africa*, vol. 2, no. 2, 1975.

Lukacs, Georg, *The Theory of the Novel* (Cambridge, Mass.: MIT Press, 1978).

—— *Writer and Critic: Essays*, ed. and trans. D. Khan (New York: Grosset and Dunlap, 1971).

Macebuh, Stanley, "African Aesthetics in Traditional African Art", *Okike*, no. 5, 1974.

Machery, Pierre and Balibar Etienne, "On Literature as an Ideological Form" in Robert Young (ed.) *Untying the Text* (Boston: Routledge & Kegan Paul, 1981).

Mao Tse-Tung, "Talks at the Yenan Forum on Literature and the Arts" in *Selected Works*, vol. 3 (Peking: Foreign Language Press, 1967).

Marx, Karl and Engels, Frederick, *On Literature and Art* (Moscow: Progress Publishers, 1976).

Mativo, Kyalo, "Ideology in African Philosophy and Literature II", *Ufahamu*, vol. 8, no. 1, 1978.

Mbiti, John, *African Religions and Philosophy* (London: Heinemann, 1969).

Ngara, Emmanuel, *Art and Ideology in the African Novel* (London: Heinemann, 1985).

Ngugi wa Thiong'o, *Homecoming: Essays* (London: Heinemann, 1972).

—— *Writers in Politics* (London: Heinemann, 1982).

—— *Barrel of a Pen* (London/Port of Spain: New Beacon, 1985).

—— "The Language of African Literature", *New Left Review*, no. 125, 1985.

Nkrumah, Kwame, *Class Struggle in Africa* (New York: International Publishers, 1970).

Nnolim, Charles, "An African Literature Aesthetic: A Prolegomena", *Bashiru*, vol. 17, 1976.

Obiechina, Emmanuel, *An African Popular Literature* (Cambridge: Cambridge University Press, 1973).

—— *Culture, Tradition and Society in the West African Novel* (Cambridge: Cambridge University Press, 1975).

Ogunba, Oyin, *The Movement of Transition* (Ibadan: University of Ibadan Press, 1975).

Ogunbiyi, Yemi (ed.) *Drama and Theatre in Nigeria* (Lagos: Nigeria Magazine, 1981).

Okpewho, Isidore, "The Aesthetics of Old African Art", *Okike*. no. 8. 1975.

—— "The Principles of Traditional African Art", *The Journal of Aesthetics and Art Criticism*, vol. 35, no. 3, 1977.

Onoge, Omafume, "The Possibilities of a Radical Sociology of African Literature" in D. I. Nwoga (ed.) *Literature and Modern West African Culture* (Benin: Ethiope, 1978).

—— "Towards a Marxist Sociology of African Literature", *Ife Studies in African Literature and the Arts* no. 2, 1984.

Shaw, Gregory, "Art and Dialectics in the Work of Wilson Harris", *New Left Review*, no. 153, 1985.

Slaughter, Cliff, *Marxism, Ideology and Literature* (London/Basingstoke: Macmillan, 1980).

Solomon, Maynard (ed.) *Marxism and Art* (New York: Vintage Books, 1973).

Soyinka, Wole, "Neo-Tarzanism: The Poetics of Pseudo-Tradition", *Transition*, no. 48, 1975.

—— *Myth, Literature and the African World* (Cambridge: Cambridge University Press, 1976).

—————— "The Critic and Society: Barthes, Leftocracy and Other Mythologies", Inaugural Lecture, University of Ife, 1980.

Taiwo, Oladele, *Culture and the Nigerian Novel* (London: Macmillan, 1976).

Thompson, Denys, *The Uses of Poetry* (Cambridge: Cambridge University Press, 1979).

Thomson, George, *Marxism and Poetry* (New York: International Publishers, 1946).

Trotsky, Leon, *Literature and Revolution* (Cambridge: MIT Press, 1965).

Vanslove, V. V., "On Content and Form as a Reflection of Life", *Marxist–Leninist Aesthetics and the Arts* (Moscow: Progress Publishers, 1980).

Vazquez, Adolfo Sanchez, *Art and Society: Essays in Marxist Aesthetics* (New York: Monthly Review Press, 1973).

Willet, John (trans. and ed.) *Brecht on Theatre* (London: Eyre Methuen, 1978).

Zed Press, *Independent Kenya* (London: Zed Press, 1982).

Index

Achebe, Chinua 122; *Arrow of God* and *Things Fall Apart* 127-8, 130-6
aesthetics 30-49, 50, 105-7, 120-1, 198
African world view, myth of 37-41, 43-4
alignment and commitment 114-17
anti-imperialist: consciousness 18, 198; struggle, nature of 6-8
art-for-art's sake criticism 21-2, 114
audience and writer 107-12
axes of criticism 13-14

bourgeois criticism 17-31, 59
Brutus, Dennis: *Stubborn Hope* 178-85

Cabral, Amilcar on national culture 89, 93-6, 134
class-ideological axis of criticism 14
class question in African literature 68-72
colonialist criticism 3, 18-21, 36
commitment 114-17, 155, 177-8
content and form 8-9, 83, 86-9, 129, 198
context 8-9, 83-5, 87-9, 129, 198
criticism, ideology and society 13-16
cultural anthropological criticism 22-3, 26

decolonization rhetoric 6-7, 33, 41, 46-9, 104
definition of African literature, quest for 2, 104-7 *see also* language question
dialectics and literary theory 77-100; categories 80-9, 129, 198
dissonant harmony of social experience 8
drama and revolution 154-74

Ekpe festival dance 14-15
ethno-criticism 23, 41, 43-6

Fanon, Frantz, on national culture: *The Wretched of the Earth* 89-93
Festac consciousness 22, 64
form and content 8-9, 83, 86-9, 129, 198

"high literature 110-11

historical materialism 60, 74-5
history: and African literature 80-3; and narrative in the African novel 125-52

ideology/ideological: affinities 12-31; analysis 4-5; and politics in African literature 56-61, 63; *see also* drama; Marxist; Ngugi; poetry
idyllic view of primitive Africa 2, 34-5, 118-19
intuitive criticism 4

language question 99-100, 112-14
liberal relativism 3-4, 36, 42-3, 46-7
linguistic indigenization 99-100, 112-14

Marxist: aesthetics 52-6; criticism of African literature 59-61; ideology and African literature 57-9, 62-3, 69; theoretical limitations of 73-4; theory and anti-imperialist struggle 10-11
Mau Mau struggle and Kenyan literature 58, 97, 115-16, 146-7, 157-61, 164, 166
messianism 29, 121

national question in African literature 61-8, 70, 126-7
Neto, Agostinho: *Sacred Hope* 185-91
Ngugi Wa Thiong'o 71; *Petals of Blood* 128, 143-52; radical ideological stance of 58, 89, 96-100, 105, 112; Ngugi and Micere Mugo: *The Trial of Dedan Kimathi* 155-61; Ngugi and Ngugi Wa Mirii: *I Will Marry When I Want* 155-6, 162-7
Nigerian Civil War literature 24-5, 65-7
non-alignment 116-17

Ofeimun, Odia: *The Poet Lied* 57, 191-5
Onitsha Market literature 25-6, 111
oral literary culture 10, 69-70, 72, 105-10, 116, 120-2, 170-1
orature 105-6

Osofisan, Femi: *Morountodun* 157, 172-4;
    Once Upon Four Robbers 57, 71, 155,
    157, 167-72; Ousmane, Sembene: *God's
    Bits of Wood* 128, 136-43

past, perceptions of the 117-20
poetry and politics 176-95
politics and ideology in African literature
    56-61, 63 *see also* drama; Marxist;
    Ngugi; poetry
popular literature 25-6, 111
popularization, need for 111-12, 156, 161-2

realism in the African novel 127-9
retrospective fixation 117-20

social commitment and alignment 114-17
socio-historical axis of criticism 13-14
sociological criticism 9, 23-7
sociology of the African novel 125-9

teaching of African literature 198-9
traditional aesthetics 30-41, 50, 104;
    pitfalls of 41-9

universalism 19-20, 35-6, 41-2, 46-7

world view, myth of 37-41, 43-4
writer: and audience 107-12; as critic 27-9;
    and critics 29-31

Institute For African Alternatives (IFAA)

Director: Ben Turok, BSc Eng, MILS, BA(SA), MA(DSM)

Prof. Bade Onimode (Nigeria) Chair　　*Prof. Abdoulaye Bathily (Senegal)*
Dr Tsehai Berhane-Selassie (Ethiopia)　*Prof. Ben Magubane (South Africa)*
Dr Fatima Babikar Mahmoud (Sudan)　　*Mr Kempton Makamure (Zimbabwe)*
Dr Kwame Ninsin (Ghana)　　　　　　　*Prof. Nzongola-Ntalaja (Zaire)*
Prof. Haroub Othman (Tanzania)　　　　*Dr E. Mwanongonze*

IFAA was established in 1986 to promote policy research and discussion on the contemporary problems of Africa. Its headquarters are located in London, UK, and consists of a suite of offices, a lecture hall, a common room and study rooms. Facilities are available for visiting Research Fellows from Africa. A network of IFAA Resource Centres is being established in seven African countries.

Conferences, Workshops, Seminars

A major annual conference is held at IFAA with invited speakers from across Africa. There is also a special conference on African women. Workshops are held on a specialist basis and seminars on particular topics. Proceedings are generally recorded and published.

Lectures and Classes

IFAA holds a series of lectures on particular topics from time to time. Classes are run on such topics as History of African Women, Problems of Development, Neocolonialism, South African Liberation etc. A residential three month course on African Women: Transformation and Development is under preparation.

IFAA is an Independent Centre of the University of London and runs joint Diploma and other courses with the Centre of Extramural Studies

Publishing

IFAA publishes its conference proceedings, books by IFAA associates, textbooks for African Universities, and occasional papers.

IFAA issues a bi-monthly newsletter IFAA NEWS, and a quarterly bibliography of African books IFAA BOOK LISTINGS.

Address: IFAA, 23 Bevenden Street, London N1 6BH, UK.
Telephone: 01-251 1503, Telex 923753 Ref W6019

ZED/IFAA CO-PUBLICATIONS

Ben Turok, AFRICA: WHAT CAN BE DONE? (1987)

Nzongola-Ntalaja, REVOLUTION AND COUNTER-REVOLUTION IN AFRICA: Essays in Contemporary Politics (1987)

Eboe Hutchful (editor), THE IMF AND GHANA: The Confidential Record (1987)

Bade Onimode, A POLITICAL ECONOMY OF THE AFRICAN CRISIS (1988)

Ahmed Samatar, SOCIALIST SOMALIA: RHETORIC AND REALITY (1988)

Chidi Amuta, THE THEORY OF AFRICAN LITERATURE: Implications for Practical Criticism (1988)

Bade Onimode (ed), THE IMF, WORLD BANK AND THE AFRICAN DEBT (1988)
   Volume 1: The Economic Impact
   Volume 2: The Socio-Political Effects